William Shakespeare's
Twelfth Night

D0060809

William Shakespeare's *Twelfth Night* is one of his most captivating plays. A comedy of mistaken identities, it has given rise to controversial debates on key issues, such as gender identities, sexual desires and social aspirations.

Taking the form of a sourcebook, this guide to *Twelfth Night* offers:

- extensive introductory commentaries on the critical and stage history of the play, from the early performances to the present;
- annotated extracts from contextual documents, reviews, critical works and the text itself;
- cross-references between extracts and other sections of the guide, in order to suggest links between texts, contexts and criticism;
- suggestions for further reading.

Part of the Routledge Guides to Literature series, this volume is essential reading for all those beginning detailed study of *Twelfth Night* and seeking not only a guide to the play but also an introduction to the wealth of contextual and critical materials that enhance our understanding of Shakespeare's text.

Sonia Massai is a lecturer at King's College London. She has published widely on Shakespeare and drama and has edited several original plays and a collection of essays on *World-Wide Shakespeares* (Routledge, 2005). She is also the author of *Shakespeare and the Rise of the Editor* (2007).

Routledge Guides to Literature

Editorial Advisory Board: Richard Bradford (University of Ulster at Coleraine), Shirley Chew (University of Leeds), Mick Gidley (University of Leeds), Jan Jedrzejewski (University of Ulster at Coleraine), Ed Larrissy (University of Leeds), Duncan Wu (St Catherine's College, University of Oxford)

Routledge Guides to Literature offer clear introductions to the most widely studied authors and texts.

Each book engages with texts, contexts and criticism, highlighting the range of critical views and contextual factors that need to be taken into consideration in advanced studies of literary works. The series encourages informed but independent readings of texts by ranging as widely as possible across the contextual and critical issues relevant to the works examined, rather than presenting a single interpretation. Alongside general guides to texts and authors, the series includes 'Sourcebooks', which allow access to reprinted contextual and critical materials as well as annotated extracts of primary text.

Already available*:

Geoffrey Chaucer by Gillian Rudd
Ben Jonson by James Loxley
William Shakespeare's The Merchant of Venice: A Sourcebook edited by S. P. Cerasano
William Shakespeare's King Lear: A Sourcebook edited by Grace Ioppolo
William Shakespeare's Othello: A Sourcebook edited by Andrew Hadfield
William Shakespeare's Macbeth: A Sourcebook edited by Alexander Leggatt
William Shakespeare's Hamlet: A Sourcebook edited by Sean McEvoy
William Shakespeare's Twelfth Night: A Sourcebook edited by Sonia Massai
John Milton by Richard Bradford
John Milton's Paradise Lost: A Sourcebook edited by Margaret Kean
Alexander Pope by Paul Baines
Jonathan Swift's Gulliver's Travels: A Sourcebook edited by Roger D. Lund
Mary Wollstonecraft's A Vindication of the Rights of Woman: A Sourcebook edited by Adriana Craciun
Jane Austen by Robert P. Irvine
Jane Austen's Emma: A Sourcebook edited by Paula Byrne
Jane Austen's Pride and Prejudice: A Sourcebook edited by Robert Morrison
Byron, by Caroline Franklin
Mary Shelley's Frankenstein: A Sourcebook edited by Timothy Morton
The Poems of John Keats: A Sourcebook edited by John Strachan
The Poems of Gerard Manley Hopkins: A Sourcebook edited by Alice Jenkins
Charles Dickens's David Copperfield: A Sourcebook edited by Richard J. Dunn

---

* Some titles in this series were first published in the Routledge Literary Sourcebooks series, edited by Duncan Wu, or the Complete Critical Guide to Literature series, edited by Jan Jedrzejewski and Richard Bradford.

William Shakespeare's
Twelfth Night
A Sourcebook

Edited by Sonia Massai

Routledge
Taylor & Francis Group

LONDON AND NEW YORK

First published 2007
by Routledge
2 Park Square, Milton Park, Abingdon, Oxon, OX14 4RN

Simultaneously published in the USA and Canada
by Routledge
270 Madison Ave, New York, NY 10016

Routledge is an imprint of the Taylor & Francis Group, an informa business

Copyright © Sonia Massai

Typeset in Sabon and Gill Sans by RefineCatch Limited, Bungay, Suffolk
Printed and bound in Great Britain by
Antony Rowe Ltd, Chippenham, Wiltshire

British Library Cataloguing in Publication Data
A catalogue record for this book is available from the British Library.

Library of Congress Cataloging in Publication Data
William Shakespeare's Twelfth night : a sourcebook / [edited by] Sonia Massai.
   p.   cm.—(Routledge guides to literature)
   Includes bibliographical references and index.
1. Shakespeare, William, 1564–1616. Twelfth night.   1. Massai, Sonia.
PR2837.W55   2007
822.3'3—dc22

                                                                    2007018152

ISBN 13: 978–0–415–30332–3 (hbk)
ISBN 13: 978–0–415–30333–0 (pbk)

ISBN 10: 0–415–30332–3 (hbk)
ISBN 10: 0–415–30333–8 (pbk)

Contents

3: Key Passages   133

Introduction   135

Key Passages   139

4: Further Reading   187

Annotations and Footnotes

Annotation is a key feature of this series. Both the original notes from reprinted texts and new annotations by the editor appear at the bottom of the relevant page. The reprinted notes are prefaced by the author's name in square brackets, e.g., [Robinson's note].

Author's note

Some of the extracts in the Contemporary Documents section are drawn from recent modernised editions, while others are drawn from the original editions and they retain early modern spelling and punctuation (please note that 'u' and 'v', and 'i' and 'y', are often used interchangeably, 'i' stands for 'i' or 'j', 'w' stands for 'w' or 'u', and that words are sometimes abbreviated through the omission of consonants signalled by wavy or straight accents placed over the preceding vowels – for, example, 'womã' for 'woman' or 'wãton' for 'wanton'). Extracts from texts originally written in foreign languages – for example, Petrarch's sonnets – are drawn from modern English translations. The extracts from early modern editions are annotated to help readers with unusual words and spellings.

Line numbers for all Shakespearean quotations and for the extracts from *Twelfth Night* included in the Key Passages section are keyed to Stanley Wells and Gary Taylor, with John Jowett and William Montgomery (eds), *The Complete Works* (Oxford: Oxford University Press, 1986).

Acknowledgements

I would like to thank Liz Thompson, Polly Dodson, the anonymous readers and the production team at Routledge. Their help and support have been invaluable at every stage of this project.

Thanks also to the following, for permission to reproduce materials:

Petrarch's Sonnets 190 and 199 are reprinted by permission of the publisher from *Petrarch's Lyric Poems: The Rime Sparse and Other Lyrics*, translated and edited by Robert M. Durling, pp. 336, 344, Cambridge, Mass.: Harvard University Press, Copyright © 1976 by Robert Durling.

Extract from Frank E. Halliday, 'Twelfth Night' (1954), in *The Poetry of Shakespeare's Plays* (London: Gerald Duckworth, 1954), pp. 122–4. Reproduced by permission of House of Stratus Ltd.

Extracts from Jonathan Bate, *Shakespeare and Ovid* (Oxford: Clarendon Press, 1993). By permission of Oxford University Press.

Extract from W. H. Auden, 'Twelfth Night' (1947), in A. Kirsch (ed.), *Lectures on Shakespeare* (London: Faber and Faber, 2000), pp. 154–5. Reproduced by permission of Faber and Faber Ltd. Copyright © 2000 by the Estate of W. H. Auden – Introduction and notes © 2000 by Arthur Kirsch. Reprinted by permission of Curtis Brown, Ltd.

Extracts from Barber, Cesar Lombardi; *Shakespeare's Festive Comedy*, Princeton, NJ: Princeton University Press, 1959 © 1959 Princeton University Press, 1987, renewed PUP. Reprinted by permission of the Princeton University Press.

Extracts from Elliot Krieger, *A Marxist Study of Shakespeare's Comedies*, Basingstoke: Macmillan, 1979. Reproduced with permission of Palgrave Macmillan and the author.

Extract from Michael Bristol, *Carnival and Theatre: Plebeian Culture and the Structure of Authority in Renaissance England*, London and New York: Routledge, 1985. Reproduced by permission of Taylor and Francis.

Extracts from Karin Coddon, '"Slander in an Allow'd Fool": *Twelfth Night*'s

Crisis of the Aristocracy.' Reprinted, with permission, from SEL *Studies in English Literature 1500–1900*, 33, 2 (spring 1993).

Extracts from '"In What Chapter of His Bosom?": Reading Shakespeare's Bodies' by Keir Elam, in Terence Hawkes (ed.), *Alternative Shakespeares 2*, London and New York: Routledge, 1996. Reproduced by permission of Taylor and Francis.

Extracts from Juliet Dusinberre, *Shakespeare and the Nature of Women*, Basingstoke: Macmillan, 1975. Reproduced with permission of Palgrave Macmillan.

Extracts from Stephen Greenblatt, 'Fiction and Friction', in *Shakespearean Negotiations: The Circulation of Social Energy in Renaissance England*, Berkeley, Calif.: University of California Press. © 1988 The Regents of the University of California and the Clarendon Press. By permission of University of California Press and Oxford University Press.

Extracts from Catherine Belsey, 'Disrupting Sexual Difference: Meaning and Gender in the Comedies', in J. Drakakis (ed.), *Alternative Shakespeares*, London and New York: Routledge, 1986. Reproduced by permission of Taylor and Francis.

Extracts from William Dodd, '"So Full of Shape is Fancy": Gender and Point of View in *Twelfth Night*', in Robert Clark and Piero Boitani (eds), *English Studies in Transition*, London and New York: Routledge, 1993. Reproduced by permission of Taylor and Francis.

Extracts from Lorna Hutson, 'On Not Being Deceived: Rhetoric and the Body in Twelfth Night', from *Texas Studies in Literature and Language* 38 (2), pp. 140–74. Copyright © 1996 by the University of Texas. All rights reserved.

Extracts from Laura Levine, *Men in Women's Clothing: Anti-Theatricality and Effeminization, 1579–1642*, Cambridge: Cambridge University Press, 1994. Reproduced by permission.

Extract from Paul Yachnin, 'Revels of Fortune', *ELH* 70 (3) (2003), pp. 776–780, 786. © The Johns Hopkins University Press. Reprinted with permission of The Johns Hopkins University Press.

Extracts from Jason Scott-Warren, 'When Theatres Were Bear-Garden's'?, *Shakespeare Quarterly* 54 (1) (2003), pp. 65–6, 74–7. © Folger Shakespeare Library. Reprinted with permission of The Johns Hopkins University Press.

Extracts from Laurie E. Osborne, *The Trick of Singularity: 'Twelfth Night' and the Performance Editions*, Iowa City, Iowa: University of Iowa Press, 1996.

Extracts from Marion F. O'Connor, 'The Theatre of the Empire', in J. E. Howard and M. F. O'Connor, *Shakespeare Reproduced: The Text in History and Ideology*, London and New York: Routledge, 1987. Reproduced by permission of Taylor and Francis.

Extract from Michael Billington (ed.), *Approaches to Twelfth Night*, London: Hern, 1990. Copyright © 1990 by Michael Billington and the Royal Shakespeare Company. Reprinted by permission of the publisher.

Extracts from Penny Gay, *As She Likes It: Shakespeare's Unruly Women*, London and New York: Routledge, 1994. Reproduced by permission of Taylor and Francis.

Extracts from Michael Dobson, 'Shakespeare Performances in England, 2002', *Shakespeare Survey* 56 (2003), pp. 258–62. By permission of Cambridge University Press.

Extract from Carol Chillington Rutter, 'Looking at Shakespeare's Women on Film', in R. Jackson (ed.), *The Cambridge Companion to Shakespeare on Film*, Cambridge: Cambridge University Press, 2000, pp. 248–50.

Every effort has been made to trace and contact copyright holders. The publishers would be pleased to hear from any copyright holders not acknowledged here, so that this acknowledgement page may be amended at the earliest opportunity.

Introduction

This study guide to William Shakespeare's *Twelfth Night: Or, What You Will* combines a selection of modernised and annotated key passages drawn from the play with two types of extracts, called 'Contexts' and 'Interpretations'. The 'Contexts' section gathers documents that influenced Shakespeare's presentation of the fictive world of the play, including its dramatic and narrative sources, contemporary pamphlets that focus on some of the central issues explored in the play, and earlier literary texts that had a tangible impact on Shakespeare's style. The 'Interpretations' section includes some of the most influential responses to *Twelfth Night* on page (critical studies), on the stage (theatrical productions) and on screen (cinematic adaptations).

The different sections into which this book is arranged are not necessarily meant to be read sequentially. Individual extracts in each section are cross-referenced to other parts of the book in order to enable readers to study specific aspects of the play and to find out how they have been interpreted by early readers, recent critics and directors. This introduction, for example, gives a preliminary overview of the play, its main characters, genre and early performance history and reception, and reflects on the relevance of the title to the events that unfold in its main plot and sub-plot. Each of these topics is cross-referenced to a wide range of documents and extracts, which are in turn prefaced by explicatory introductions and commentary notes.

One central document for readers interested in the performance history of the play is a short entry in John Manningham's *Diary* (see Contextual Overview, p. 7). Manningham was a law student at the Middle Temple[1] when *Twelfth Night* was performed in its great hall on 2 February 1602. His diary entry represents an invaluable and rare contemporary eyewitness account of a Shakespearean production in the Elizabethan period. Also worth noting is that Manningham singled out the steward Malvolio, a character in the sub-plot, and his downfall, as the most enjoyable and memorable features of the play as a whole.[2] Recent critics and audiences tend to regard Malvolio as a sympathetic, or even as a potentially tragic, character (see Interpretations, p. 43 and The Work in Performance,

---

1 The Middle Temple is one of the four Inns of Court which have traditionally served as centres of legal and collegiate activities for London barristers and law students.
2 A plot summary is provided in the Key Passages Section, pp. 135–7.

pp. 106–7). However, the stratagems through which Malvolio's feelings for his mistress, the Lady Olivia, are exposed and ridiculed are undoubtedly funny. Unsurprisingly, then, when *Twelfth Night* was printed as part of the first collected Folio edition of Shakespeare's dramatic works in 1623, it was grouped with other plays described as 'Comedies'. If the sub-plot, with Malvolio's deception at its centre, can best be described as satirical, or even farcical, the main plot features all the main elements which distinguish Shakespeare's 'romantic comedy' from other types of comedy. The main plot revolves around the incidents generated by the Orsino–Viola–Olivia love triangle: Orsino is in love with Olivia, who spurns him and falls in love with Viola disguised as Cesario, who, in turn, falls in love for her master Orsino. Viola decides to conceal her identity when, after surviving a shipwreck, she is cast ashore in a foreign land, called Illyria. She therefore fashions a new identity for herself, by imitating the looks and mannerisms of her twin brother Sebastian, who was travelling with her at the time of the shipwreck and who is now believed to have perished at sea. Sebastian, like Viola, has in fact survived the shipwreck and will also arrive in Illyria in Act 3, thus providing a resolution to the emotional impasse generated by Olivia's unrequited feelings for Viola, by Orsino's unrequited feelings for Olivia and by Orsino's growing attachment to Viola.

Twelfth Night is also commonly described as one of Shakespeare's 'mature' comedies, both because it was written and performed towards the end of Elizabeth's reign, when Shakespeare was already an established and successful playwright, and because it departs from the pre-eminently farcical quality of some of his early comedies, including *The Comedy of Errors* and the sub-plot in *The Taming of the Shrew*. Shakespeare's 'mature' or 'romantic' comedies, which include, besides *Twelfth Night*, *As You Like It* and *Much Ado about Nothing*, are also radically different from other plays generally described as 'problem plays', or 'dark comedies', such as *Measure for Measure*, *All's Well that Ends Well* and *Troilus and Cressida*. In these plays potentially tragic situations remain unresolved and undermine the sense of resolution typically associated with the ending of a comedy. However, *Twelfth Night* is not wholly devoid of darker tones. In fact, despite the successful matching of the lovers and Sir Toby and Maria's wedding, the ending is tarnished by Malvolio's pledge to be revenged on his persecutors, by the presence of disappointed suitors, like Sir Andrew, and by unfulfilled passions, including the deep attachment which the sea captain Antonio develops for Sebastian after rescuing him at sea. Overall, *Twelfth Night* represents one of Shakespeare's most complex comedies, because it skilfully re-employs the satirical elements of earlier comedies while anticipating the darkness and melancholy associated with the later comedies and the great tragedies of the early Jacobean period.

Besides blending satirical and romantic elements with light touches of discomfort, unease and sadness, *Twelfth Night* also draws on another dramatic form and tradition, as suggested by its title. *Twelfth Night* is the only play in the Shakespearian canon which refers explicitly to one of the main holidays in the Christian calendar, the twelfth night after Christmas, otherwise known as the Epiphany. Its title has, therefore, led some scholars to regard *Twelfth Night* as a 'festive comedy', that is, as a play directly associated with real-life holidays and popular festivals, which were celebrated by over indulging in drink, dance, music and fun. *Twelfth Night* does indeed usher the audience into a world shaped by the pursuit of pleasure and the fulfilment of gastronomic and sexual appetites. However, the relation between Twelfth Night, traditionally celebrated on 6 January, and Shakespeare's play is far from straightforward and uncontroversial, as suggested by the enigmatic subtitle, *What You Will*. Samuel Pepys, the late-seventeenth-century diarist who recorded a visit to the theatre to see *Twelfth Night* on 6 January 1663, famously described it as 'a silly play and not relating at all to the name or day'.[3] Conversely, mid-twentieth-century critic Leslie Hotson argued that Shakespeare chose this title because *Twelfth Night* was the play performed before the Queen and one of her notable guests, the Count Don Virginio Orsino, at Whitehall, on the night of 6 January 1601.[4] Hotson's theory has been refuted by scholars who believe that *Twelfth Night* was in fact written towards the end of 1601, but is still valuable because it draws attention to the fact that the fictive world of the play resembles in many ways Queen Elizabeth's court. All the main characters in the plot and sub-plot are members of the aristocracy, and Olivia's undisputed rule over her large household has been read as an oblique reference to the Queen's role at Court. Queen Elizabeth was also renowned for the lavish entertainments that she commissioned to celebrate Twelfth Night, and the title could therefore be interpreted as a tribute that Shakespeare paid to the Queen for a play that he may have written with her court in mind just before the Christmas period of 1601–2. One may wonder, though, whether the Queen would have been flattered by being associated with an aristocratic young woman who, after resisting Duke Orsino's advances, is overwhelmed by her infatuation for a stranger, who is, at least apparently, a mere servant.

The connection between the play and Twelfth Night is ultimately intriguing and worth keeping in mind, and not only in relation to Elizabeth's court, but also in relation to its significance as a Christian holiday. As mentioned above, the twelfth night after Christmas is also known in religious terms as the Epiphany. Etymologically, the word 'epiphany' comes from the Greek and suggests the act of becoming manifest, of shining forth. In Christian theology, it describes the revelation of God to mankind through the birth of his son Jesus Christ and, more specifically, the arrival of the Wise Men in Bethlehem. Viola and Sebastian's reunion at the end of the play does indeed conjure a sense of wonder. Orsino's line, 'One face, one voice, one habit, and two persons' in the last scene conveys a sense of quasi-religious mystery. The lengthy recognition sequence (see Key Passages, **pp. 181–3**), where Viola and Sebastian realise that they are both alive, reinforces the other-worldly quality of the final scene. Even at plot level, the association between this play and the twelfth night after Christmas, which officially brings the Christmas period to an end, seems in keeping with the somber register of the final lines, which follow the recognition sequence. Malvolio, Sir Andrew and Antonio are left empty-handed and feeling betrayed and disappointed, while the audience return to a world where, as Feste's song reminds them, desires may not always be fulfilled, 'For the rain it raineth every day' (see Key Passages, **pp. 184–5**).

---

3   *The Diary of Samuel Pepys*, edited by Robert Latham and William Matthews, vol. IV (London: Bell, 1971), p. 6.
4   Leslie Hotson, *The First Night of 'Twelfth Night'* (London: Rupert Hart-Davis, 1954).

1

Contexts

Contextual Overview

Introduction

When John Manningham saw *Twelfth Night* performed at the Middle Temple Hall on 2 February 1602, he noted the following in his diary:

> At our feast wee had a play called "Twelue Night, or What You Will," much like the Commedy of Errores, or Menechmi in Plautus, but most like and neere to that in Italian called *Inganni*.[1] A good practise in it to make the Steward beleeve his Lady widdowe was in love with him, by counterfeyting a letter as from his Lady in generall termes, telling him what shee liked best in him, and prescribing his gesture in smiling, his apparaile, &c., and then when he came to practise making him beleeue they tooke him to be mad.[2]

Manningham understood *Twelfth Night* both in relation to classical and foreign literary models, which are less well known to us than they were to Shakespeare's learned audience at the Middle Temple, and in relation to some key aspects of Elizabethan society, which gave Malvolio's downfall a special topical resonance likely to be lost on modern readers and theatre-goers. This opening section, therefore, aims to introduce users of this study guide to a selection of contemporary documents that shed light on relevant but potentially unfamiliar aspects of the literary and social contexts within which *Twelfth Night* was first written and performed.

---

1 Manningham is probably referring to *Gl'Ingannati* (*The Deceived*), one of Shakespeare's main sources, rather than two later Italian plays called *Inganni* (see Contemporary Documents, pp. 26–8).

2 *Diary of John Manningham, of the Middle Temple, and of Bradbourne, Kent, Barrister-at-Law, 1602–3*, ed. John Bruce (London: J.B. Nichols and Sons, 1868), p. 18.

'To Be Count Malvolio': Marriage and Fantasies of Social Mobility

Modern audiences and readers may be struck by Orsino's assumption that Olivia should not feel too distraught about marrying the wrong twin, since Sebastian's blood is, after all, 'right noble' (see Key Passages, **p. 183**). Is Shakespeare implying that belonging to the same social group makes Olivia's mistake less upsetting or humiliating? Is rank more important than compatibility? How would Shakespeare's contemporaries answer these questions, and to what extent were their views on marriage different from our own?

English society had changed dramatically since the Tudors had come to power towards the end of the fifteenth century. As historian Christopher Dyer has pointed out, 'Edmund Dudley, writing in 1509, divided the commonwealth into the three orders of nobles, clergy and peasants, as William Langland had done in the 1370s and Aelfric soon after 1000'.[3] However, William Harrison, the author of *A Description of England* (1577),[4] a detailed contemporary account of social life under Queen Elizabeth, listed four orders of people in the English commonwealth. The new order, or the 'middling sort', later to be called the middle classes, was made up of merchants and professionals, who often became as wealthy as, if not wealthier than, the gentry, and sometimes successfully purchased a title, as Shakespeare himself did in 1596. Besides increased wealth and a consequent widening of access to education, marriage was also seen as a means to attain status and patrimony. Wealthy widows (or, less often, heiresses like Olivia) represented a prime target for well-educated but poor or destitute gentlemen like John Manningham, the law student who saw *Twelfth Night* performed at the Middle Temple in February 1602. Interestingly, his account of the production at the Middle Temple erroneously refers to Olivia as Malvolio's 'lady-widow', by far the most accessible category of independent, well-to-do women who could secure their new husbands a good income. However, other cultural, religious and historical forces were contributing to qualify this predominantly monetary and self-interested attitude to marriage.

In medieval times, when England was a Catholic country, the Church discouraged even those who married from regarding sexual relations as a source of mutual love and intimacy. Besides, biblical texts like Genesis supported the view that women were physically and morally weaker than men and, therefore, implied that husband and wife were not equal partners. Consequently, the institution of marriage sanctioned the husband's supremacy over the other members of the family, including his children, his servants (if there were any) and his wife. The rise of humanism, a cultural movement which flourished in fourteenth- and fifteenth-century Europe, played a crucial role in changing early modern attitudes

---

3   Christopher Dyer, *Making a Living in the Middle Ages: The People of Britain, 850–1520* (London: Penguin, 2003), p. 363. Edmund Dudley (c. 1462–1510) was a famous lawyer and statesman during the reign of King Henry VII; William Langland (c. 1325–c. 1390) was a poet, mostly known for his poem *The Vision of Piers Plowman*; Aelfric was Archbishop of Canterbury between 995 and 1005.

4   William Harrison, *The Description of England*, ed. Georges Edelen (Washington, DC and New York: Folger Shakespeare Library and Dover Publications, 1968).

to marriage. Humanists believed in men *and* women's ability to improve themselves through education and that only harmony and companionship would ensure a happy and fulfilling married life. After King Henry VIII declared the Church of England's independence from Rome in the early 1530s, Protestant and Puritan theologians, pamphleteers and social commentators like Edmund Tilney (see Contemporary Documents, **pp. 19–21**) appropriated humanist views on marriage in order to take their distance from the legacy of medieval Catholicism. It is, however, worth stressing that, despite being progressive and enlightened in some respects, humanist and Puritan views on marriage were still deeply affected by a patriarchal bias against women, as the extracts from Tilney's tract *The Flower of Friendship* (1568) clearly show. Although Tilney regards equality in 'yeares, . . . giftes of nature, and fortune' as the basis for 'matrimoniall amitie', he also believes that 'concord' in matrimony is achieved only if the wife willingly submits to her husband, since 'both divine, and humaine lawes, in our religion giveth the man absolute aucthorities, over the woman in all places'. Similarly, in *A Godly Form of Household Government* (1598), Robert Cleaver warns the husband that 'as God created the womā, not of the head, & so equall in authoritie with [him]: so also hee created her not of *Adams* foote, that she should be troden downe and despised'. However, Robert Cleaver adds that if a 'noble woman' happens to unwisely marry a

> man of base estate . . . she ought to consider, that no distinction or difference of birth and nobilitie, can be so great, but that the league, which both Gods ordinance and nature hath ordaineth betwixt [them], farre exceedeth it: for by nature woman was made mans subiect.[5]

What the documents included in this section collectively show is that there was no linear progression in the social and cultural changes that affected the institution of marriage from the medieval to the early modern period. The Catholic model gave way to conflicting views on marriage, which encouraged matrimonial amity, while reinforcing hierarchical power relations within the family and class boundaries within the community. Literary and dramatic works from the period explore the tensions surrounding the matching of socially unsuitable partners. The transgressive marriage between the Duchess and her steward Antonio in John Webster's *The Duchess of Malfi* (1612–14), for example, leads to a bloody and tragic resolution. Conversely, Jack's marriage to his master's widow, which allows him to become a successful and wealthy clothier in Thomas Deloney's *Jack of Newbury* (1597), has no tragic implications because Jack, unlike Malvolio, has no desire for social elevation. Despite the different outcomes of their marriages, both Antonio and Jack voice their concerns about marrying wealthier women. They both seem familiar with Tilney's position, according to which, when that happens, 'a man hath gotten in steed of a wyfe, a husband, and she of him a wyfe, a straunge alteration, a wonderfull metamorphosis' (see Contemporary Documents, **p. 20**). The documents in this section can, therefore, help us understand why Orsino expects to become the 'one self king' of Olivia's affections, once she

---

5   Robert Cleaver, *A Godly Form of Household Government* (1598), pp. 210, 146.

gives in to his amorous advances (see Key Passages, p. 142) and why Olivia, who enjoys the highly unusual privilege of being fully in control of her own life and fortunes, keeps rejecting him. As Sir Toby explains, 'She'll none o'th'Count', because she is determined not to 'match above her degree, neither in estate, years, nor wit' (1.3.105–6). While the ending of *Twelfth Night* attempts to restore normative sexual and social relations, by focusing on Malvolio's public humili-ation, on Viola and Sebastian's 'noble blood' and on Cesario's announced meta-morphosis into Viola, the play as a whole allows characters to play out their wildest fantasies of erotic and social fulfilment. Their fantasies imply new modes of being, which were made possible partly by the changes discussed above and partly by specific theories about the body, which strongly affected how the Eliza-bethans understood gender differences and the impact of such differences on the circulation of sexual desire, as explained in the next section.

'One Face, One Voice, One Habit, and Two Persons': Early Modern Views on Gender and Sexuality

The reunion of the twins at the end of *Twelfth Night* represents the dramatic climax of the play and its most intriguing conundrum. When they finally appear on stage together in Act 5, Scene 1, Viola and Sebastian are wearing the same clothes and they look and sound identical. As Antonio puts it, 'An apple cleft in two is not more twin / Than these two creatures' (see Key Passages, p. 181). When Sebastian challenges Viola to admit that there may be a crucial difference between them – 'Were you a woman . . . I should say "Thrice welcome, drownèd Viola"' – she fails to identify herself as Viola. Even ten lines later, when Viola refers to her disguise as 'masculine usurped attire', identification is deferred to a time when Viola can change into her 'maiden weeds'. Her admission 'That I am Viola' is presented as a verifiable hypothesis, which is, however, never put to the test. Viola and Sebastian continue to look identical despite the fact that they are paired off to form two normative heterosexual couples with Orsino and Olivia. The final scene in *Twelfth Night* is clearly devised to make 'real' and 'feigned' masculinity look identical until and beyond the end of the play. Viola's failure to discard her disguise is partly due to the fact that women were not allowed to act on the early modern stage and that the conventional use of boy actors to play female roles (see The Work in Performance, pp. 113–15) prevented Viola from ever coming clean about her sexual identity. However, what even all-male modern productions can-not recover is the connection between this staging practice and early modern theories about human physiology, which blurred gender distinctions.

The predominant model through which Shakespeare's contemporaries under-stood the human body was first introduced by a Greek physician called Galen in the second century A D. According to Galenic physiology, male and female sexual organs were structurally similar. Anatomically, the neck of the womb and the ovaries were believed to mirror the penis and the testicles. What changed was the position of these organs, which was determined by the different temperature of the male and female body. The hotter and drier make-up of the male body allowed the sexual organs to protrude, while the sluggish and colder female body was thought to lack the strength to develop and its sexual organs remained help-lessly stranded within. Gail Kern Paster has usefully pointed out that William Harvey's discovery of the female *ovum* in 1651 and Regnier de Graf's discovery of the ovarian follicle in 1672 would ultimately disprove the Galenic model.[6] However, at the beginning of the seventeenth century, sexual difference was still believed to be one of degree rather than kind. Differential dress and behavioural codes, whereby men and women are taught how to experience their bodies, were therefore regarded as crucially important to uphold gender differences. This is why pamphleteer Philip Stubbes (see Contemporary Documents, **pp. 25–6**) con-demned cross-dressing as a threat against natural and social order. Clothes were in turn seen not simply as external signifiers revealing essential gender differences but rather as key elements in the construction of masculinity and femininity (see also The Work in Performance, **pp. 113–15**). Or, as Stubbes put it, 'to weare the apparell of another sexe, is to participate with the same, and to adulterate the veritie of his owne kinde' (see Contemporary Documents, **p. 26**).

The twins' reunion at the end of *Twelfth Night* does not only reveal the ultimate instability of gender distinctions but also a fantasy world where marriage does not supplant but develops from same-sex friendships that border upon homo-erotic attachments. Both *Twelfth Night* and some of its narrative and dramatic sources (see Contemporary Documents, **pp. 26–30**) foreground the desirability of the heroine in disguise, who, thanks to her adopted male persona, establishes strong bonds of mutual friendship and respect with her future partner. The fact that Orsino addresses Viola as 'boy' even after she has promised to change into her 'maiden weeds' can be read as a symptom of the cultural and social uneasiness attached to the transition between same-sex friendship, which is based on mutual respect and affection, to marriage, which was still a strongly hierarchical institu-tion, as explained in the previous section. Tellingly, after Orsino asks Viola to marry him, they hardly speak again. The hasty pairing off of the lovers at the end of *Twelfth Night* seems particularly noteworthy in a play that literally forges a new language of love, as explained in the next section.

'Where Lies Your Text?': Reinventing the Language of Love

Seduction in *Twelfth Night* is predominantly aural. If both Orsino and Olivia are attracted by Viola's androgynous looks, they seem equally charmed by her rhet-orical skills. After Viola's 'willow cabin' speech in Act 1, Scene 5, Olivia meta-phorically elevates her status by granting her a 'five-fold blazon', thus emphasising Cesario's eligibility as a husband. Orsino similarly takes an interest in Viola when the latter remarks that music 'gives a very echo to the seat / Where Love is throned' (see Key Passages, **p. 162**). The sheer power of these lines convinces Orsino that

6 For more details, see Gail Kern Paster, *The Body Embarrassed: Drama and the Disciplines of Shame in Early Modern England* (Ithaca, NY and London: Cornell University Press, 1993), pp. 23–63.

Viola is in love and that she must, therefore, understand the depth of his own feelings for Olivia. What makes Viola's language so special?

Two influential literary models affected the way in which early modern poets, including Shakespeare, wrote about love. The Roman poet Publius Ovidius Naso, better known as Ovid (43 BC–AD 18), and the Italian poet Francesco Petrarca (henceforth Francis Petrarch, 1304–74), were widely imitated by Shakespeare and his contemporaries, who found in their work not only powerful images and sophisticated conceits but also radically different views on the effects of love and sexual desires on our sense of self. Ovid and Petrarch did not simply translate a range of familiar emotions into literary language; like expert craftsmen, they used language to forge new modes of being in love (or, subject positions), which were simply unimaginable, because unspeakable, before them.

Ovid specialised in the exploration of physical love and the effects of sexual desire on the body and the mind. In *Metamorphoses*, a collection of myths and stories in verse, which was first translated into English by Arthur Golding in 1567, Ovid describes the changes brought about by the sheer power of sexual desire, both when desire is allowed to manifest itself and when it is shunned or repressed. Ovid's work was used in the early modern period as a storehouse of stories and characters associated with psychological states ranging from aggressive and destructive lust, peevish self-love and self-preserving chastity, to the frustration experienced as a result of sexual jealousy, enforced separation or unrequited love. Although change in Ovid often translates into a transformation of a person, or even a god, into something less than human, like a flower, a tree, a bull or a nightingale,[7] change does not necessarily imply a moral fall and cannot be automatically translated into a warning against the perils of sex and sexual experience. Change is rather a symptom of the overwhelming power of desire, which literally shatters *and* transforms the self. In this respect, *Twelfth Night* is thoroughly Ovidian. Olivia, for example, compares the power and the sudden arousal of her feelings for Viola to the devastating effects of the plague: 'Even so quickly may one catch the plague?' (see Key Passages, **p. 151**) – while even the sombre steward Malvolio is literally transformed into a bambling fool, sporting yellow stockings and garters, by his consuming desire to please Olivia.

The play is also awash with allusions to Ovidian myths: as Jonathan Bate has shown, the two Ovidian myths of 'Actaeon' and 'Narcissus and Echo' are 'among the controlling structures of the play' (see Modern Criticism, **pp. 59–63**). The myth of 'Actaeon and Diana', for example, is explicitly invoked by Orsino in the opening scene. In Ovid, the hunter becomes the hunted when the goddess Diana turns the huntsman Actaeon into a hart for spying on her while she is bathing in a sylvan pool. Actaeon dies when his dogs, the embodiment of his desire for the beautiful goddess, tear him to pieces. Orsino, as Bate explains, compares himself to Actaeon, when he reminisces about the first time he saw Olivia: 'That instant was I turned into a hart / And my desires, like fell and cruel hounds, / E'er since pursue me' (see Key Passages, **p. 142**).

---

7   See, for example the stories of 'Narcissus and Echo', Book III, 343–513, 'Apollo and Daphne', Book I, 450–568, 'Jupiter and Europa', Book II, 834–75, or 'Tereus, Procne, and Philomela', Book VI, 412–677, in *Metamorphoses*, translated by A. D. Melvill and annotated by E. J. Kenney (Oxford: Oxford University Press, 1986).

If language, plot and characterisation in *Twelfth Night* undoubtedly gain resonance and psychological depth through extensive allusions to Ovidian myths, the innovative quality of Shakespeare's dramatic and poetic vision in *Twelfth Night* cannot be fully appreciated without a clear sense of how he appropriated and departed from another influential poetic tradition associated with Francis Petrarch. If Ovidian poetry ascribes agency to sexual desire as an *external* force that can alter, transform and redefine the boundaries of the self, Petrarchan poetry focuses on the poet's obsessive exploration of the changes brought about by desire within the *internal* landscape of the poet's own soul. If Ovid focuses on the *shattering* of the self under the influence of sexual desire, Petrarch spent over forty years weaving his '*scattered* rhymes' (Sonnet 1, my emphasis) into a revolutionary sequence of poems, known as *Il Canzoniere* (songbook), which many now associate with one of the earliest literary manifestations of the modern self in Western Europe. Petrarch envisages his own subjectivity as poised between a yearning for the beloved, but unattainable, Lady Laura and the opposite urge to cherish interiority as the ultimate source of personal identity. If Orsino in Act 1, Scene 1 uses the Ovidian myth of Actaeon and Diana to explain how his first meeting with Olivia transformed him into a prey of his own desires (see Key Passages, **p. 142**), Petrarch's construction of his poetic persona in *Il Canzoniere* provides Shakespeare with the primary model for Orsino's character.

Although English poets from Thomas Wyatt to John Donne were inspired by Petrarch, Petrarchan conventions had been so widely imitated by the time Shakespeare wrote *Twelfth Night* that they were starting to seem modish and outdated rhetorical postures. The poems included in the Contemporary Documents section highlight the development which a popular Petrarchan trope, the hunting metaphor, and a Petrarchan convention, the blazon (literally, an armorial bearing or heraldic sign; by analogy, a detailed catalogue, or poetical anatomy, of the beloved's physical attributes),[8] had already undergone by the time Shakespeare used them in *Twelfth Night*. In Petrarchan poems, the lady is often seen as a beautiful creature for the onlooker to contemplate or for the hunter to pursue (see Contemporary Documents, **pp. 30–5**). Olivia's rejection of Orsino's suit and Sir Toby's allusion to the fact that Olivia will 'not match above her degree, neither in estate, years, nor wit' (1.3.105–6) may suggest that Olivia is not quite comfortable in the conventional role of the hunted deer made available by the Petrarchan tradition. Her active wooing of Viola/Cesario confirms that she is more inclined to chase the object of her desires than to be 'hunted' by Orsino. Olivia's description of her face in Act 1, Scene 5 as '*item*, two lips, indifferent red; *item*, two grey eyes, with lids to them; *item*, one neck, one chin, and so forth' (see Key Passages, **p. 150**) effectively illustrates the sinister implications of the Petrarchan vogue for the blazon, which conventionally compares female physical attributes to precious stones, flowers or dainty foods, thus turning the body of the woman into a commodity. The last group of poems included in this section also shows how the pornographic gaze of the male poet turns the female body into an object by listing and itemising its parts. This last group of poems is particularly useful in relation

---

8   For more details on the ideological implications of the popularity of the blazon in early modern culture, see, for example, Jonathan Sawday, *The Body Emblazoned: Dissection and the Human Body in Renaissance Culture* (London: Routledge, 1995).

to the first meeting between Olivia and Cesario in Act 1, Scene 5, which can be read both as a turning point within the fictive world of the play *and* as a poetic manifesto, through which Shakespeare skilfully revises and reinvents Petrarch's language of love and interiority. Olivia's rejection of Orsino's love as 'feigned' and 'bookish' signals Shakespeare's consciously revisionary attitude towards his literary models. Cesario's famous 'willow cabin' speech is a masterly display of rhetorical skills on Shakespeare's part, because, despite depending on Ovidian myth and the Petrarchan trope of the frustrated lover, it comes across as an outburst of raw emotions unmediated by poetic tradition.

Overall, the sociological, the medical and the literary contexts explored in this opening chapter can help us understand the significance of aspects of this play which would otherwise be lost on contemporary readers and theatre-goers. What was familiar to Shakespeare's original audiences – early modern beliefs about the material basis of emotions, literary conventions used to express or to reform ways of being and ways of feeling in love, and the growing phenomenon of upward mobility within a resiliently hierarchical world – can be recovered through careful investigation of a wide range of documents, including the representative selection gathered in the 'Contemporary Documents' section, which follows below after a brief chronology of Shakespeare's life.

Chronology

Bullet points indicate events in Shakespeare's life, and asterisks indicate historical and literary events which occurred in or around Shakespeare's lifetime.

1538
* Publication of Accademia degli Intronati, *The Deceived*

1558
* Coronation of Queen Elizabeth I

1564
• Shakespeare born in Stratford-upon-Avon (baptised 26 April; birthday traditionally celebrated 23 April)

1567
* Publication of Arthur Golding's translation of Ovid's *Metamorphoses*; first permanent theatre, the Red Lion, built in London

1568
* Publication of Edmund Tilney's *The Flower of Friendship*

1576
* James Burbage builds the Theatre in Shoreditch, where Shakespeare's plays were later to be staged, 1593–7

1577
* Publication of *The Description of England* by William Harrison; opening of the Curtain in Shoreditch, where Shakespeare's plays were later to be staged, 1598–9

1581
* Publication of Barnaby Rich's *His Farewell to Militarie Profession*

1582

- Shakespeare marries Anne Hathaway, who is eight years older than him and pregnant

1583

- Shakespeare's first child, Susanna, born (baptised 26 May)
- * Publication of Philip Stubbes' *The Anatomy of Abuses*

1584

- * Masters at Middle Temple ban the practice of electing a 'Lord of Misrule', appointed by students to preside over riotous holiday period from Christmas to Candlemas (2 February)

1585

- Shakespeare's twins, Hamnet and Judith, born (baptised 2 February)

1587

- * Philip Henslowe builds the Rose Theatre in Southwark

1588

- Shakespeare begins career as actor-playwright in London around this time
- * Defeat of Spanish Armada

1592

- * Outbreak of plague; London theatres closed until May 1594

1593

- First edition of *Venus and Adonis*, published by Shakespeare's fellow-Stratfordian, printer and publisher Richard Field, dedicated to Henry Wriothesley, Earl of Southampton

1594

- Shakespeare becomes a member of newly formed acting company, the Lord Chamberlain's Men, also including clown Will Kemp and tragedian Richard Burbage (son of James Burbage); publication of *Titus Andronicus*, first Shakespearian play to reach the press and *The Rape of Lucrece*, second narrative poem which Shakespeare dedicated to Southampton; possible allusion to a performance of *The Comedy of Errors* at Gray's Inn (28 December)
- * Francis Langley builds the Swan Theatre

1595

- * Publication of Edmund Spenser's *Amoretti* and *Epithalamion*

1596

- Hamnet dies; Shakespeare successfully applies for coat of arms on father's behalf and acquires New Place, one of the largest houses in Stratford; *The Merchant of Venice* (approximate date of composition)

1597

- First Quarto edition of *Romeo and Juliet*
- *A Proclamation Enforcing Statutes and Proclamations of Apparel* issued, whereby Elizabeth I updates sumptuary laws passed by Parliament under Henry VIII in 1530s and 1540s and under Mary in 1550s; publication of Thomas Deloney's *Jack of Newbury*

1598

- Shakespeare's name appears for first time on title page of *Love's Labour Lost* (First Quarto), *Richard II* (Second Quarto) and *Richard III* (Second Quarto)
- John Manningham enrols at Middle Temple; publication of Emanuel Ford's *Parismus*

1599

- The Burbages and other members of the Chamberlain's Men including Shakespeare dismantle the Theatre in Shoreditch and use the timber to build the Globe Theatre on the South Bank in Southwark; comedian Will Kemp leaves company and replaced in 1600 by Robert Armin, who played Feste in *Twelfth Night; As You Like It* (approximate date of composition)
- Publication of Richard Hakluyt's *The Principal Navigations, Voyages, Traffiques and Discoveries of the English Nation*

1600

- *Hamlet* (approximate date of composition); publication of *The Merchant of Venice*
- Philip Henslowe and Edward Alleyn build the Fortune Theatre; the East India Company established

1601

- Shakespeare's father dies; *Twelfth Night* (approximate date of composition)
- Don Virginio Orsino, Duke of Bracciano (Lazio, Italy), entertained at White Hall on Twelfth Night; Earl of Essex's attempted rebellion and execution; Shakespeare's company questioned at Essex's trial

1602

- First recorded performance of *Twelfth Night* at Middle Temple Hall (2 February)

1603

- Publication of first Quarto edition of *Hamlet*
- Outbreak of plague; death of Elizabeth I; King James VI of Scotland crowned King James I of England and Scotland (25 July); new king grants royal patronage to Shakespeare's company, renamed the King's Men

1604

- *Othello* (approximate date of composition); first recorded performance at Banqueting House, Whitehall (1 November). Publication of second Quarto edition of *Hamlet*
- Peace treaty with Spain signed at Somerset House

1609

- Shakespeare's mother dies; publication of *Pericles, Troilus and Cressida* and *The Sonnets*; Shakespeare's company start performing at new indoor theatre in Blackfriars

1611

- Shakespeare moves back to Stratford; *The Tempest* (approximate date of composition and first recorded performance on 1 November at Whitehall)

1616

- Shakespeare dies in Stratford-upon-Avon (23 April); buried in Holy Trinity Church
* King James I and Ben Jonson publish their collected works

1618

* 'The King's Book of Sports' issued to regulate 'Lawful Sports to be Used on the Sabbeth Day'

1620

* Publication of *Hic Mulier, or The Man-Woman* and *Haec-Vir, or The Womanish Man*

1622

- Publication of *Othello*

1623

- Publication of the First Folio edition of *Mr. William Shakespeares comedies, histories, & tragedies*, including, among other previously unpublished plays, first editions of *Twelfth Night, The Comedy of Errors, As You Like It* and *The Tempest*
* Publication of John Webster's *The Duchess of Malfi*

1633

* Charles I reissues James I's 'Book of Sports'; aggravation of political tension between King and bishops led by Archbishop Laud, on one hand, and Puritan and Parliamentary opposition groups, on the other

1642

* Outbreak of Civil War; theatres closed down and 'Book of Sports' publicly burned

Contemporary Documents

Changing Views on Marriage

From **Edmund Tilney, *The Flower of Friendship*** (1568) ed. V. Wayne
(Ithaca, NY and London: Cornell University Press, 1992), pp. 105, 108, 112, 134

Edmund Tilney (1535/6–1610) was a courtier under Queen Elizabeth I, the
dedicatee of his popular tract on marriage, *The Flower of Friendship* (1568).
Tilney's attempt to impress the Queen and gain a position at court paid off, and
he was appointed Master of the Revels in 1579. As Master of the Revels
between 1579 and 1610, Tilney arranged courtly entertainments, decided which
plays written for the public stage were to be performed at court and licensed all
plays staged in London, including *Twelfth Night*.

Tilney's tract drew heavily on earlier humanist tracts on marriage, such as
Erasmus's *Coniugium* (1523) and Pedro di Luxan's *Coloquios matrimoniales*
(1550), which provide both its subject matter and the names of the fictional
characters engaged in the learned conversation informing its structure. In the
extracts below Erasmus, Master Pedro and Lady Julia (from Eulalia, the virtuous
wife in Erasmus's *Coniugium*) endorse humanist views according to which husband and wife should love and respect each other as companions. Lady Aloisa
(from Heloise, the medieval author of the famous correspondence to her former lover and husband Pierre Abelard) is firmly associated with a medieval
distrust of marriage, while Lady Isabel (Spanish for Elizabeth) finds flaws in
humanist views, which are still strictly patriarchal. Isabel's arguments in favour of
true equality are criticised by Master Pedro and the latter's comments suggest
the extent to which Elizabeth's own position on the throne of England and her
failure to marry were perceived as deeply anomalous and disruptive by her
contemporaries.[1]

---

1   Recent scholarship has suggested that Elizabeth did not refuse to marry, as has often been argued,
     and that her failure to do so depended more on diplomatic and political obstacles rather than
     on 'psychological motives or political reasons associated with her gender'. From Susan Doran,
     Monarchy and Matrimony: The Courtships of Elizabeth I (London and New York: Routledge,
     1996), p. 11.

Tilney himself married late in life. Although his *Flower of Friendship* champions the humanist precept according to which wives should be chosen for their virtues and not for their dowries, he married a wealthy widow, called Lady Mary Bray. Tilney proved luckier than Malvolio, but, ironically, he failed to secure his wife's patrimony after her death and was financially destitute when he died in 1610. Romance and cynical self-interest lived side by side in Shakespeare's London, as much as in Shakespeare's Illyria.

[MASTER PEDRO] [I]f antiquitie may give any worthinesse, what is more auncient than this honourable estate,[2] which God himself the founder of all ordayned and consecrated? What is more honorable, and praise worthie, than thys that Christ with hys mother in Canaan did not onely with his presence make honorable, but also wyth miracles did sanctifie the same?[3] What is more just, than to render that to oure posteritie, which we of our predecessors have before receyved? What thing is more in humaine, than for man to contemne that as profane which the eternall hath halowed, and nature hir selfe bewtified? Christ our Lorde commaundeth, that man shall forsake Father and Mother and cleave to his welbeloved Spouse, and what is more holy than love towards parentes, which God in the commaundementes, hath rewarded with the longnesse of lyfe, yet matrimony is preferred before the same. What is then more necessarie than Matrimonie, which containeth the felicity of mans life, the *Flower of Friendship*, the preservation of Realmes, the glorie of Princes, and that which is most of all, it causeth immortalitie. [. . .]

[T]he Ladie *Julia* desireth to heare of our friendly *Flower*, wherto now I returne, and saye, that equalitie is principally to be considered in this matrimoniall amitie,[4] as well of yeares, as of the giftes of nature, and fortune. For equalnesse herein, maketh friendlynesse.

Pitachus Mityleneus one of the seaven sages of *Greece*, being demaunded of a yong man, whome he should take to wyfe, aunswered, go, and learne of the children, that play togither, and they will informe thee. For they had a game among them, wherin they often repeated, *take to thee thy peere*.[5] Marry not a superiour, saith *Plutarch*. For in so doing, in steede of kinsfolkes, thou shalt get thee maisters, in whose awe thou must stande, and a riche woman, that marieth a poore man, seldome, or never, shake off the pride from hir shoulders. Yea *Menander* sayth, that suche a man hath gotten in steed of a wyfe, a husband, and she of him a wyfe, a straunge alteration, a wonderfull metamorphosis. [. . .]

In this long, and troublesome journey of matrimonie, the wise man maye not be contented onely with his spouses virginitie, but by little and little must gently

---

2   Master Pedro is here referring to the institution of marriage.
3   According to the Gospel of Saint John (2:1–11), Jesus performed his first miracle while attending a wedding in Cana in Galilee, where he turned water into wine. Master Pedro is therefore arguing that by performing his first miracle at a wedding, Christ meant to 'sanctifie' marriage.
4   Friendship.
5   Choose your equal.

procure that he maye also steale away hir private will, and appetite, so that of two bodies there may be made one onelye hart, which she will soone doe, if love raigne in hir, and without this agreeable concord matrimonie hath but small pleasure, or none at all, and the man, that is not lyked, and looved of his mate, holdeth his lyfe in continuall perill, his goodes in great jeopardie, his good name in suspect, and his whole house in utter perdition. [. . .]

[LADY ISABELLA] But what say you to the custome which *Dionysius Alicarnasseus*, wryteth of the *Numidians*, and *Lydians*, where the women commaunded within doores, and the men without.

Yea marie quoth the Ladye *Aloisa*, that was a just law, where the commaunding was equall.

Not so, quoth the Lady *Julia*. For though it were better than the other two: yet not tollerable amongest us, neyther was the soveraignetie so equallye devided, as you thinke. For if the woman keepe alwaies hir house, as dutye is, the man standeth ever at hir commaundement. For as long as she is within, though he commaund hir without, this lawe byndeth hir not to obey. Wherfore in my opinion al those *Barbarian* customes are to be disanulled, and contemned of Christians.

Ye say well, Madam, quoth M. *Erasmus*. For in deede both divine, and humaine lawes, in our religion giveth the man absolute aucthoritie, over the woman in all places.

And, quoth the Lady *Julia*, as I sayde before, reason doth confirme the same, the man being as he is, most apt for the soveraignetie being in government, not onely skill, and experience to be required, but also capacity to comprehende, wisdome to understand, strength to execute, solicitude to prosecute, pacience to suffer, meanes to sustayne, and above all a great courage to accomplishe, all which are commonly in a man, but in a woman verye rare: Then what blame deserve those men, that doe permit their wyves to rule all, and suffer themselves to be commaunded for company.

From **Thomas Deloney, *Jack of Newbury*** (1597), in P. Salzman (ed.), *An Anthology of Elizabethan Prose Fiction* (Oxford: Oxford University Press, 1987), pp. 320, 329–30

Thomas Deloney (1543?–1600?) was a silk weaver, who became popular as a writer of historical ballads. Towards the end of his life he turned to prose fiction and wrote three innovative works, *Jack of Newbury, The Gentle Craft* and *Thomas of Reading*, which departed from the contemporary fashion for Italian *novelle* or medieval romances and focused instead on the everyday life of weavers, clothiers and shoemakers.

Jack of Newbury provides a utopian view of social harmony at a time of radical change. By marrying his master's widow, Jack becomes rich enough to send an army of 150 men to the war and to organise a lavish banquet to entertain King Henry VIII during his progress through Berkshire. Although Jack effectively carries out duties traditionally associated with the aristocracy, he refuses to be knighted. Unlike Malvolio, Jack the weaver has no desire to wear 'branched velvet gown[s]' (see Key Passages, **p. 168**); on the contrary, Jack, who 'would always keep himself in comely and decent apparel',[1] beseeches the king 'to let [him] rest in [his] russet coat a poor clothier to his dying day'.[2] In the extract below, he initially resists, and then cautiously accepts, the widow's advances, when he realises that he cannot safely reject her. Also interesting is the contrast between Malvolio's wish to control higher-rank members in Olivia's household, like Sir Toby, and Jack's conciliatory attitude towards his fellow servants once he becomes their master. Because of his lack of social ambition, Jack's reasons for marrying his master's widow are radically different from Malvolio's erotic fantasies, which are fuelled by his desire to attain patrimony and status.

And in the mean space, John [Jack] got him up into his chamber and there began to meditate on this matter, bethinking with himself what he were best to do; for well he perceived that his dame's affection was great toward him. Knowing therefore the woman's disposition, and withal that her estate was reasonable good, and considering beside that he should find a house ready furnished, servants ready taught, and all other things for his trade necessary, he thought it best not to let slip that good occasion, lest he should never come to the like. But again, when he considered her years to be unfitting to his youth, and that she that sometime had been his dame would (perhaps) disdain to be governed by him that had been her poor servant, that it would prove but a bad bargain, doubting many inconveniences that might grow thereby, he therefore resolved to be silent rather than to proceed further. Wherefore he got him straight to bed, and the next morning settled himself close to his business. [. . .]

John, seeing no remedy, consented because he saw the matter could not otherwise be amended, and married they were presently. When they were come home, John entertained his dame with a kiss, which the other servants seeing thought him something saucy. The widow caused the best cheer in the house to be set on the table, and to breakfast they went, causing her new husband to be set in a chair at the table's end with a fair napkin laid on his trencher. Then she called out the rest of her servants, willing them to sit down and take part of their good cheer. They, wondering to see their fellow John sit at the table's end in their old master's chair, began heartily to smile and openly to laugh at the matter, especially because their dame so kindly sat by his side. Which she perceiving asked if they were all the manners they could show before their master. 'I tell you,' quoth she, 'he is my husband, for this morning we were married, and therefore henceforward look you acknowledge your duty towards him.'

The folks looked one upon another, marvelling at this strange news. Which when John perceived he said 'My masters muse not at all, for although by God's providence and your dame's favour I am preferred from being your fellow to be your master, I am not thereby so much puffed up in pride that any way I will forget my former estate. Notwithstanding, seeing I am now to hold the place of

1   Thomas Deloney, *Jack of Newbury*, in P. Salzman (ed.), *An Anthology of Elizabethan Prose Fiction* (Oxford: Oxford University Press, 1987), p. 314.
2   Deloney, *Jack of Newbury*, p. 356.

a master, it shall be wisdom in you to forget what I was and to take me as I am; and in doing your diligence you shall have no cause to repent that God made me your master.' The servants hearing this, as also knowing his good government before time, passed their years with him in dutiful manner.

From **John Webster,** *The Duchess of Malfi* (1612–14), ed. E. M. Brennan (London and New York: Black and Norton, 1993), Act 2, Scene 5, lines 1–80 and Act 3, Scene 2, lines 248–98

John Webster (1578/80–1638?) wrote two famous tragedies, *The White Devil* (1612) and *The Duchess of Malfi* (1612–14), which focus on two charismatic, if morally ambiguous, female characters. Vittoria Corombona in *The White Devil* fulfils her sexual desires outside wedlock, while the Duchess in *The Duchess of Malfi*, like Olivia, actively woos and secretly marries Antonio, a virtuous man, whose status is below her rank. The Duchess thus flouts the authority of her two brothers, Ferdinand and the Cardinal, who have forbidden her to remarry after the death of her first husband. In the second half of the following extract, the treacherous courtier Bosola, hired by the Cardinal, tricks her into revealing the name of her husband by extolling Antonio's virtues. His exorbitant praise of the Duchess's decision to value virtue over rank barely conceals contemporary anxieties about social mobility, as suggested by Bosola's startling image of Turks and Moors turning Christians to serve the Duchess. (Turks and Moors were regarded as fearsome enemies, due to the growing military and economic power of the Muslim Ottoman Empire during the fifteenth and sixteenth centuries.) By secretly marrying the Duchess, Antonio achieves the same type of social elevation to which Malvolio aspires. While in *Twelfth Night* Malvolio's fantasies are brutally shattered and Orsino conveniently reassures Olivia that Sebastian's blood is 'right noble' (see Key Passages, **p.183**), the Duchess's secret marriage to Antonio is viewed as a treacherous offence by her two brothers, who are prepared to have their own sister killed in order to defend the family's good name. Ferdinand's plan to 'purge' his sister's 'infected blood' can be usefully compared to the ritual blood-letting performed at the end of *The Changeling* (1623), another Jacobean tragedy where the adulterous Beatrice-Joanna dies shedding the blood that would otherwise defile her father and her husband's reputations.

Act 2, scene 5, lines 1–26

[*Enter*] CARDINAL, *and* FERDINAND, *with a letter.*

FERDINAND
    I have this night digg'd up a mandrake.[1]

---

1 [Brennan's note.] The mandrake, a plant of the genus Mandragora, has a forked root and thus resembles the human form. It was supposed to grow under the gallows and was said to shriek when pulled from the ground. Moreover, plucking it would lead to madness.

CARDINAL   Say you?

FERDINAND
    And I am grown mad with't.

CARDINAL   What's the prodigy?

FERDINAND
    Read there, a sister damn'd, she's loose, i'th' hilts:[2]
    Grown a notorious strumpet. [. . .]

CARDINAL   Is't possible?
    Can this be certain?

FERDINAND   Rhubarb,[3] oh for rhubarb
    To purge this choler; here's the cursed day
    To prompt my memory, and here't shall stick
    Till of her bleeding heart I make a sponge
    To wipe it out.

CARDINAL   Why do you make yourself
    So wild a tempest?

FERDINAND   Would I could be one,
    That I might toss her palace 'bout her ears,
    Root up her goodly forests, blast her meads,
    And lay her general territory as waste,
    As she hath done her honour's.

CARDINAL   Shall our blood?
    The royal blood of Aragon and Castile,
    Be thus attainted?

FERDINAND   Apply desperate physic,[4]
    We must not now use balsamum,[5] but fire,
    The smarting cupping-glass,[6] for that's the mean
    To purge infected blood, such blood as hers. [. . .]

Act 3, scene 2, 250–90

BOSOLA
                         [. . .] He was an excellent
    Courtier, and most faithful; a soldier, that thought it
    As beastly to know his own value too little,
    As devilish to acknowledge it too much;
    Both his virtue and form deserv'd a far better fortune:
    His discourse rather delighted to judge itself, than show itself.
    His breast was fill'd with all perfection,

---

2   [Brennan's note.] unreliable (here in the sense of unchaste)
3   [Brennan's note.] Considered to be choleric itself, rhubarb was a recognized antidote for an excess
    of choler.
4   Remedy.
5   [Brennan's note.] aromatic healing ointment
6   'A glass vessel applied to the skin' (*Oxford English Dictionary, attrib.* 4) 'in the operation of
    drawing blood . . . by applying a cup or cupping-glass the air in which is rarified by heat . . .'
    (*Oxford English Dictionary, vbl. sb.* 1).

And yet it seem'd a private whisp'ring room:
It made so little noise of't.

DUCHESS   But he was basely descended.

BOSOLA
Will you make yourself a mercenary herald,
Rather to examine men's pedigrees, than virtues?
You shall want him: [. . .]

DUCHESS
Oh, you render me excellent music.

BOSOLA   Say you?

DUCHESS
This good one that you speak of, is my husband.

BOSOLA
Do I not dream? Can this ambitious age
Have so much goodness in't, as to prefer
A man merely for worth: without these shadows
Of wealth, and painted honours? possible?

DUCHESS
I have had three children by him.

BOSOLA   Fortunate lady,
For you have made your private nuptial bed
The humble and fair seminary of peace.
No question but many an unbenefic'd[7] scholar
Shall pray for you, for this deed, and rejoice
That some preferment in the world can yet
Arise from merit. The virgins of your land,
That have no dowries, shall hope your example
Will raise them to rich husbands. Should you want
Soldiers, 'twould make the very Turks and Moors
Turn Christians, and serve you for this act.

Gender and Clothing

From **Philip Stubbes, *The Anatomy of Abuses*** (1583), ed. M. J. Kidnie
(Tempe, Ariz.: Renaissance English Text Society, 2002), p. 118

In his popular work *The Anatomy of Abuses* (1583), London pamphleteer Philip
Stubbes (c. 1555–1610?) attacked cross-dressing as a dangerous threat against
divine and social order (see also The Work in Peformance, **pp. 113–15**). Cross-
dressing was a staple convention on the early modern stage, because the

---

7   Ecclesiastial property and land granted in feudal tenure were generally referred to as 'benefices'
    (*Oxford English Dictionary, sb.* 1 and 2); Bosola is therefore associating Antonio with a socially
    recognisable type, namely, the erudite but destitute scholar, who despite having a good education,
    was forced to seek service in order to earn a living.

exclusion of women from the acting profession forced theatrical companies to cast boy actors to play female roles. Stubbes and other contemporary writers report that cross-dressing was also practised on the streets of London. In *The Description of England* (1587), for example, William Harrison claims to 'have met with some of these trulls in London, so disguised, that it hath passed my skill to discern whether they were men or women. Thus it is now come to pass that women are become men and men transformed into monsters'.[1] In the following extract from *The Anatomy of Abuses*, the speaker is Philiponus, who has travelled across Ailgna (Anglia, that is, England, spelled backwards) for seven years to observe the infamous customs of its inhabitants. Cesario's reference to disguise as a 'wickedness' (see Key Passages, **p. 155**) echoes the moral views advocated by early modern writers like Stubbes and Harrison.

Doublets for Women in England.

Philo. The women also there haue Doublets and Ierkins, as men haue here, buttoned vp the breast, and made with wings, weltes and pinions on the shoulder pointes, as mans apparel is in all respectes, and although this be a kind of attire, proper onely to man, yet they blush not to wear it: and if they could as wel change their sexe, and put on the kind of man, as they can weare apparell assigned only to man, I thinke they would as verily become men indeed, as now they degenerate from godly sober women, in wearing this wãton leud kind of attire, proper only to man. It is written in the **22.** of **Deuteronomy, that what man so euer weareth womans apparell is accursed, and what woman weareth mans apparell, is accursed also.** Now whether they be within the compasse of that curse, let they themselues iudge. Our apparell was giuen as a signe distinctiue, to discerne betwixt sexe and sexe, and therfore one to weare the apparell of another sexe, is to participate with the same, and to adulterate the veritie of his owne kinde. Wherefore these women may not improperly bee called **Hermaphroditi**, that is Monsters of both kindes, halfe women, half men. Who if they were naturall women, and honest Matrones, woulde blush to go in such wanton & leud attire, as is incident only to man.

Androgyny and Homoeroticism

From **Accademia degli Intronati, The Deceived** (1531), in G. Bullough (ed.), *Narrative and Dramatic Sources of Shakespeare*, Vol. II (London and New York: Routledge & Kegan Paul and Columbia University Press, 1960), pp. 292–6

> *Gl' Ingannati* (*The Deceived*), a bawdy comedy of mistaken identity, was written and performed by a literary society called Accademia degli Intronati (the

---

1   William Harrison, *The Description of England*, ed. Georges Edelen (Washington, DC and New York: The Folger Shakespeare Library and Dover Publications, 1968), p. 147.

'Thunderstruck') in Siena in 1531. Parallels in plot devices and character names suggest that Shakespeare was influenced by this play, or, as Manningham points out in his diary entry (see Contextual Overview, **p. 7**), by two later Italian comedies based on it, both called *Gl' Inganni*, by Niccolò Secchio (1562) and Curzio Gonzaga (1592). Viola's arraignment of disguise as a 'wickedness' (see Key Passages, **p. 155**) can be usefully contrasted to Lelia's more pragmatic assessment of the risks and benefits involved in adopting a male disguise. The following extract, where Lelia explains to her maid Clemezia how she started serving Flamminio (Orsino) disguised as Fabio (Cesario), shows suggestive parallels between Viola's growing intimacy with Orsino (see Key Passages, **pp. 144–5 and 161–4**) and Flamminio's interest in Fabio's androgynous looks, their intense friendship and the sexual connotations attached to the services provided by Fabio to his master.

Scene III

Lelia dressed as a young man, calling herself Fabio; and Clemenzia the Nurse

LELIA   It is indeed very rash of me, when I think of it, to come out in the streets so early, considering the wild practices of these licentious youths of Modena. Oh, how awful it would be if one of these young scapegraces seized me by force, and, dragging me into a house, wanted to make sure whether I am a man or a woman! They'd teach me to leave home so early in the morning! But the cause of it is the love I feel for that ungrateful, cruel Flamminio. O what a fate is mine! I love a man who hates me, who always scorns me; I serve one who does not know me; and to make things worse I help him in his love for another (though, if it should become known, nobody surely could believe it); all without any hope other than of feasting my longing eyes by seeing him all day as I please.

[*Enter Clemenzia*]

[. . .]

CLEM.   Is it possible that you did not fall dead with shame?

LELIA   Love aiding me I replied frankly that I was a Roman, and being poor was seeking my fortune. He looked me up and down from head to foot so closely that I feared he would recognize me; then he said that if I would care to work for him he would employ me, treating me well and like a gentleman. Though I felt a little ashamed I answered, Yes.

CLEM.   If I'd heard that I'd have wished never to have been born. And what use do you see in committing this madness?

LELIA   What use? Do you think a woman in love is unhappy to see her beloved continually, to speak to him, touch him, hear his secrets, observe his habits, discuss things with him, and be certain at least that, if she doesn't enjoy him, nobody else does either?

CLEM.   A mad girl's notions! And isn't it only adding fuel to the fire if you are not certain that by doing all this you will please your beloved? In what ways do you serve him?

LELIA   At table, in his room; and I know that in this fortnight while I have served him I have pleased him so much that if it had happened to me in my true person, how happy I should be!

CLEM.   Tell me this now: Where do you sleep?

LELIA   Alone; in his antechamber.

CLEM.   And if some night, seized with the accursed temptation, he called you in to sleep with him, what would you do?

LELIA   I don't want to think of evil before it comes. When this occurred I should reflect on it and decide what to do.

From **Emanuel Ford, Parismus** (1598), in G. Bullough (ed.), *Narrative and Dramatic Sources of Shakespeare*, Vol. II (London and New York: Routledge & Kegan Paul and Columbia University Press, 1960), pp. 366–7, 369–71

In writing *Twelfth Night*, Shakespeare was influenced by two English romances as much as by the Italian comedies discussed in the previous head-note. Barnaby Rich's prose tale of 'Apollonius and Silla', for example, which is included in his *Riche his Farewell to Militarie Profession* (1581), provided Shakespeare with many details of plot and characterisation. Far more interesting and subtle are the similarities between Emanuel Ford's *Parismus* (1598) and Shakespeare's emphasis on Viola (Adonius)'s androgynous appeal, which both Olivia (Laurana) and Orsino (Parismus) find overwhelmingly irresistible (see Key Passages, **pp. 146–52**) and uncannily alluring (see Key Passages, **pp. 161–4**). Interestingly, the name Adonius conjures memories of Ovid's lovely Adonis – 'Then a most lovely infant, then a youth, / And now a man more lovely than the boy'[1] – and of Shakespeare's 'rose-cheeked Adonis' in *Venus and Adonis*.[2]

The following extract focuses on Violetta's disclosure of her real identity and can be usefully compared to Viola and Sebastian's reunion in Act 5, Scene 1 (see Key Passages, **pp. 181–3**). Unlike Viola, Violetta does not marry Parismus, the Orsino figure, but his friend Pollipus whom she had brutally rejected as Violetta, and then tenderly served him as his page Adonius. The male disguise gives Violetta a chance to appreciate the depth of Pollipus's feelings for her, while Pollipus finds solace in Adonius's friendship. This extract shows the level of intimacy and familiarity enjoyed by master and servant: Pollipus and Adonius do not only share a bed but they also 'oftentimes . . . imbraced' *before* Violetta reveals her true identity. Pollipus, like Orsino at the end of *Twelfth Night*, appears slightly reluctant to accept the fact that the kind Adonius, who 'had done [him]

1   *Ovid, Metamorphoses*, trans. A. D. Melville, ed. E. J. Kenney (Oxford: Oxford University Press, 1986), Book X, pp. 520–1.
2   William Shakespeare, *Venus and Adonis* (1593), 3.

manifold pleasures', is, in fact, his beloved but cruel Violetta, 'considering how unlikely it is she should be so kind to [him]'.

Violetta, who hearing that Parismus was departing towards his owne countrey, determined to venter her life and credit to go with him, and therefore fitted herselfe in Pages apparrell, which so well became her, that she seemed to be the artificiallest workmanshippe that ever nature had framed, her sute being greene Satten, her buskins of the finest Spanish lether, fastned to her daintie legge with Christall buttons, her haire wreathed with a carnatian Ribbin, and all things else so neate and so comelie uppon her delicate body, that shee was most comely to beholde, and in this sort apparelled, shee secretly stole from her Fathers house, and soone gat to the Pallace [. . .] where shee continued many dayes together, in which time shee laboured by all meanes to bee entertayned by Parismus. And on a time espying him with Laurana, walking privately in the Garden, on a sodaine shee came towardes them, who beholding her comely shape and delicate complection, deemed her to be rather a divine then a mortall creature, who beeing come neare them, Parismus demanded whose Page hee was. My Lords, sayde Violetta, as yet I have no maister, but I would gladly bee entertayned: quoth hee then, would you attend on Laurana and myselfe, if it please her to like you. I am (quoth shee) in all humble dutie readie at your command. Many questions Laurana asked the Boy (as shee supposed) demanding his name, his Countrey, and parentage. Violetta aunswered, my name is Adonius, my countrey Greece, and my parents all dead, and the fame of the noblenesse of this Court, made me travaile into this Countrey with the Emperour, with determination to gette myselfe some good service, which you have vouchsafed me, & herein my dutie, and indevour, shall be such, as I trust you shall hereafter well like of. Which speeches poore Violetta uttered, with so pretie a grace, that they both tooke great delight in her behaviour, whome now wee will call by the name of Adonius. [. . .]

But when [Violetta, disguised as Adonius] had tenderly coucht her selfe by [Pollipus's] manly side, she could not devise how to grow into conference with him, being strooken with such a delightful fear, to discover her selfe, as she had never felt the like. At last she said, [. . .] I am that Violetta you so earnestly enquire after, I am the partie that have so long time procured your discontent, and I am shee whose absence you have so oft bewayled, and nowe I am constrained to manifest myselfe unto you, desiring you to pardon my hardheartednesse that have so long concealed my selfe, and thereby procured your disquiet. Pollipus hearing her speeches, could not tell what to say, being halfe perswaded it was she, by remembring her countenance, and the behavior she had used in all their travels: as also calling to mind her kindnes, & nowe at length her own speeches, could not resolve what to do, for that his fancie still perswaded him it was not Violetta. And on the other side he had a mightie perswasion it might be she; at last he said, I know not what to conjecture, nor howe to behave my selfe, nor whether I should call you Adonius, or Violetta, considering how unlikely it is she should be so kind to me, and how certaine I am that Adonius hath done me manifold pleasures. Then sweete Violetta (if you are she) resolve me of this my doubt, being thereby driven to that hopefull dispaire, that I know not whether my fortune be better or worse then it was. Violetta thinking a little back, said, Pardon me deere Pollipus, for I am your unworthie friend Violetta, that have in this disguise, made trial of my fortune, & your friendship. Pollipus then tooke her most lovingly in his arms [. . .]. Yet he was in a doubt still, & could not bee quiet, until he had used such kind meanes (yet far from dishonour) as thereby he found shee was a virgine, and no Page, and therefore assured himselfe it was Violetta: and foulding her delicate and tender body in his manlike armes (which he had oftentimes before imbraced, but not with such kindnes, banishing all sadnesse from his sorrowfull heart) with sweete and delightful content, hee imbraced her with that kindnesse that long parted lovers enjoy.

Petrarchan Conventions I: The Hunting Metaphor

Francis Petrarch, 'Sonnet 190' (1334–74), in *Petrach's Lyric Poems*, trans. and ed. Robert M. Durling (Cambridge, Mass.: Harvard University Press, 1976), p. 336

Francis Petrarch (1304–74), prominent Italian poet and humanist scholar, wrote a famous collection of love poems, called *Il Canzoniere*, which was widely imitated from the end of the fifteenth to the first half of the seventeenth century in most Western European countries, including England.

The onlooker in 'Sonnet 190', smitten by the beauty of the white doe, anticipates several of Orsino's traits. The doe, like Olivia, is ultimately unattainable, and the onlooker's fall into the river signals impotence and self-oblivion, thus providing an interesting counterpart to Orsino's description of his passion for Olivia as a spirit that 'Receiveth as the sea' (see Key Passages, p. 141). More generally, the onlooker's fascination with the doe, a symbol for Laura, earthly fame (laurel) and divine perfection, is reflected in Orsino's obsessive passion for Olivia and the devotional language he uses to praise her in the final scene. More specifically, note Orsino's lines, where he greets Olivia by saying 'Here comes the Countess. Now heaven walks on earth' and where he describes his courtship as 'the faithfull'st off'rings . . . That e'er devotion tendered' (see Key Passages, p. 180).

A white doe on the green grass appeared to me, with two golden horns, between two rivers, in the shade of a laurel, when the sun was rising in the unripe season.

Her look was so sweet and proud that to follow her I left every task, like the miser who as he seeks treasure sweetens his trouble with delight.

"Let no one touch me,"[1] she bore written with diamonds and topazes[2]
around her lovely neck. "It has pleased my Caesar[3] to make me free".

And the sun had already turned at midday; my eyes were tired by
looking but not sated, when I fell into the water, and she disappeared.

Thomas Wyatt, 'Who so list to hounte I know, where is a hynde' (c. 1530), in British Library, MS Egerton 2711

Thomas Wyatt (c.1503–42), courtier and poet, lived during the turbulent years
of Henry VIII's divorce from Katherine of Aragon and is believed to have
developed strong feelings for Anne Boleyn before she became the King's mistress and then his queen in 1533. His fortunes at court were indeed marred by
Anne's own demise in 1536. Wyatt was arrested and committed to the Tower
of London, from where he watched Anne's execution on 19 May 1536.

Wyatt was the first poet to translate Petrarch into English and to imitate his
sonnets. The following sonnet transforms the onlooker's contemplative stance
in Petrarch's Sonnet 190 into a frustrating chase, which anticipates Shakespeare's use of the hunting metaphor in *Twelfth Night*. Wyatt adds to Petrarch
the new motif of worldly competition by stressing that the deer (Anne Boleyn?)
is now unattainable not because it embodies a spiritual ideal but because it
happens to be the private possession of a much more powerful hunter (the
King?). Although Orsino refuses to go hunting, he similarly imagines a time when
Cupid's 'golden shaft' will kill all other affections in Olivia's heart (Orsino's main
competitor at this point in the play being Olivia's memories of her dead
brother) and will instate him as its supreme ruler, its 'one self king' (see Key
Passages, **p. 142**).

Who so list[1] to hounte I know, where is a hynde.
but, as for me: helas,[2] I may no more.
the vayne travail[3] hath wried[4] me so sore.
I ame of theim, that farthest cometh behinde.
yet, may I, by no meanes, my weried maynde
Drawe from the Diere: but as she fleeth afore
fayntyng I folowe. I leve of[5] therefore:
Sithens in a nett I seke to hold the wynde.

1 [Durling's note.] According to Solinus (third century A.D.) three hundred years after Caesar's death
  white stags were found with collars inscribed "Noli me tangere, Caesaris sum" (Do not touch me, I
  am Caesar's). See also note 7 on page 32.
2 [Durling's note.] Emblems of steadfastness and chastity, respectively.
3 [Durling's note.] Probably God.

1 Wishes.
2 Alas.
3 Labour, toil.
4 Wearied, tired, fatigued.
5 I give up the chase.

Who list her hount: I put him owte of dowbte:
as well, as I: may spend his tyme in vain:
and, graven[6] with Diamondes, in letters plain:
There is written, her faier neck rounde abowte:
Noli me tangere:[7] for Cesars I ame:
and wylde for to holde: though I seme tame.

Edmund Spenser, 'Sonnet 67' (1595), in *Amoretti and Epithalamion*
(London: William Ponsonby, 1595), E3r

Edmund Spenser (1552?–1599), who translated poems by Petrarch when he was still a student, wrote his own sonnet sequence, called *Amoretti*, when he met Elizabeth Boyle, who became his wife in 1594. The sonnet became for Spenser a vehicle to record a very different experience from that of the stereotypical Petrarchan lover, since Elizabeth proved ultimately attainable, as suggested by the fact that the deer in the following sonnet gives itself up spontaneously.

In this respect, Shakespearean comedy is closer to Spenser than to Petrarch. Leonard Tennenhouse has effectively explained this important difference between the Petrarchan model and Shakespeare's reworking of it:

Petrarchan writing always situates us outside of the community of blood. By definition it always fixes the gaze on that which is metaphysically other than the gazer as the male attempts to make himself desirable to a female of a significantly higher station by representing his desire for her in extravagant terms. By way of contrast, Shakespearean comedy foregrounds the instrumentality of female desire. The multiple marriages at a comedy's conclusion make it seem as if desire had brought about a politically homogenous community. At the same time, desire also preserves the sexual hierarchy, for the subordination of wife to husband invariably invokes that of subject to king.[1]

According to Tennenhouse, the ending of *Twelfth Night*, like Spenser's sonnet, marks the re-establishment of patriarchal order, although patriarchal double standards are softened by the fact that, 'having passed into the body of a woman [Shakespeare's Olivia, or Spenser's Elizabeth, or Queen Elizabeth I], power becomes her gift to give'.[2] Hence, Spenser's fantasy of the woman–deer, who does not only become attainable but *chooses* to give herself up, and Sebastian's eagerness to accept the unsolicited advances of the rich and powerful lady Olivia in *Twelfth Night*, shortly after he meets her in Act 4.

---

6   Engraved.
7   Latin for 'touch me not', the words spoken by Jesus to Mary Magdalen as he resurrected from the dead (see The Gospel of Saint John, 20:17).

---

1   Leonard Tennenhouse, *Power on Display: The Politics of Shakespeare's Genres* (New York and London: Methuen, 1986), p. 62.
2   Tennenhouse, *Power on Display*, p. 68.

Lyke as a huntsman after weary chace,
Seeing the game from him escapt away:
sits downe to rest him in some shady place,
with panting hounds beguiled of their pray.

So after long pursuit and vaine assay,[3]
when I all weary had the chace forsooke,
the gentle deare returnd the selfe-same way,
thinking to quench her thirst at the next brooke.

There she beholding me with mylder looke,
sought not to fly, but fearelesse still did bide:[4]
till I in hand her yet halfe trembling tooke,
and with her owne goodwill hir fyrmely tyde.

Strange thing me seemd to see a beast so wyld,
so goodly[5] wonne with her owne will beguyld.

Petrarchan Conventions II: The Blazon

Francis Petrarch, 'Sonnet 199' (1334–74), in *Petrach's Lyric Poems*, trans. and ed. Robert M. Durling (Cambridge, Mass.: Harvard University Press, 1976), p. 344

This sonnet provides a representative example of the Petrarchan convention of the blazon: the poet's obsessive focus on the beloved's hand is reverential but at the same time possessive and patronising, as suggested by the combination of the vocabulary of religious praise and of economic gain ('sweet spoils'). Also typical of this convention is the attribution of ideal beauty to specific body parts, which are also endowed with the ability to hurt the poet. The beloved's hand is a beautiful hand, which is, however, clutched tightly around his heart, and her nails, although as beautiful as oriental pearls, have the power to inflict harsh and cruel wounds. These aspects of the Petrarchan convention of the blazon are particularly prominent in *Twelfth Night*, where Orsino praises Olivia's 'sweet perfections' while hoping to rule over her as 'one self king' (see Key Passages, **p. 142**), or in a later passage where he compares her cruel aloofness to 'a raven's heart within a dove' (see Key Passages, **p. 181**).

O beautiful hand that grasps my heart and encloses in a little space all
   my life, hand where Nature and Heaven have put all their art and all
   their care to do themselves honor,

3   Attempt (to capture the deer).
4   Wait.
5   Conveniently.

neat soft fingers, the color of five oriental pearls, and only bitter and cruel to wound me: to make me rich, Love now opportunely consents that you be naked.

White, light, and dear glove, that covered clear ivory and fresh roses: who ever saw in the world such sweet spoils?

Would I had again as much of that lovely veil! Oh the inconstancy of human life! Even this is theft, and one is coming who will deprive me of it.

Edmund Spenser, 'Epithalamion' (1595), in Amoretti and Epithalamion (London: William Ponsonby, 1595), G8v

Spenser wrote 'Epithalamion' ('marriage song') when he married Elizabeth Boyle in 1594. Through his marriage to Elizabeth, Spenser added new land to his share of the plantation of Munster in Ireland, which had been confiscated from the Irish in 1586. In 'Epithalamion', Spenser compares Elizabeth to precious stones and consumables rather than to landed property, possibly because, like Orsino, he disclaimed an interest in the 'dirty lands ... that fortune hath bestowed' (see Key Passages, **p. 163**) upon his beloved Elizabeth. However, both Orsino's reference to Olivia as his 'queen of gems' (see Key Passages, **p. 163**) and Spenser's use of the blazon reveal the proprietary claims that early modern husbands and hopeful suitors could lay upon the *objects* of their affections.

[...] TEll me ye merchants daughters did ye see
So fayre a creature in your towne before,
So sweet, so louely, and so mild as she,
Adornd with beautyes grace and vertues store,
Her goodly eyes lyke Saphyres shining bright,
Her forehead yuory white,
Her cheekes lyke apples which the sun hath rudded,[1]
Her lips lyke cherryes charming men to byte,
Her brest like to a bowle of creame vncrudded,[2]
Her paps[3] lyke lyllies budded,
Her snowie necke lyke to a marble towre,
And all her body like a pallace fayre,
Ascending vppe with many a stately stayre,
To honors seat and chastities sweet bowre. [...]

---

1   Made red.
2   Uncurdled.
3   Nipples or breasts.

William Shakespeare, 'Sonnet 130' (1609), in *Shake-speares Sonnets, Neuer before Imprinted* (London, 1609), H4r

Olivia's ironic allusion to the blazon in Act 1, Scene 5 (see Key Passages, **p. 150**) is not the only occasion when Shakespeare parodied this Petrarchan convention in order to emphasise, by contrast, the genuine, unmediated quality of his own language of praise. By pointing out how different his beloved (the so-called 'Dark Lady') is from the hackneyed Petrarchan ideal, Shakespeare makes her, and his feelings for her, seem more real.

MY Mistres eyes are nothing like the Sunne,
Currall[1] is farre more red, then her lips red,
If snow be white why then her brests are dun:[2]
If haires be wiers,[3] black wiers grow on her head:
I haue seene Roses damaskt,[4] red and white,
But no such Roses see I in her cheekes,
And in some perfumes is there more delight,
Then in the breath that from my Mistres reekes.
I loue to heare her speake, yet well I know,
That Musicke hath a farre more pleasing sound:
I graunt I neuer saw a goddesse goe,
My Mistres when shee walkes treads on the ground.
   And yet by heauen I thinke my loue as rare,
   As any she beli'd with false compare.[5]

1   Coral.
2   Dull greyish brown.
3   Wires.
4   A variety of rose imported from Damascus.
5   Showed to be false, artificial, by comparison.

2

Interpretations

Critical History

The Rise of the Critical Tradition

Seventeenth-century readers and theatre-goers had eyes only for Malvolio. As mentioned above, John Manningham's short eyewitness account of the production that took place on 2 February 1602 in the Great Hall at the Middle Temple (see Contextual Overview, p. 7) pays almost undivided attention to the 'good practice' perpetrated by Maria and her associates at Malvolio's expenses. Also significant is the fact that in King Charles I's copy of the Second Folio edition of Shakespeare's plays (1632) the title is crossed out and replaced by Malvolio's name. Similarly, when Leonard Digges, an admirer of Shakespeare who had contributed a dedicatory poem to the First Folio of 1623, wrote more prefatory verses for Benson's 1640 edition of Shakespeare's *Poems*, he reported that 'The Cockpit[1] Galleries, Boxes, all are full / To heare *Maluolio* that crosse garter'd Gull'.[2] Malvolio's popularity was at least partly due to the rise of the so-called 'comedy of humours', a dramatic form first introduced by Shakespeare's fellow dramatist Ben Jonson in the early 1600s, which aimed to expose the *psychological* excesses induced by a *physiological* imbalance in the bodily fluids identified by Galenic medical lore as 'humours' (see Contextual Overview, pp. 10–11).

Most of Shakespeare's plays, including *Twelfth Night*, lost their appeal in the second half of the seventeenth century, due to the rise of neo-classical standards of dramatic decorum, which demanded uniformity of tone, register and subject matter. Lofty and sombre style was accordingly deemed suitable for tragedies, while light-hearted humour, colloquialisms and informal dialogue were to be used only in comedies. Shakespeare's *Twelfth Night* mingles Viola's poetical lines with Feste's popular songs and Viola and Olivia's bereavement with Sir Toby's penchant for cakes and ale. Predictably, when late-seventeenth- and eighteenth-century critics wrote about *Twelfth Night*, they found it disconcertingly inadequate, because of its failure to comply with the current taste for a decorous distinction between tragedy and comedy, high and low style, serious and humorous characters. When, for example, French author and philosopher Voltaire (1694–1778)

---

1   London theatre, also known as 'The Phoenix', built in 1617 in Drury Lane.
2   William Shakespeare, *Poems* (London, 1640), *4r, ll. 10–11.

wrote about Shakespeare, he famously argued that he 'had a genius full of force and fecundity, of the natural and the sublime, without the least glimmer of good taste and without the least knowledge of [neo-classical] rules'.[3] Samuel Johnson, prominent eighteenth-century scholar and man of letters, promoted more moderately neo-classical views and praised Shakespeare for the strength of his poetic imagination but faulted him for his lack of stylistic sophistication. He was particularly unimpressed by the main characters in *Twelfth Night* and famously referred to Viola as an 'excellent schemer, never at a loss'.[4] Charlotte Lennox anticipated Johnson's views on *Twelfth Night* by dismissing its main characters as 'unaccountable', 'improbable' and 'ridiculous' (see Early Criticism, **pp. 50–1**).

And yet, even while eighteenth-century writers and critics were busy establishing how Shakespeare fell short of neo-classical standards of formal and stylistic decorum, popular pressure groups, such as the 'Shakespeare Ladies Club', actively campaigned to revive Shakespeare's popularity on the stage. As early as the 1730s, Shakespeare started to be identified as the poet who best represented the values and aspirations of the English middle classes. The appropriation of Shakespeare in the eighteenth century, while involving a radical rewriting of his plays on the stage and a decorous normalisation of their language in a string of collected editions, went hand in hand with the rise of Bardolatry, the cult of Shakespeare as national poet.[5] The erection of a monument to Shakespeare in Poets' Corner in Westminster Abbey in 1741 and the Jubilee organised by the famous Shakespearian actor, David Garrick, in Stratford-upon-Avon in 1769 were symptomatic of a wider attempt to challenge neo-classicism, which was intimately associated with French political and cultural supremacy in Europe. The Romantic movement, especially in England and Germany at the turn of the eighteenth and the nineteenth century, developed in conscious opposition to French neo-classicism and saw in Shakespeare the champion of a national literature which derived its strength and originality from native traditions as opposed to classical models.[6] Hence, the emphasis that Romantic critics, like A. W. Schlegel, T. S. Coleridge, William Hazlitt (see Early Criticism, **pp. 51–2**), Anna Jameson (see Early Criticism, **pp. 52–3**) and Charles Lamb placed on Shakespeare's ability to overcome the artificial confines of artistic categories that distort or overlook far more important truths belonging to the realm of nature and the imagination. While Hazlitt highlighted the beauty and psychological depth of Viola's character, Jameson was the first critic to draw attention to her moral and psychological stature, which challenges a patriarchal understanding of women's innate inferiority to men. The Romantics also changed the way in which Malvolio's character

---

3   Voltaire, *Lettres philosophiques* (1734), quoted in Jonathan Bate (ed.), *The Romantics on Shakespeare* (London: Penguin, 1992), pp. 3–4.

4   Samuel Johnson (ed.), *The Plays of William Shakespeare, in eight volumes, with the corrections and illustrations of various commentators; to which are added notes by Sam. Johnson*, Vol. II (London, 1765), p. 358. Johnson justifies his view of Viola's character as follows: 'Viola seems to have formed a very deep design with very little premeditation: she is thrown by shipwreck on an unknown coast, hears tht the prince is a batchelor, and resolves to supplant the lady whom he courts' (p. 357).

5   For more details, see Michael Dobson, *The Making of the National Poet: Shakespeare, Adaptation and Authorship, 1660–1769* (Oxford: Clarendon Press, 1992).

6   For more details, see Jonathan Bate, *The Romantics on Shakespeare* (London: Penguin, 1992), especially pp. 1–35.

had been understood by earlier critics and theatre audiences. Charles Lamb, for example, saw Malvolio as a tragic, rather than a farcical, misfit. In his 'Essay on Some of the Old Actors' (1822),[7] he explains that his views on Malvolio were profoundly affected by Robert Bensley's sympathetic interpretation of this role some twenty years earlier. Scholars have now demonstrated that Lamb was either misremembering Bensley's performance, which he saw some twenty years before he wrote his famous essay, or he was deliberately changing what he saw to support his reading of Malvolio's character. Whether or not Lamb's account of Bensley's performance was a misrepresentation of what he saw, his views on Malvolio proved profoundly influential towards the end of the nineteenth century, when Henry Irving performed Malvolio as a tragic and dignified character (see The Work in Performance, p. 104) and in the second half of the twentieth century, when Malvolio's suffering became an integral element of increasingly dark productions of *Twelfth Night* (see The Work in Performance, pp. 106–7). The cult of Viola was also extremely influential throughout the nineteenth century. As a result, later critics like Émile Montégut and William Archer (see Early Criticism, pp. 53–6) developed a tendency to privilege the poetic and philosophical aspects of *Twelfth Night* over its comic elements.

The cult of Shakespeare as the national poet and the popularity of character studies introduced by the Romantics lasted well into the twentieth century. A. C. Bradley combined a biographical interest in Shakespeare and a critical interest in his characters by claiming that Feste represents Shakespeare's own viewpoint in the world of the play.[8] Although now dated, this approach retains a strong popular appeal, as Trevor Nunn's 1996 film clearly shows (see The Work in Performance, pp. 111 and 130–1). The attention that Romantic critics had paid to the plays of Shakespeare as poetry rather than drama proved even more resilient and played a crucial role in the rise of an influential movement, called New Criticism. Critics like G. Wilson Knight (1932) paid an unprecedented level of attention to Shakespeare's use of recurrent images, symbols and verbal and thematic patterns in *Twelfth Night*, which gave the play a sense of organic unity.[9] While harking back to the Romantic period, the New Critics' interest in Shakespeare's language anticipated later critics, who, like Feste – Olivia's 'corrupter of words' (see Key Passages, p. 175) – highlighted a fundamental instability in the language of the play. If a new critical appreciation of the complex but ultimately harmonic quality of Shakespeare's poetic vision survived in mid-twentieth-century critics like Frank Halliday (see Modern Criticism, pp. 57–9), recent critics have tended to focus on the ways in which *Twelfth Night* challenges and deconstructs linguistic *and* social categories, like class and gender. Although, as the next section explains, much recent criticism of *Twelfth Night* has focused on these two issues, Shakespeare's language has continued to attract critical attention. A representative example is Jonathan Bate's perceptive exploration of Ovidian influences on Shakespeare's dramatic imagination (see Modern Criticism, pp. 59–63).

7   Extracts of this essay are reproduced in D. J. Palmer (ed.), *Shakespeare: Twelfth Night* (Basingstoke: Macmillan, 1972), pp. 36–48.
8   A. C. Bradley, 'Feste the Jester', in *A Book of Homage to Shakespeare*, ed. Israel Gollancz (Oxford: Humphrey Milford, 1916), pp. 164–9.
9   G. Wilson Knight, *The Shakespearian Tempest* (London: Humphrey Milford, 1932), especially pp. 121–30.

Modern Critical Approaches

The distinction between early and modern critical responses to Shakespeare's *Twelfth Night* is inevitably arbitrary because, as pointed out above, early critics often anticipated later approaches. However, a conceptual and ideological break did occur when Shakespeare's representation of gender and class distinctions started to be regarded as inherently problematic and unstable. In 1947, poet and essayist W. H. Auden explicitly connected the fact that 'society in *Twelfth Night* is beginning to smell gamey' to the dominant role that women play in it: 'the women', he disconcertingly argued, 'are the only people left who have any will, which is the sign of a decadent society' (see Modern Criticism, **pp. 63–4**). Auden was not alone in starting to wonder whether Illyria had far more to do with a permanent state of disorder than with the festive inversions associated with seasonal holidays, such as the twelfth night after Christmas (see Introduction, **pp. 2–3**), throughout the middle ages and at the beginning of modernity. Holiday periods routinely ushered in the temporary subversion of the social hierarchy, which involved the appointment of a Lord of Misrule, but was then followed by the re-establishment of order and normality.[10] Even C. L. Barber's famous study on *Shakespeare's Festive Comedy*, which overtly argues that *Twelfth Night* celebrates the clarification of mistaken identities and misdirected passions after a period of disorder and licentiousness, betrays some anxiety about the assumed stability of gender distinctions. While Barber sees disguise as 'playful' and ultimately 'benign', he welcomes Sebastian's willingness to fight in Act 4 as a salutary contrast to Viola's inability to live up to a traditional ideal of aggressive masculinity: 'To see this manly reflex is delightful – almost a relief' (see Modern Criticism, **p. 65**). The parenthetical remark introduced by the dash suggests the extent to which Barber is troubled by the prospect that gender districtions may not be safely re-established by the end of the play. Class is also a sore point for Barber. His reference to Malvolio as a 'profane intruder' was soon to be challenged by later critics who came to regard *Twelfth Night* as a radical exploration of social tensions and class struggle in Elizabethan England.

To Be 'as Hungry as the Sea': Class and the Circulation of Material Desires

Mid-twentieth-century critics like John W. Draper started to point out that *Twelfth Night* is less a play about love than a play about economic matters and social security.[11] If the opening scene ushers readers and spectators into a world of courtly leisure and pastimes, the second scene foregrounds Viola's destitution and her need to find suitable employment. In Act 1, Scene 2, Orsino

---

10 Other readings of *Twelfth Night* as a dark comedy abound in the next two decades. See, for example, Jan Kott, *Shakespeare Our Contemporary* (London: Methuen, 1964) and Clifford Leech, *Twelfth Night and Shakespearean Comedy* (Toronto: University of Toronto Press, 1965).
11 John W. Draper, *The Twelfth Night of Shakespeare's Audience* (Stanford, Calif.: Stanford University Press, 1950).

and Olivia are identified as potential patrons, and Viola's 'worth' is measured according to her ability to entertain, divert and please the rich and powerful. Similarly, Feste expects to receive food and shelter from Olivia and money from the other characters who show appreciation for his wit. Viola's remark about Feste in Act 3, Scene 1 – 'This fellow is wise enough to play the fool' (see Key Passages, p. 176) – suggests that Feste's character belongs to the humanist tradition associated with Erasmus, the author of a seminal book called *The Praise of Folly* (1509), who championed the paradox according to which true wisdom stems from the realisation of the limitations of rational knowledge. However, Feste is also a professional entertainer, and, as Viola realises, his wit is 'full of labour' and he must adjust it to '[t]he quality of persons and the time' and the mood of those 'on whom he jests' (see Key Passages, p. 176). In an influential article written in 1969, Muriel Bradbrook argued that Feste, like the professional clown in Shakespeare's theatre, 'was no longer a challenger but a servant'.[12]

Still focussing on the social fabric of Shakespeare's comic vision, Elliot Krieger pointed out how the level of economic and social power enjoyed by Shakespeare's characters in *Twelfth Night* determines the play's outcome. Far from reflecting universal values like love, truth and natural harmony, as many Romantic critics had claimed in the nineteenth century, the comic resolution in *Twelfth Night* reflects the specific interests of those who have the power to impose their fantasies on others. According to Krieger, 'there is no fundamental difference between Malvolio's fantasy of narcissistic withdrawal into a world in which he can be Count Malvolio . . . and Orsino's narcissistic withdrawal into the Petrarchan conventions and the beds of flowers'. Their fantasies, as Krieger continues, 'differ only in the social reaction and response that they elicit' (see Modern Criticism, p. 69). Krieger takes his distance from C. L. Barber's conclusion that Malvolio is a 'profane intruder' and the structure of Shakespearean comedy a ritualistic 'release' of disruptive energies leading to 'clarification'. 'The conclusion', as Krieger explains, 'confirms the aristocratic fantasy . . . that clarification is achieved when people are released from indulgence and restored to the degree of greatness with which they were born' (see Modern Criticism, p. 70). Krieger's approach has in turn been queried by critics who no longer regard class as an absolute determinant of subjectivity. Cristina Malcolmson, for example, believes that 'Viola is never simply a noble person masquerading as a gentle person without wealth' and that 'her rendition of masculine gentility subtly suggests that all social roles can be impersonated'.[13] However, the approach championed by Draper, Bradbrook and Krieger had a strong influence on what Penny Gay describes as the 'dark' productions of *Twelfth Night* in the 1980s (see The Work in Performance, pp. 106–7), which interpreted the play as a realistic exploration of ambition, greed and narcissistic desire.

Despite the popularity of increasingly dark and realistic productions focusing

12 Muriel Bradbrook, 'Robert Armin and *Twelfth Night*', in *Shakespeare the Craftsman* (London: Chatto & Windus, 1969), p. 232.
13 Cristina Malcolmson, ' "What You Will": Social Mobility and Gender in *Twelfth Night*', in Valerie Wayne (ed.), *The Matter of Difference: Materialist Feminist Criticism of Shakespeare* (Hemel Hempstead: Harvester Wheatsheaf, 1991), p. 37.

on issues of social rank and power, the 1980s ushered in a new critical approach inspired by Russian theorist Mikhail Bakhtin, who regarded the carnival and carnivalesque elements in late medieval and early modern literature as crucial sources of transgressive energy through which society cyclically allowed temporary outbursts of disorder and excess in order to release social tensions and regenerated itself.[14] Michael Bristol, for example, associated the rowdy and sanguine Sir Toby with the principle of Carnival, which celebrates the material aspects of existence connected to eating and drinking over the purely intellectual and moral life of the mind, and the dour steward Malvolio, with the principle of Lent, which curbs bodily excesses and enforces restraint. According to Bristol, disorder in *Twelfth Night* is never completely exorcised by the re-establishment of order at the end of the play. As he puts it, 'the battle of angry Carnival and sullen, vindictive Lent is not concluded in the represented world of Illyria, nor is it ever concluded in the world offstage' (see Modern Criticism, p. 73). Even before Bakhtin's utopian views on the regenerative and reforming function of carnival were applied to Shakespearian drama, they had been radically qualified by seminal studies, according to which carnival traditions, far from expressing the autonomy of popular culture, were carefully regulated by the elite to reinforce social solidarity.[15] As a result early modern scholars since the mid-1980s have been far more cautious in identifying carnivalesque disorder with genuine transgression.[16] Some of them have usefully pointed out how festivity in Elizabethan and Jacobean England was becoming increasingly divorced from the lower classes. David Wiles, for example, has noted that 'the land-owing aristocracy began to use rites associated with the land to lay claim to authentic Englishness in opposition to the urban and bourgeois Puritan movement'.[17] In London, traditional festivities were also associated with the ruling elite. Crucially, King James I issued a proclamation in 1618, now commonly known as 'The Book of Sports', in order to protect and preserve popular holidays and pastimes from the polemical attacks of increasingly powerful Puritan and Parliamentary groups, thus showing the extent to which the ruling elite had appropriated festivity for its own political ends. These revisionist theories about the function of carnivalesque elements in Shakespeare's plays account for apparent 'anomalies', including the fact that Sir Toby, the closest counterpart to the Lord of Misrule who was appointed to preside over the festivities during periods of seasonal holidays in the middle ages and

---

14 Bakhtin's best-known study of late medieval carnivals and popular culture is *Rabelais and His World*. For accessible introductions to Bakhtin, see Sue Vice, *Introducing Bakhtin* (Manchester: Manchester University Press, 1997), Simon Dentith, *Bakhtinian Thought: An Introductory Reader* (London: Routledge, 1995) and Pam Morris (ed.), *The Bakhtin Reader: Selected Writings of Bakhtin, Medvedev and Voloshinov* (London: Arnold, 1994). See also Modern Criticism, pp. 70–3.

15 See, for example, Peter Burke, *Popular Culture in Early Modern Europe* (London: Temple Smith, 1978), and Emmanuel Le Roy Ladurie, *Le Carnaval de Romans* (1979), recently reissued in translation as *Carnival in Romans: Mayhem and Massacre in a French City*, trans. Mary Feeney (London: Phoenix, 2003).

16 See, for example, Peter Stallybrass and Allon White, *The Politics and Poetics of Transgression* (London: Methuen, 1986).

17 David Wiles, 'The Carnivalesque in *A Midsummer Night's Dream*', in Ronald Knowles (ed.), *Shakespeare and Carnival: After Bakhtin* (Manchester: Manchester University Press, 1998). Other essays in this collection usefully explore the benefits and limitations of a Bakhtinian approach to Shakespeare.

early modern period, is a member of the aristocracy, while Malvolio, who polices and curbs Sir Toby's excesses, is a steward in Olivia's household. Other scholars, like Karin Coddon and Keir Elam, have similarly shown that the notion of carnivalesque disorder and the grotesque body can be rewardingly applied to *Twelfth Night*, provided that enough attention is paid to the social and cultural context within which such categories were used. Coddon, for example, points out that Malvolio and Feste are indeed even more transgressive and disruptive than Sir Toby, who is overtly associated with the Carnival principle (see Modern Criticism, **pp. 73–5**). Elam instead continues to celebrate the utopian potential of Sir Toby's grotesque body but points out that Orsino's equally indecorous appetites effectively feminise and degrade him, since 'the "appetite" charge . . . was an essential ingredient of early modern misogyny' (see Modern Criticism, **pp. 75–80**).

In the light of Coddon's and Elam's studies, one could add that if *Twelfth Night* is not an entirely festive comedy, it is not an entirely conservative social fantasy either. Sir Toby and Maria's marriage transgresses social boundaries; Feste's refusal to account for his whereabouts highlights an interesting site of social resistance; and Orsino's reassurance that Sebastian's blood is 'right noble' (see Key Passages, **p. 183**) seems a slightly belated attempt to gloss over the differences in rank and status between the twins and their aristocratic partners. Cristina Malcolmson has interestingly observed that Orsino's remark signals the need to neutralise social instability rather than its successful containment. Malcolmson also reflects on the fact that *Twelfth Night* is a play that 'relentlessly excludes the figure of the merchant, although in the sources, the father of Viola and Sebastian is almost always a merchant'.[18] As explained in 'Contextual Overview', an increasingly large and powerful group of merchants and professionals achieved social status through wealth rather than lineage in Shakespeare's time, thus challenging traditional social distinctions. Malcolmson is certainly right in regarding the absence of merchants in a play like *Twelfth Night* as a remarkable and significant omission. However, Malcolmson overlooks the fact that Antonio is quite clearly Orsino's enemy because of the role he played in what the First Officer describes as a trade war in Act 1, Scene 5: 'this is that Antonio / That took the *Phoenix* and her freight from Candy . . . / When your young nephew Titus lost his leg' (see Key Passages, **p. 178**). Besides, *Twelfth Night* is strewn with references to the fabulous wealth accumulated by merchants who traded with the Middle East and Far East Asia. Sir Toby refers to Maria as 'my metal of India' (see Key Passages, **p. 167**), while Maria describes the unnatural grin on Malvolio's face at Act 3, Scene 2, lines 74–5 by referring to a new map of the East Indies. After the gulling of Malvolio, Fabian stresses how much he looks forward to seeing the dour steward courting his lady Olivia in yellow stocking and cross-gartered by saying that he would 'not give [his] part of this sport for a pension of thousands to be paid from the Sophy' (2.5.173–4). The Sophy was the title used to refer to the Shah of Persia. The fabulous wealth of his court and his generosity towards Western merchants had been the subject of two contemporary reports about Sir Anthony Shirley, who worked as the Sophy's ambassador between 1599

---

18 Malcolmson, p. 50. For a full bibliographical reference, see Further Reading, **p. 192**.

and 1601, and a collaborative play called *The Travels of the Three English Brothers*, which was published in 1607. More generally, Illyria (modern-day Croatia) was under Venetian influence, and early modern Venice was one of the most powerful trading centres in Europe, a liminal city geographically and culturally poised between the Christian West and the Muslim East.

The cumulative effect of the frequent references to the East included in *Twelfth Night*, combined with the recurrent imagery of the sea, of shipwrecks and sudden changes of fortune, should not be underestimated. Feste's sarcastic allusion to the fact that the uncertain lifestyle of merchants who accumulate and lose large fortunes at sea would suit Orsino's inconstancy of character (see Key Passages, **p. 163**) establishes yet another connection between the world of trade and commerce. It is, therefore, worth wondering whether, rather than repressing or exorcising anxieties about upward mobility in Elizabethan England, *Twelfth Night* in fact defies any mechanical association between status and fortune, social and personal powers, rank and self-worth.

'I Am Not What I Am': Gender and Sexual Identity

In 1959, C. L. Barber had interpreted Shakespeare's 'handling of boy actors playing women, and playing women pretending to be men' in *Twelfth Night* as a 'playful aberration' safely neutralised by Sebastian's timely arrival in the second half of the play (see Modern Criticism, **p. 65**). What struck Barber in 1959 as a providential turn in the plot seemed to Juliet Dusinberre a regrettable fall from grace in 1975. According to Dusinberre, Viola 'is diminished by a return to a world where she must be Orsino's lady', because her male disguise granted her a 'momentary freedom' from the constraints imposed by society upon women (see Modern Criticism, **p. 82**). Dusinberre also anticipated later critics included in this guide by pointing out that both Sir Andrew's and Viola's reluctance to fight in Act 3, Scene 4 shows that '[b]reaches of themselves bestow no bravery on either the natural inmate [Sir Andrew] or the usurper [Viola]' and that '[b]oth "men" need instruction in manhood' (see Modern Criticism, **p. 81**).

Adopting a new historicist approach,[19] Stephen Greenblatt argued that gender categories are indeed a cultural construct and that *Twelfth Night* should be read alongside other early modern legal, medical and religious texts, which affected how gender distinctions were perceived by Shakespeare's contemporaries. Greenblatt noticed that gender and sexual instabilities were not confined to the fictive world of Shakespeare's Illyria and to Shakespeare's appropriation of the classical model of the comedy of mistaken identities. According to the Galenic model of human physiology (see Contextual Overview, **pp. 10–11**), male and female sexual organs were structurally identical, and sexual identity was

---

19 New historicism is a recent critical approach, which regards literary (and dramatic) *texts* as *historical*, that is, intrinsically bound to the context within which they were first written (and performed), and *history* as a *text*, or, as the collective body of documents interpreted by historians in order to make sense of the past, which is inevitably *reconstructed* from the historians' own standpoint, rather than objectively *recovered* (see also Modern Criticism, **pp. 82–3**).

determined by 'differential homology',[20] that is by the different outcome of the struggle between male and female principles within the same individual. As Greenblatt explains, 'predominance' rather than 'exclusion' of one of the two principles determined sexual identity, and 'predominance was never . . . absolute'. This implied, in Greenblatt's own words, 'the persistent doubleness, the inherent twinship of all individuals' (see Modern Criticism, **p. 88**) Greenblatt believes that *Twelfth Night* exploits the Galenic model of 'differential homology' between the sexes not only by allowing two persons, one male and one female, to have 'One face, one voice, one habit' (see Key Passages, **p. 181**), but also by procrastinating Cesario's metamorphosis into Viola beyond the final scene. While Dusinberre regretted such transformation, Greenblatt pointed out that it is never enacted. Furthermore, still according to Greenblatt, the congenital superiority which Galenic physiology granted to the male body and the early modern practice of casting boy actors to play female roles are jointly responsible for the fact that *Twelfth Night*, in particular, and early modern drama, in general, reinforce a cultural bias towards the emergence of male identity and 'an apparent homoeroticism in all sexuality' (see Modern Criticism, **p. 90**).

Greenblatt's views have proved tremendously influential. However, later critics have departed in interesting ways from his influential essay, either by qualifying his approach or by proposing alternative models of analysis. Those who qualify Greenblatt's approach have pointed out how Galenic medical discourse may not necessarily be the most relevant context for a better and historically sound understanding of Shakespeare's representation of gendered and sexual identity in *Twelfth Night*. Lorna Hutson, for example, believes that

> the capacity to plot, write, and *be able to make use* of the erudition and wit of a comedy such as *Twelfth Night* might in itself be more central to sixteenth- and seventeenth-century conceptions of what it meant to 'be a man' than any theory derived from Galen (see Modern Criticism, **pp. 97–100**).

It is worth stressing that Shakespeare's rhetorical abilities and his successful career as a playwright and shareholder of his acting company allowed him to earn enough money to apply for a coat of arms and to buy New Place, the largest property in Stratford in 1596. Shakespeare, like Viola, used his rhetorical skills to secure the good will of powerful patrons, including Henry Wriothesley, 3rd Earl of Southampton, the dedicatee of *Venus and Adonis* (1593) and *The Rape of Lucrece* (1594), and the Earls of Pembroke and Montgomery, the dedicatees of the First Folio (1623), who apparently bestowed 'much favour' upon the author when he was still alive.

Other critics have qualified Greenblatt's approach to *Twelfth Night* by identifying further contexts that shed light on Shakespeare's representation of gender and sexual identity. Elizabeth I's long reign (1558–1603), for example, challenged contemporary views according to which women were unfit to rule. In some cases,

---

20 Stephen Greenblatt, 'Fiction and Friction', p. 81. For a full bibliographical reference, see Modern Criticism, **p. 82**.

the presence of a female monarch on the English throne exacerbated patriarchal double standards. Even Edmund Tilney, who dedicated *The Flower of Friendship* (see Contemporary Documents, **pp. 19–21**) to Queen Elizabeth, refuted the radical views about marriage voiced by Isabella (Spanish for Elizabeth). His dedication can, therefore, be read both as a tribute aimed at gaining the Queen's patronage and protection and as an indirect comment on her repeated failure to marry. Far less diplomatic was John Knox's treatise, *A Blast of the Trumpet against the Monstrous Regiment of Women* (1558), which was untimely published shortly before Elizabeth's accession to the throne. However, Elizabeth's long reign was also a catalyst for a contentious debate, the so-called Woman Controversy, which produced countless pamphlets and tracts, polemical statements and rebuttals about the role of women in early modern society. One of these pamphlets, called 'Jane Anger, Her Protection of Women' (1589), offers an interesting context for Orsino and Cesario's exchange in Act 2, Scene 4. As Cristina Malcolmson has pointed out, this pamphlet tackles similar issues, as it endeavours to prove that women can love as passionately as men, while condemning 'men's stomachs' for being 'so queasy, as do they taste but twice of one dish they straight surfeit'.[21]

Changing views on the family (see Contextual Overview, **pp. 8–10**) represent another interesting area of inquiry for scholars interested in reading *Twelfth Night* historically. Catherine Belsey, for example, considers how 'the contest for the meaning of the family . . . momentarily unfixed the existing system of differences' upon which gender distinctions had traditionally rested. Unlike Greenblatt, Belsey believes that, rather than supporting a patriarchal bias towards the emergence of male identity, *Twelfth Night* grants its readers and audiences a glimpse of 'a mode of being, which is not a-sexual, nor bi-sexual, but which disrupts the system of differences on which sexual stereotyping depends' (see Modern Criticism, **p. 92**). William Dodd reinforces Belsey's conclusion by drawing attention to the fact that the twins' reunion represents the climactic focus of the dramatic action, thus encouraging the audience to see neither heterosexual nor homoerotic attachments, but rather the 'reciprocal enthralment of an androgynous sister and an androgynous brother' (see Modern Criticism, **p. 95**), as an ideal mode of being, narcissistically poised before gendered and sexual individuation.

This introduction has placed a considerable amount of emphasis on aspects of *Twelfth Night* which are directly related to distinctions of gender, sexuality and class because they have attracted sustained attention since the mid-twentieth century. However, other significant studies than the ones discussed here or included in the extracts in the next section are listed in the annotated bibliography provided at the end of this guide (see Further Reading, **pp. 189–94**). Although the role played by the circulation of desire and by the interplay between erotic attraction, rank and lineage is still central to current readings of *Twelfth Night*,[22] another emerging area of interest is the range of economic, political and religious connotations associated with the geographical location of the play in the

---

21 Malcolmson, p. 40. For a full bibliographical reference, see Further Reading, **p. 192**.
22 See, for example, David Schalkwyk, 'Love and Service in *Twelfth Night* and *The Sonnets*', *Shakespeare Quarterly*, 56 (2005), pp. 76–100.

north-eastern basin of the Mediterranean Sea.[23] This development in current critical responses to *Twelfth Night* is at least partly in keeping with a more general tendency to reconsider Shakespeare and early modern drama in relation to contemporary representations of literal and metaphorical borders between East and West, and between Islam and Christianity.

23 See, for example, Goran Stanivukovic, 'Illyria Revisited: Shakespeare and the Eastern Adriatic', in Tom Clayton, Susan Brock, Vincente Forès (eds), *Shakespeare and the Mediterranean* (Newark, Del.: University of Delaware Press, 2004), pp. 400–15.

Early Criticism

From **Charlotte Lennox, Shakespear Illustrated: Or the Novels and histories, on which the Plays of Shakespear are Founded . . .** (1753), 3 vols (London: Millar, 1753), Vol. I, pp. 243–50

Charlotte Lennox, née Ramsay (1730/31?–1804), was a prolific writer, translator and critic, who famously argued that some of Shakespeare's sources were better structured than his plays and that his characters and plot lines often lacked credibility. Lennox's critical views on Shakespeare were affected by eighteenth-century literary and moral standards, which privileged the neo-classical rules of probability and decorum over invention. The following extract also shows that the neo-classical tenet, according to which Art should imitate Nature, reflects aesthetic as well as political assumptions which may no longer seem 'natural' to us. Lennox, for example, deems 'the Passion of *Olivia* [. . .] for the disguised Lady' and 'the Violence of [Antonio]'s Friendship for Sebastian' as 'unnatural', and therefore 'highly improbable', 'unaccountably extravagant', and ultimately 'ridiculous'. Lennox's views on *Twelfth Night* can, therefore, help us understand not only how notions of what seems 'natural' or 'unnatural' have changed, but also how Nature is often invoked to legitimise sets of values, which, far from being 'natural' are, in fact, the product of a specific historical and cultural context.

[. . . Viola] all of a sudden takes up an unaccountable Resolution to serve the young Batchelor-Duke in the Habit of a Man. . . .

A very natural Scheme this for a beautiful and virtuous young Lady to throw off all at once the Modesty and Reservedness of her Sex, mix among Men, herself disguised like one; and, prest by no Necessity, influenced by no Passion, expose herself to all the dangerous Consequences of so unworthy and shameful a Situation.

[. . .]

But what are *Viola's* Motives for so rash an Enterprize? She is neither in love with or abandoned by the Duke, and cannot reasonably propose to herself any Advantage by thus hazarding her Virtue and Fame: His Person she had never seen;

his Affections she was informed were engaged; what then were her Views and Designs by submitting to be his Attendant?

[. . .]

The Passion of *Olivia*, the Duke's Mistress, for the disguised Lady, is attended with Circumstances that make it appear highly improbable and ridiculous: She is represented as a noble and virtuous Lady, overwhelmed with Grief for the Death of a beloved Brother; her Grief indeed is of a very extraordinary Nature. . . .

This sorrowful Lady, however, makes her first Appearance in the Company of a Jester, with whom she is extremely diverted; and notwithstanding her Vow which we are told of in another Place, not to admit the Sight or Company of Men, she permits the Duke's Page to approach her, shews him her Face, and bandies Jests and smart Sentences with all the lively Wit of an airy Coquet.

Then follows her sudden Passion for the supposed Youth, which is as suddenly declared, without any of those Emotions that Bashfulness, Delicacy, and a Desire of preserving the Decorum her Sex and Birth oblige her to observe, must raise in the Mind of a Woman of Honour.

Had *Shakespear*, by mixing so much Levity in the Character of *Olivia*, designed a Satire on the Sex, he would have certainly led us by some Reflexions on the Inconsistency of her Behaviour to have made that Inference; but this is not the Case; for *Olivia* is every where highly extolled for her Virtues.

[. . .]

[W]hy should the Duke, a sovereign Prince who so passionately adored *Olivia*, all at once take a Resolution to marry *Viola*, a Stranger whom he had never seen in her proper Garb, because she had served him in Disguise; 'tis absurd to suppose he could in a Moment pass from the most extravagant Passion imaginable for *Olivia*, to one no less extravagant, for a Person, whom till then he had always believed to be a Boy; and 'tis also highly improbable that a great Prince would so suddenly resolve to marry a Girl, who had no other Title to his Favour than an imprudent Passion, which had carried her greatly beyond the Bounds of Decency.

[. . .]

Antonio, a Sea Captain, delivers *Sebastian* from the Fury of the Waves; the Youth being obstinately determined to go to the Court, *Antonio*, who in a Sea-fight had done great Mischief to the Duke's Galleys, resolves, out of the Violence of his Friendship, to follow him thither, notwithstanding he knew his Life would be in manifest Danger if he was seen in *Illyria*.

How unaccountably extravagant is this Kindness in a Stranger?

From **William Hazlitt, 'Twelfth Night: Or, What You Will'**, in *Characters of Shakespear's Plays* (London: Hunter, 1817), pp. 257–9

William Hazlitt (1778–1830), Romantic essayist, critic and commentator, openly repudiated the neo-classical legacy of eighteenth-century commentators, such as Charlotte Lennox and Samuel Johnson, and argued that Shakespeare's greatest achievement in *Twelfth Night* was not his exposition of Malvolio's overweening ambition but the poetic 'sweetness' of Viola's lines and the 'unchecked' quality of the lovers' passions. Hazlitt found in Shakespeare's comedy a congenial representation of love as a type of folly which infects the body like the plague but brings enlightenment and fires the imagination. While estranged from his first wife, Hazlitt fell in love with Sarah Walker. Contemporary accounts by those who knew him and Hazlitt's own writings describe his feelings for Sarah as a blinding passion, which verged on madness and distraction. Like Orsino, Hazlitt pursued Sarah to great personal and emotional costs; like Orsino, he ended up marrying somebody else. Hazlitt's philosophical beliefs, his literary taste and his first-hand experience of the ravaging power of erotic infatuation made him one of the most sympathetic readers of *Twelfth Night* of his generation.

[. . .] Shakespear's comedy is of a pastoral and poetical cast. Folly is indigenous to the soil, and shoots out with native, happy, unchecked luxuriance. Absurdity has every encouragement afforded it; and nonsense has room to flourish in. Nothing is stunted by the churlish, icy hand of indifference or severity. The poet runs riot in a conceit, and idolises a quibble. His whole object is to turn the meanest or rudest objects to a pleasurable account. The relish which he has of a pun, or of the quaint humour of a low character, does not interfere with the delight with which he describes a beautiful image, or the most refined love. The clown's forced jests do not spoil the sweetness of the character of Viola; the same house is big enough to hold Malvolio, the Countess, Maria, Sir Toby, and Sir Andrew Ague-cheek. [. . .] Much as we like Shakespear's comedies, we cannot agree with Dr Johnson that they are better than his tragedies; nor do we like them half so well. If his inclination to comedy sometimes led him to trifle with the seriousness of tragedy, the poetical and impassioned passages are the best parts of his comedies. The great and secret charm of *Twelfth Night* is the character of Viola. Much as we like catches and cakes and ale, there is something that we like better.

From **Anna Jameson, Characteristics of Women** (London, 1833), pp. 245–7, 250–1

Anna Brownell Jameson, née Murphy (1794–1860), enjoyed a long career as a travel writer, biographer, critic and public advocate for the advancement of women through better education and fairer professional opportunities. Like Hazlitt and other Romantic critics of her generation, Jameson praised 'the genuine sweetness and delicacy of [Viola's] character' and took her distance from her predecessor, Charlotte Lennox, who had criticised her rash and unaccountable passion for Orsino as unseemly and improbable. Like Hazlitt, Jameson insisted that the genuine, poetical quality of Viola's feelings is more important than their probability or their moral implications. Unlike Hazlitt, though, Jameson sensed that the aesthetic beauty and intensity of Shakespeare's vision could also be interpreted as a radical political statement. Jameson was the first critic to remark on the gap between the moral and intellectual strength of Shakespeare's heroines and the hampering limitations imposed on women who lived in Shakespeare's time. She therefore juxtaposed 'artificial society', where man-made laws and regulations prevent women from fully expressing themselves personally and professionally, to Shakespeare's Illyria, where 'truth' and 'nature' prevail. Interestingly, while Charlotte Lennox believed that social and aesthetic order mirrored nature, Jameson impeached 'artificial society' and celebrated nature as the prime site of radical dissent.

We are left to infer, (for so it is hinted in the first scene,) that this Duke—who with his accomplishments and his personal attractions, his taste for music, his chivalrous tenderness, and his unrequited love, is really a very fascinating and poetical personage, though a little passionate and fantastic—had already made some impression on Viola's imagination; and when she comes to play the confidante, and to be loaded with favours and kindness in her assumed character, that she should be touched by a passion made up of pity, admiration, gratitude, and tenderness, does not, I think, in any way detract from the genuine sweetness and delicacy of her character, for *'she never told her love.'*

Now all this, as the critic[1] wisely observes, may not present a very just picture of life; and it may also fail to impart any moral lesson for the especial profit of well-bred young ladies: but is it not in truth and in nature? [. . .]

The distance of rank which separates the Countess from the youthful page—the real sex of Viola—the dignified elegance of Olivia's deportment, except where passion gets the better of her pride—her consistent coldness towards the Duke—the description of that 'smooth, discreet, and stable bearing' with which she rules her household—her generous care for her steward Malvolio, in the midst of her own distress,—all these circumstances raise Olivia in our fancy, and render her caprice for the page a source of amusement and interest, not a subject of reproach. *Twelfth Night* is a genuine comedy—a perpetual spring of the gayest and the sweetest fancies. In artificial society men and women are divided into castes and classes, and it is rarely that extremes in character or manners can approximate. To blend into one harmonious picture the utmost grace and refinement of sentiment and the broadest effects of humour, the most poignant wit and the most indulgent benignity, in short, to bring before us in the same scene Viola and Olivia, with Malvolio and Sir Toby, belonged only to Nature and to Shakespeare.

From **Émile Montégut, 'Twelfth Night'** (1867). Reprinted in H. H. Furness (ed.), *A New Variorum Edition of Shakespeare*, Vol. XIII, *Twelfth Night: Or, What You Will* (Philadelphia, Pa.: Lippincott Company, 1901), pp. 382–4

Émile Montégut (1825–95), a French critic who specialised in the study of Shakespeare and English literature, was the first early commentator to argue

---

1   Jameson is here referring to earlier critics, who, like Charlotte Lennox, objected to Shakespeare's breach of the neo-classical rules of decorum and probability (see Early Criticism, **pp. 50–1**).

that the title of *Twelfth Night* highlighted a connection between Shakespeare's comedy and early modern festive traditions, such as the appointment of a Lord of Misrule, who presided over annual holidays, like Christmas (and Twelfth Night), Candlemas and Shrove Tuesday. Montégut's approach affected mid-twentieth-century critics like C. L. Barber (see Modern Criticism, **pp. 64–7**) and Michael Bristol (see Modern Criticism, **pp. 70–3**). However, the distinction he draws between 'a graceful and poetic madness', which affects those characters whose desires are ultimately fulfilled, and 'a grotesque and trivial madness', which affects those characters whose dreams and aspirations are bitterly disappointed, reveals a strong prejudice against *some* passions, which, as in Lennox's extract, are deemed 'unnatural'. Once again, Nature is elected to act as supreme judge of what constitutes acceptable sexual inclinations. And, once again, moral perversions are associated with aesthetic flaws, as Montégut explains how Nature 'thrusts aside as a revolt and a sin, every dream wherein ugliness intrudes'.

[. . .] *Twelfth Night* is a masquerade, slightly grotesque, as befits a play whereof the title recalls one of those festivals which were most dear to the jocund humour of our forbears. This festival was the day whereon in every family a king for the nonce was crowned after he had been chosen by lot, sometimes it fell to a child to be the ruler over the whole family, again a servant was crowned by his master, for the moment it was the world turned upside down, a rational hierarchy topsy-turvy, authority created by chance, and the more grotesque the surprise, the merrier the festival. [. . .] The whole episode of the wild orgy of Toby and of the crotchety Malvolio is drawn incomparably to the life; Shakespeare has there, so to speak, surpassed himself, for he has there shown himself a consummate master of a species of composition which has been many a time denied to him, namely, comedy. That Shakespeare, in the comedy of fancy, of caprice, of adventure, is without a peer is acknowledged by every one; but he has been gravely reproached with not being able to stand a comparison with those masters who draw their resources exclusively from those faculties whence alone true comedy springs; in a word, with not being sufficiently in his comedies exclusively comic. The episodes of Sir Toby and Malvolio correct this judgement of error; Rabelais[1] is not more of a buffoon, and Molière[2] not more exclusively comic than Shakespeare in these two episodes.

The sentimental and romantic portions of the play are stamped with that inimitable grace which especially characterises Shakespeare; but even here this comedy remains faithful to its title of *Twelfth Night*; for ambiguity still reigns sovereign mistress there, and treats the real world under its double form, the reality of nature and that of society, like a carnival farce. [. . .]

---

1 François Rabelais (1494–1553) was a famous French humanist scholar and author of *Gargantua and Pantagruel*, an influential satirical novel, which inspired, among others, Mikhail Bakhtin in the twentieth century (see Critical History, **p. 44**).
2 French playwright Jean-Baptiste Poquelin, better known as Molière (1622–73), who wrote famous satirical comedies, including *Tartuffe* (1664), *The Misanthrope* (1666) and *The Miser* (1668).

In Shakespeare's plays philosophy is rarely lacking; is there then a philosophy in this poetic masquerade? Ay, there is one here, and to its fullest depth. In two words it is: we are all, in varying degrees, insane; for we are all the slaves of our defects, which are genuine chronic follies, or else we are the victims of dreams which attack us like follies at an acute stage. Man is held in leash by his imagination, which deceives him even to the extent of reversing the normal conditions of nature and the laws of reality. An image, ordinary but true, of man in every station is this silly Malvolio, whose folly unavowed and secretly cherished, bursts forth on a frivolous pretext. Malvolio is, no question, a fool, but this sly waiting woman who ensnares him by an all revealing strategem, is she herself exempt from the folly of which she accuses Malvolio? and if the steward believes himself beloved by his mistress, does she not pursue the same ambitious dream of making a match with Sir Toby, who, however degraded and drunken, is at least a gentleman and the uncle of Olivia? It is the same dream under very different conditions which Viola pursues,—a dream which would never have come true, if luck had not extricated her from the *cul de sac* whither her temerity had led her. What is to be said of Olivia but that her imagination, suddenly smitten, could go so far astray as to stifle in her the instinct which should have revealed to her that Viola was of her own sex? The friendship of Antonio for Sebastian,—a friendship which involves him in perils so easily foreseen,—is a sentiment exactly twin with the love of Olivia for Cesario-Viola. All dream, all are mad, and differ from another only in the kind of their madness,—some have a graceful and poetic madness, others a madness grotesque and trivial. And after all, some of these dreams come true. Must we ascribe the honour of success to the good sense of the happy ones who see their secret desires crowned? Ah no, we must ascribe it to nature. We all dream,—it is a condition of humanity; but in this multitude of dreams, Nature accepts only certain ones which are in harmony with grace, with poesy, and with beauty; for Nature is essentially platonic, and thrusts aside as a revolt and a sin, every dream wherein ugliness intrudes.

From **William Archer, 'Twelfth Night at the Lyceum'** (1884), *Macmillan's Magazine*, 50 (298). Reprinted in L. L. Harris (ed.), *Shakespearean Criticism* 1 (1984), pp. 558–9

William Archer (1856–1924), journalist, translator and theatre critic, introduced Henrik Ibsen's plays to the London stage. Ibsen wrote radically innovative plays by focusing on social issues, such as the role of women and children within the Victorian family, and portrayed his characters in a shockingly realistic way. His plays represented a radical departure from late Victorian theatre, which relished spectacle and entertainment over Ibsen's commitment to furthering social change through playwriting. Despite his admiration for Ibsen, Archer's impatience with the gulling of Malvolio and with Feste's wordplay is indicative of an enduring bias first introduced by Romantic critics at the beginning of the nineteenth century, which favoured the sweetness of Viola's lines over the exploration of social prejudice.

The elements of beauty and of humour are kept very much apart in *Twelfth Night*. It contains two actions in one frame—a romantic intrigue borrowed from Italy, and a pair of practical jokes, or "good practices," as Mr. Manningham hath it,[1] invented by Shakespeare. These two actions can be said really to touch at only one point, and then, as it were, unwillingly; for it is where Viola's blade crosses Sir Andrew's. . . . The play has just as much unity as two spheres in contact.
    [. . .]
So much for the fairy tale: now for the farce. Its construction is entirely Shakespeare's, and affords a good specimen of his manner. Given the pompously fatuous character of Malvolio, the "practise" put upon him is a very simple invention. Much more ingenuity is shown in the second practical joke of the duel, with its recoil upon the head of its perpetrator through the intervention of Sebastian. All these scenes—the scene of the letter, of the cross-garters, of the duel and its consequences—are theatrically effective by reason of their skilful dialogue, which a little judicious pruning renders fairly comprehensible to modern ears. On the other hand there are many passages which can at no time have been reasonably good dialogue—such as the first meeting between Maria and Sir Andrew, and several of the scenes in which the Clown is concerned. Such inane word-strainings may have been true to nature, since the professional fools of the day, bound to be funny at all hazards, must often have resorted to them; but they are none the less puerile, and should drop away on the modern stage to the great advantage of all concerned. Feste is, on the whole, one of the shallowest of Shakespeare's jesters. When he says of himself that he is not Olivia's fool, but her corrupter of words, there is more than a spice of truth in the remark. Compared with Touchstone,[2] he sinks into absolute insignificance. The parts can scarcely have been written for the same actor; Touchstone was probably designed for a comedian of authoritative genius, Feste for a mere singing clown.

---

1   See Contextual Overview, p. 7.
2   The jester in Shakespeare's *As You Like It*.

Modern Criticism

Language and Myth

From **Frank E. Halliday, 'Twelfth Night'**, in *The Poetry of Shakespeare's Plays* (London: Gerald Duckworth, 1954), pp. 122–4

> Frank E. Halliday (1903–82) was profoundly influenced by the New Critical methods championed, among others, by F. R. Leavis. The following extract shows the extent to which the legacy of nineteenth-century Romantic critics affected New Critical approaches to Shakespeare in the first half of the twentieth century. Like William Hazlitt, Halliday describes Viola's language as 'celestial music' and, like other New Critics of his generation, he insists that 'Shakespeare was above all things a poet',[1] thus reinforcing a Romantic aversion against the stage. Halliday's analysis of the famous 'willow cabin' speech in Act 1, Scene 5 (see Key Passages, **pp. 150–1**) shows how the New Critical approach privileged Shakespeare's poetic diction over other aspects of the play. Halliday regards this speech quite literally as a musical set piece, and is more interested in establishing *how* this speech works than *what* Viola actually says.

[. . .] it is not for the prose of Beatrice and Rosalind that we have been waiting since Shakespeare wrote the last scene of *The Merchant of Venice*, it is for dramatic verse that by some miracle will be imbued with a poetry comparable to that celestial music. As soon as we hear Viola speak we know that the miracle has been accomplished; her very first words have the pure and piercing quality that we come to realize as peculiar to her speech, and we cannot read or hear without a thrill:

> *Enter Viola, a Captaine, and Saylors*
> *Vio.* What Country (Friends) is this?
> *Cap.* This is Illyria Ladie.

1   Halliday, 'Twelfth Night', p. 14.

> *Vio.* And what should I do in Illyria?
> My brother he is in Elizium,
> Perchance he is not drown'd: What think you saylors?
>
> (2.1.1–5)

Perhaps the strange music is imparted by the thin and clear music of the *i*'s and *y*'s, a sound that enchanted Orsino's ear:

> thy small pipe
> Is as the maiden's organ, shrill and sound.
>
> (see Key Passages, **p. 145**)

Partly, perhaps, it is the association of Viola with the sea, and with the sea-change suffered by so many of the later heroines. She is at once the last of the heroines of the middle comedies, and the first of those of the romances; Marina[2] is born at sea, Perdita[3] lost and found on the sea-coast of Bohemia, Miranda[4] washed ashore on the magic island, and Viola cast up on the Illyrian coast.

Her first interview with Olivia begins in stilted prose, but when they are left alone and Olivia unveils, Viola unaffectedly exclaims,

> 'Tis beauty truly blent, whose red and white
> Nature's own sweet and cunning hand laid on:
> Lady, you are the cruell'st she alive,
> If you will lead these graces to the grave
> And leave the world no copy.
>
> (see Key Passages, **pp. 149–50**)

Here is the dramatic poetry that we have been waiting for, a poetry in which almost every word is related to character and action, and at the same time harmonically related to the other words throughout the passage. Less obvious than the earlier lyricism, because no longer static and repetitive in pattern, more natural, or more seeming-natural, therefore, and for that reason again more dramatic, it is the beginning of the perfected Shakespearean counterpoint, in which rhythm and assonance are complementary and interdependent, making a pattern which, though based on the linear structure, is coextensive with the speech. A reversed rhythm is suggested by *beauty truly*, emphasized by *Nature's . . . laid on*, *Lady*, and further developed by the other verbal trochees, related to them and to one another both by juxtaposition and assonance, so that this apparently simple speech is really a passage of the most intricate harmony in which almost every syllable is involved.

Before she goes, Viola describes the depth and constancy of her own love for Orsino in terms of his love for Olivia; it is the music of the nightingale, all the liquids welling up to the climax of 'Olivia':

---

2 The daughter of Pericles, King of Tyre, in *Pericles*, a later play now believed to have been written collaboratively by Shakespeare and George Wilkins.
3 Leontes's daughter in Shakespeare's late play *The Winter's Tale*.
4 Prospero's daughter in Shakespeare's late play *The Tempest*.

Make me a willow cabin at your gate,
And call upon my soul within the house;
Write loyal cantons of contemned love
And sing them loud even in the dead of night;
Halloo your name to the reverberate hills,
And make the babbling gossip of the air
Cry out 'Olivia!'

(see Key Passages, **pp. 150–1**)

Beatrice and Rosalind are creatures of prose, and their adventures much ado about nothing, but Viola is of another and a rarer element, the first of the heroines whom Shakespeare brought fully to life in verse, and he treated her predicament with a corresponding gravity. He never forgot her, and many years later was to describe the heroine of *Pericles* in terms of her of *Twelfth Night*:

thou dost look
Like Patience gazing on kings' graves, and smiling
Extremity out of act.

(see Key Passages, **p. 164**)

In another sense he never forgot her, for she is one with her poetry, and as Shylock[5] taught Shakespeare to write dramatic verse, so did Viola teach him to write dramatic poetry.

From **Jonathan Bate, *Shakespeare and Ovid*** (Oxford: Clarendon Press, 1993), pp. 145–50

Jonathan Bate's reading of *Twelfth Night* rests on the assumption that 'mythological allusion pervades Elizabethan and Jacobean writing' and that reading in the Renaissance 'meant reading with a consciousness of the classics'.[1] Given Ovid's centrality to the classical training of early modern readers and writers, Bate also believes that 'every individual connection [he] make[s] could have been perceived by an educated Elizabethan'.[2] His reading of a selection of scenes and speeches from the play certainly shows the pervasiveness of Ovidian myth in Shakespeare's dramatic imagination. Whether *all* references to Ovid which Bate highlights would have been identified by Shakespeare's audiences and readers is more arguable. However, Bate's splendid account of Ovidian influences in *Twelfth Night* does help modern readers, who are undoubtedly less familiar with the classics, to capture resonances in Shakespeare's language and complexities in his characters that would otherwise go unnoticed. Also useful is Bate's suggestion that Shakespeare's Ovidian allusions emphasize the

---

5 The Jewish money-lender in Shakespeare's *The Merchant of Venice*.

1 Bate, *Shakespeare and Ovid*, pp. 11, 13.
2 Bate, *Shakespeare and Ovid*, p. 13.

destructive nature of sexual desire, as it is represented in Ovid's *Metamorphoses*. Interestingly, then, Bate's views on the dark qualities of the play match influential interpretations offered by other mid- to late-twentieth-century critics, who are discussed later on in other sections of this chapter and in The Work in Performance, especially **pp. 107–9**.

Twelfth Night is pervaded by a sense of mutability; constancy and inconstancy in love shape both the twists of the plot and the preoccupations of the characters. The tone is set by Orsino's opening speech in which he changes his mind about whether or not he wants more music, and compares the spirit of love to the ebb and flow of the sea. 'So full of shapes is fancy, / That it alone is high fantastical' (see Key Passages, **p. 141**): the language signals entry into that world of the imagination and its inconstant shapes which Shakespeare explored most fully in *A Midsummer Night's Dream*. So it is that certain myths ... of the *Metamorphoses*, in particular those of Actaeon and of Narcissus and Echo ... are among the controlling structures of the play.

The image of metamorphosis is introduced openly when Orsino speaks of the effects of his seeing Olivia:

> That instant was I turned into a hart,
> And my desires, like fell and cruel hounds,
> E'er since pursue me.

> (see Key Passages, **p. 142**)

The figure of Actaeon is so embedded in this trope that he is not mentioned by name. [. . .]

In comparing himself to Actaeon, Orsino implicitly compares Olivia to Diana; thus, when he explicitly compares Cesario to Diana (see Key Passages, **p. 145**), we know that (s)he is replacing Olivia as the Duke's idealized object of desire. Diana is above all the goddess of chastity: it is because of Olivia's pose of chastity that Orsino's suit is unsuccessful and the pursuit of love turns self-destructively inward. Orsino is in love with the idea of being in love, and that is a state approaching the self-love of Narcissus. The abundant desire which surfeits on itself and so dies is that of Narcissus. Not only do many of the play's dilemmas and potential disasters arise from the narcissism of Olivia and Orsino: the comic plot reiterates and emphasizes the motif. Malvolio is 'sick of self-love' (1.5.86) and 'practis[es] behaviour to his own shadow' (see Key Passages, **p. 167**) in the manner of Ovid's Narcissus, who is to be seen 'gazing on his shadow still with fixed starting eyes'.[3] He is gulled into wearing yellow, the colour of the flower into which Narcissus is transformed.

Malvolio also presents a different angle on the Actaeon pattern. If the noble Orsino is to be read as Actaeon in that he is hunted by the dogs of his own desires, the steward may be viewed in terms of the myth's implication that it is dangerous

---

3   W. H. D. Rouse (ed.), *Shakespeare's Ovid* (1904, repr. 1961), Vol. III, p. 524.

to lift one's eyes above one's rank. In the box-tree scene, instead of seeing Actaeon spying on Diana, we watch an Actaeon figure being spied on himself as he fantasizes about his Diana's desire for him. As Malvolio interprets the meaning of the 'I' in the letter, Fabian remarks, 'Ay, an you had any eye behind you, you might see more detraction at your heels than fortunes before you' (see Key Passages, **p. 171**). The pun concentrates the double identity of Malvolio as Narcissus (the self-obsessed 'I') and Actaeon (the desiring 'eye'). The dogs are watching him – even Sir Andrew is 'dog at a catch' and, as Feste says, 'some dogs will catch well' (see Key Passages, **p. 159**) – and already snapping at his heels. The 'detraction' which comes to him is the play's version of the fate of Actaeon. Given this, it is tempting to read his final cry of vengeance as an image of Actaeon turning the story around and beating off the pursuing hounds: 'I'll be revenged on the whole *pack* of you' (see Key Passages, **p. 184**).[4] It may therefore be that Shakespeare is making one of his characteristic fusions of high and low culture: the educated audience reads Malvolio as Actaeon and simultaneously the illiterate spectator – who does not view the theatre so differently from the bear-pit – sees him as a bear. [. . .]

If all the characters in *Twelfth Night* were perpetually self-centred, it would be no comedy. It is above all Viola who effects a release from naricissism. When she first appears as Cesario, she too seems to be a Narcissus: the ambivalence suggested by ''Tis with him in standing water, between boy and man' (see Key Passages, **p. 147**) associates Cesario with the sixteen-year-old Narcissus, who 'seemde to stande beetweene the state of man and Lad'.[5] As Cesario attracts both Orsino and Olivia, so with Narcissus, 'The hearts of divers trim yong men his beautie gan to move, / And many a Ladie fresh and faire was taken in his love'.[6] But Viola redeems the play because she proves to be selfless, not selfish, in love. She becomes Echo instead of Narcissus.

When Olivia asks Cesario what he would do if he were in love with her, the boy departs from the script which Orsino has given him, with its enumeration of the conventional courtly lover's groans and sighs, and speaks instead with an authenticity and intensity that immediately strike a chord in Olivia ('You might do much', she murmurs approvingly in reply):

> Make me a willow cabin at your gate
> And call upon my soul within the house,
> Write loyal cantons of contemned love,
> And sing them loud even in the dead of night;
> Halloo your name to the reverberate hills,
> And make the babbling gossip of the air
> Cry out 'Olivia!' O, you should not rest
> Between the elements of air and earth,
> But you should pity me.
>
> (see Key Passages, **pp. 150–1**)

---

4 [Bate's note.] (my italic). *OED*'s first usage of 'pack' for a company of hounds kept for hunting is 1648, but Shakespeare does sometimes use the word in contexts suggesting violent collective pursuit: 'God bless the Prince from all the pack of you! / A knot you are of damnèd bloodsuckers' (*Richard III*, 3.3.4–5); 'Hence; pack! . . . Out, rascal dogs!' (*Timon of Athens*, 5.1.111, 114).

5 Rouse, *Shakespeare's Ovid*, Vol. III, p. 438.

6 Rouse, *Shakespeare's Ovid*, Vol. III, p. 439–40.

The 'babbling gossip of the air' is an explicit allusion to Echo, prepared for by the images of reverberating hills and of hopeless love – Echo's love is condemned because Narcissus loves only himself. Shakespeare's adjective was probably determined by Golding's 'A babling Nymph that *Echo* hight'.[7] Cesario seems to speak authentically because it is really Viola speaking of her own secret love for Orsino; her plight, which requires silence and concealment of her feelings, appears to be like Echo's. So it is that when she is with Orsino, Viola implicitly compares herself to Echo by speaking of an imaginary sister, really herself, whose history is a 'blank',

> she never told her love,
> But let concealment, like a worm i'th'bud,
> Feed on her damask cheek. She pined in thought,
> And with a green and yellow melancholy
> She sat like patience on a monument,
> Smiling at grief. Was not this love indeed?
>
> (see Key Passages, **p. 164**)

[. . .] But not all the associations of Echo are melancholy. She functions in Ovid as an alternative to self-love: had Narcissus responded to her love, neither of them would have been destroyed. Viola's function is to enable characters to respond, to see that love requires echoing instead of narcissism. Here the mythological pattern is transformed into a metaphorical one. This process is at work earlier in the scene with Orsino. After speaking of the instability of lovers, 'Save in the constant image of the creature / That is beloved', Orsino asks Cesario how he likes the music that is playing:

> VIOLA.   It gives a very *echo* to the seat
>   Where love is throned.
> DUKE.   Thou does speak masterly.[8]
>
> (see Key Passages, **p. 162**)

Viola has given words to Orsino's own thought: they echo each other in the belief that music echoes love. Viola harmonizes Illyria by teaching its inhabitants to echo and thus to love. Cesario, through being two natures in one, shows the others that their true selves are to be found by looking at others instead of contemplating their own images in the manner of Narcissus. The moment of greatest harmony occurs in the visual echo when Viola faces Sebastian, love is doubled, and the plot resolved.

Yet the resolution is by no means complete. Malvolio is still a Narcissus or an Actaeon, and Viola must be split from Cesario. *Twelfth Night* recognizes the fragility of Echo and the pervasiveness of Narcissus. [. . .] *Twelfth Night* is and is not a benign rewriting of the myth, in which Narcissus recants of his narcissism, Echo is re-embodied and wins his love, and they live happily ever after. Quite apart from the little local problem of Malvolio's detention of the captain who

---

7   Rouse, *Shakespeare's Ovid*, Vol. III, p. 443.
8   [Bate's note.] (my italic).

holds the symbolic key to Viola's reassumption of feminine identity, the tonality of the final song is not that of living happily ever after: it is of the wind and the rain [. . .].

Darkening Shakespeare's Festive Comedy

From **W. H. Auden, 'Twelfth Night'** (1947), in A. Kirsch (ed.), *Lectures on Shakespeare* (London: Faber and Faber, 2000), pp. 154–5

Poet and essayist W. H. Auden (1907–73) delivered his Shakespeare lectures at the New School for Social Research in Greenwich, New York, in 1946–7. Auden's dark views on *Twelfth Night* seem to reflect the bleak outlook of a generation that was still coming to terms with the extent of the devastation caused by the Second World War. However, his scathing remarks about the cynical, self-interested quality of Shakespeare's characters in *Twelfth Night* re-emerged fifteen years later, when in his essay called 'Music in Shakespeare' he wrote:

> I have always found the atmosphere of *Twelfth Night* a bit whiffy. I get the impression that Shakespeare wrote the play at a time when he was in no mood for comedy, but in a mood for puritanical aversion to all those pleasing illusions which men cherish and by which they lead their lives. The comic convention in which the play is set prevents him from giving direct expression to this mood, but the mood keeps disturbing, even spoiling, the comic feeling. One has a sense, and nowhere more strongly than in the songs, of there being inverted commas around the "fun".[1]

What seems most remarkable about the 1947 lecture is the extent to which Auden associates decadence, deception, lack of self-knowledge and true love, to a world where 'women have become dominant . . . [and] get what they want'.

[. . .] [T]here is cynicism about money in *Twelfth Night*, an awareness that services must be paid for, that people can be bought, and that money can get you what you want. There are many examples of this attitude. Sir Toby says Sir Andrew Aguecheek is "as tall a man as any's in Illyria" because "he has three thousand ducats a year" (1.3.18–20). Viola assures the Sea Captain she will pay him "bounteously" (1.2.48) for his help in presenting her in disguise as Cesario to Duke Orsino. And Olivia, when she falls in love with Cesario, thinks of what she can "bestow of him" to win him, "For youth is bought more oft than begg'd or borrow'd" (3.4.3).

Women have become dominant in *Twelfth Night* and take the initiative. Malvolio lacks self-confidence and self-control and is weak, and with the exception of Antonio, the other men are passive. The women are the only people left

---

1 W. H. Auden, 'Music in Shakespeare', *The Dyer's Hand* and *Other Essays* (New York: Random House), p. 520.

who have any will, which is the sign of a decadent society. Maria, in love with Sir Toby, tricks him into marrying her. Olivia starts wooing Cesario from the first moment she sees him, and Viola is a real man-chaser. All the ladies in this play get what they want.

The society in *Twelfth Night* is beginning to smell gamey. The characters in the play are out for gain, they are generally seedy, and they are often malicious. Unlike Falstaff,[2] who also drinks and is idle, and who might at first seem comparable, especially to Sir Toby, they are neither wise and intelligent, nor full of self-knowledge, nor capable of real love. The turnabouts in the marriages at the end are emblematic. The Duke, who up till the moment of recognition had thought himself in love with Olivia, drops her like a hot potato and falls in love with Viola on the spot, and Sebastian accepts Olivia's proposal of marriage within two minutes of meeting her for the first time. Both appear contemptible, and it is impossible to imagine that either will make a good husband. Unlike Falstaff, these people emerge victorious and have their nasty little triumph over life. Falstaff is defeated by life.[3]

From **C. L. Barber, 'Testing Courtesy and Humanity in *Twelfth Night*'**, in *Shakespeare's Festive Comedy: A Study of Dramatic Form and Its Relation to Social Custom* (Princeton, NJ: Princeton University Press, 1959), pp. 245, 245–7 and 255–6

C. L. Barber established a connection between the social form and function of Elizabethan holidays, including Candlemas (2 February), Shrove Tuesday (the last day of Carnival before Ash Wednesday), May Day (1 May), Midsummer Eve (21 June), Harvest-Home (or Midautumn, 21 September) and the twelve days of Christmas ending with Twelfth Night, and the 'saturnalian[1] pattern' in Shakespeare's festive comedies.[2] Central to Barber's understanding of festivity is the assumption that the inversions brought about by saturnalian release actually reinforce the norms which they temporarily suspend. For all the attention he paid to festivity, Barber overlooked other aspects of Elizabethan culture, which *Twelfth Night* clearly addresses, and which found no resolution or clarification either on or off stage. When, for example, he refers to Olivia as a 'spoiled and dominating young heiress' and explains her determination to shun Orsino and woo a young page as an attempt to retain her position of power and privilege, he dismisses this trait in her character by claiming that 'it was not the habit of Shakespeare's age to look for such implications'. Texts included in the Contemporary Documents section (see, for example, **pp. 19–25**) suggest otherwise.

---

2   Prince Hal's rowdy companion in Shakespeare's *1 and 2 Henry IV*.
3   Auden is here referring to Hal's rejection of Falstaff, once he becomes King Henry V at the end of *2 Henry IV*.

---

1   From 'Saturnalia', important Roman festival dedicated to Saturn and characterised by revelry, carnivalesque inversions in the role of masters and their slaves, excessive eating and drinking.
2   Other comedies examined by Barber include *A Midsummer Night's Dream, As You Like It, The Merchant of Venice* and *Love's Labour's Lost*.

The most fundamental distinction the play brings home to us is the difference between men and women. To say this may seem to labor the obvious; for what love story does not emphasize this difference? But the disguising of a girl as a boy in *Twelfth Night* is exploited so as to renew in a special way our sense of the difference. Just as a saturnalian reversal of social roles need not threaten the social structure, but can serve instead to consolidate it, so a temporary, playful reversal of sexual roles can renew the meaning of the normal relation. One can add that with sexual as with other relations, it is when the normal is secure that playful aberration is benign. This basic security explains why there is so little that is queasy in all Shakespeare's handling of boy actors playing women, and playing women pretending to be men. [. . .] Olivia's infatuation with feminine qualities in a youth takes her, doing 'I know not what', from one stage of life out into another, from shutting out suitors in mourning for her brother's memory, to ardor for a man, Sebastian, and the clear certainty that calls out to 'husband' in the confusion of the last scene.

We might wonder whether this spoiled and dominating young heiress may not have been attracted by what she could hope to dominate in Cesario's youth – but it was not the habit of Shakespeare's age to look for such implications. And besides, Sebastian is not likely to be dominated; we have seen him respond to Andrew when the ninny knight thought he was securely striking Cesario:

> *Andrew.* Now, sir, have I met you again? There's for you!
> *Sebastian.* Why, there's for thee, and there, and there!
>
> (4.1.23–5)

To see this manly reflex is delightful – almost a relief – for we have been watching poor Viola absurdly perplexed behind her disguise as Sir Toby urges her to play the man: 'Dismount thy tuck, be yare in thy preparation. . . . Therefore on, or strip your sword naked; for meddle you must, that's certain' (3.4.218–19 and 3.4.243–4). She is driven to the point where she exclaims in an aside: 'Pray God defend me! A little thing would make me tell them how much I lack of a man' (3.4.293–4). What she lacks, Sebastian has. His entrance in the final scene is preceded by comical testimony of his prowess, Sir Andrew with a broken head and Sir Toby halting. The particular implausibility that there should be an identical man to take Viola's place with Olivia is submerged in the general, beneficent realization that there is such a thing as a man. Sebastian's comment when the confusion of identities is resolved points to the general force which has shaped particular developments:

> So comes it, lady, you have been mistook.
> But nature to her bias drew in that.
>
> (see Key Passages, pp. 182–3)

Over against the Olivia–Cesario relation, there are Orsino–Cesario and Antonio–Sebastian. Antonio's impassioned friendship for Sebastian is one of those ardent attachments between young people of the same sex which Shakespeare frequently presents, with his positive emphasis, as exhibiting the loving and lovable qualities later expressed in love for the other sex. Orsino's fascination with Cesario is more complex. In the opening scene, his restless sensibility can find no object: 'nought enters there, . . . / But falls into abatement . . . / Even in a minute' (see Key Passages, **p. 141**). Olivia might be an adequate object; she at least is the Diana the sight of whom has, he thinks, turned him to an Actaeon torn by the hounds of desires.[3] When we next see him, and Cesario has been only three days in his court, his entering question is 'Who saw Cesario, ho?' and already he has unclasped to the youth 'the book even of [his] secret soul' (see Key Passages, **p. 144**). He has found an object. The delight he takes in Cesario's fresh youth and graceful responsiveness in conversation and in service, is one part of the spectrum of love for a woman, or better, it is a range of feeling that is common to love for a youth and love for a woman. For the audience, the woman who is present there, behind Cesario's disguise, is brought to mind repeatedly by the talk of love and of the differences of men and women in love. 'My father had a daughter loved a man . . .'

> She never told her love,
> But let concealment, like a worm i' th' bud,
> Feed on her damask cheek.
>
> (see Key Passages, **p. 164**)

This supremely feminine damsel, who 'sat like patience on a monument', is not Viola. She is a sort of polarity within Viola, realized all the more fully because the other, active side of Viola does not pine in thought at all, but instead changes the subject: '. . . and yet I know not. / Sir, shall I to this lady? – Ay, that's the theme' (see Key Passages, **p. 164**). The effect of moving back and forth from woman to sprightly page is to convey how much the sexes differ yet how much they have in common, how everyone who is fully alive has qualities of both. Some such general recognition is obliquely suggested in Sebastian's amused summary of what happened to Olivia:

> You would have been contracted to a maid;
> Nor are you therein, by my life, deceiv'd:
> You are betroth'd both to a maid and man.
>
> (see Key Passages, **p. 183**)

The countess marries the man in this composite, and the count marries the maid. He too has done he knows not what while nature drew him to her bias, for he has fallen in love with the maid without knowing it.

[. . .]

In 'loving' his mistress, as Cesario her master, he [Malvolio] is a kind of foil, bringing out her genuine, free impulse by the contrast he furnishes. He does not desire Olivia's person; *that* desire, even in a steward, would be sympathetically regarded, though not of course encouraged, by a Twelfth-Night mood. What he wants is 'to be Count Malvolio', with 'a demure travel of regard, telling them I know my place, as I would they should do theirs' (see Key Passages, **p. 168**). His secret wish is to violate decorum himself, then relish to the full its power over

---

3 For further details about the Ovidian myth of 'Actaeon and Diana', see Modern Criticism, pp. 60–1.

others. No wonder he has not a free disposition when he has such imaginations to keep under! When the sport betrays him into a revelation of them, part of the vengeance taken is to make him try to be festive, in yellow stockings, and cross-gartered, and smiling 'his face into more lines than is in the new map with the augmentation of the Indies' (III ii 74–5). Maria's letter *tells* him to go brave, be gallant, take liberties! And when we see him 'acting this in an obedient hope' (as he puts it later), he is anything but free: 'This does make some obstruction in the blood, this cross-gartering . . .' (3.4.19–20).

In his 'impossible passages of grossness', he is the profane intruder trying to steal part of the initiates' feast by disguising himself as one of them – only to be caught and tormented for his profanation. As with Shylock,[4] there is potential pathos in his bafflement, especially when Shakespeare uses to the limit the conjuring of devils out of a sane man, a device which he had employed hilariously in *The Comedy of Errors*.[5] There is no way to settle just how much of Malvolio's pathos should be allowed to come through when he is down and out in the dark hole. Most people now agree that Charles Lamb's[6] sympathy for the steward's enterprise and commiseration for his sorrows is a romantic and bourgeois distortion.

Power, Class and Carnivalesque Disorder

From **Elliot Krieger, *A Marxist Study of Shakespeare's Comedies***
(London: Macmillan, 1979), pp. 1, 4–5, 121 and 122–5

Elliot Krieger's use of the terms 'primary world' and 'second world' to define the fictive and the ideal worlds conjured by Shakespearean comedy is directly related to the Marxist distinction between 'base' and 'superstructure'. According to Marxist theorists, subjectivity is determined by specific relations to labour and to the material conditions of economic production (the 'base'), while social and ideological superstructures, including literature, simply reflect those relations. The main merit of Krieger's approach is that it reveals an interesting collusion between Malvolio's persecutors and those critics like C. L. Barber who regard Malvolio as a 'profane intruder' (see Modern Criticism, **p. 67**). In this respect, Krieger's Marxist analysis of *Twelfth Night* represents an interesting and valuable development in the history of the critical reception of

---

4   As pointed out above (p. 59), Shylock is the Jewish money-lender in Shakespeare's *The Merchant of Venice*. Like Malvolio, Shylock threatens to upset the power relations between the dominant consituency of Christian merchants and the Venetian Jews, when a Christian merchant, called Antonio, fails to repay his loan to him and Shylock claims a pound of his flesh in compensation.

5   Act 4, Scene 2 in *Twelfth Night*, when Malvolio is locked up in a dark room and is challenged by Sir Topas the curate (Feste in disguise) to prove that he is not mad, has a close counterpart in Shakespeare's earlier play, *The Comedy of Errors*, where a conjuring schoolmaster called Doctor Pinch attempts to exorcise Antipholus and Dromio of Ephesus, who are believed to be insane, simply because they are mistaken for their twins, Antipholus and Dromio of Syracuse.

6   Charles Lamb (1775–1834), writer and essayist, who, with his sister Mary, rewrote some of Shakespeare's plays into prose narratives suitable for children. Both Charles's and Mary's lives were blighted by bouts of madness. Charles's first-hand experience of mental illness may have influenced his sympathetic response to Malvolio's ordeal in Act 4, Scene 2.

this play. However, his distinction between 'base' and 'superstructure', 'primary' and 'second world', has been radically revised by post-Marxist critics who no longer believe that literature is a mere reflection of the dominant ideology generated by specific relations of economic production and class divisions.

In each of Shakespeare's comedies one of two things happens. Either (a) the protagonists move from one location, in which the action begins, to another, in which it concludes, or (b) the action begins as a group of characters arrive in a new location. Critics refer to the location toward which the characters, hence the action, move as the "second world"; the location either in which the action begins or from which the characters have departed critics call the "primary world". [. . .]

[. . .] Although the protagonists release their private fancy or vision from its limitations, the boundaries of the individual consciousness, and enact the fancy as a second world, a clarified image that determines social and historical relations, other people experience the second world as a restriction on their own autonomy. The transforming and regenerative effect of the second world [. . .] can only apply with qualifications: at the same time that the protagonists experience the second world as a retreat, withdrawal, or replacement, others experience the second world as a domination, an exhibition of authority. Any character—Malvolio, for example—can abandon the actual environment in order to retreat to fantasy and abstraction. But only a protagonist who has social degree, and power, can develop a second world in which personal whims organize the social experience of others, in which the needs of the subject's ego replace the history of the primary world.

The development of a second world manifests aristocratic privilege: this is an idea so obvious that it has probably never been stated. But without stating the obvious we are liable to separate the second-world strategy from the material conditions, the specific class structure and social hierarchy, that make the strategy possible and successful. The second world does not emerge from a vacuum but from, and partially in response to, primary-world social conditions. When critics separate the second world from the primary-world social conditions, the second-world strategy appears to be a universal solution to the problems of the primary world. The second world then appears to produce an abstract moral condition such as "harmony" or "concord", beneficial to all of the characters save perhaps one or two (e.g. Jaques,[1] Shylock,[2] Malvolio) who may be excluded from the comic resolution for "balance". But the interests, needs, and fantasies of the different characters differ, and the differentiation has in part to do with social degree. Inasmuch as the second world develops from the primary-world social structure, the second-world strategy cannot lead to universal good: to the extent that the second world clarifies the subjective interests of the members of one social class, it is antagonistic to the interests of other classes. In implicitly denying that different social classes develop opposed interests, the idea of universal good is by

---

1   A melancholy character in Shakespeare's *As You Like It*.
2   See Footnote 4 on **p. 67**.

its nature a revisionist fantasy, a way of interpreting and acknowledging only the comfortable and progressive aspects of a given situation. Uncomfortable finding class struggle and class interests dramatized in Shakespeare's comedies, many critics abstract the concrete motives, solutions, and themes of the plays from the particular class interests that these qualities serve; many critics place the comedies on the refined level of the universals of human nature, within which the class interests are absorbed and obscured. These critics argue that the plays articulate "neutral" themes such as "love's truth", the value of the imagination, or the need for mercy. They see that the clarified image reveals a world of holiday leisure, but they do not see that without servants, no leisure time would be available for the protagonists. They see that the plays celebrate hierarchy in society and correspondence between nature and society, but they do not see that those who formulate the celebration correspond only to the highest level of nature. They see that the second world enables the protagonists to discover their true identities and to assert their autonomy, but they do not see that others must discover their "true identity" by abandoning autonomy and devoting themselves to service. These critics, in short, find universal truths rather than class interests in Shakespeare's comedies. [. . .]

Ultimately, there is no fundamental difference between Malvolio's fantasy of narcissistic withdrawal into a world in which he can be Count Malvolio, sitting in state, "having come from a day-bed" (see Key Passages, **p. 168**) and Orsino's [narcissistic] withdrawal into the Petrarchan conventions and the beds of flowers.[3] The two second-world fantasies differ only in the social reaction and response that they elicit. Those near Orsino confirm his withdrawal from time: they echo his language and thereby subordinate the world and their autonomy in the world to the Duke's ego, they assure Orsino that he is neither solitary nor mad. The social reaction to Malvolio's second world is just the opposite: others cut Malvolio off from the world, imprison him in darkness; they disconfirm his sense perceptions and accuse him of being mad. Certainly, madness pervades the play, but whereas Sir Toby and Orsino use madness as an indulgence, and Sebastian and Olivia find their wishes fulfilled in their madness, only Malvolio confronts madness as a restriction and a limitation.

Malvolio's imprisonment marks the limit that class status imposes on the "morality of indulgence". The fantasy that leads to Malvolio's imprisonment— his love for Olivia and his vision of himself as a Count—is not in the abstract ridiculous or perverse. Only when we apply the ruling-class assumptions about degree and decorum does it seem that Malvolio is sick of self-love, whereas Orsino and Olivia seem to engage in healthy, therapeutic folly and deceit. [. . .]

A ruling-class ideology operates within the play and prevents Malvolio from creating his own antithetic second world. The second world that Malvolio tries to create, however, is not antithetic to that ideology, for Malvolio accepts and supports the aristocratic assumptions about the need for respect, decorum, and propriety. The charge against Sir Toby—"Is there no respect of place, persons, nor time in you?" (see Key Passages, **p. 160**) – is retained, emphatically, in Malvolio's fantasy: "telling them I know my place as I would they should do theirs" (see Key

---

3   See Contextual Overview, **pp. 12–14.**

Passages, **p. 168**). It is quite wrong to see Malvolio's fantasy as egalitarian or as a bourgeois opposition to aristocratic norms. Malvolio attends scrupulously to each aspect of aristocratic behavior, and in fact part of what he would hope to accomplish as Count Malvolio would be the "amendment" of Sir Toby's behavior, the restoration of Olivia's family to normality and decorum. Barber wrongly says that Malvolio has a "secret wish . . . to violate decorum himself".[4] Rather, hoping to achieve the stature into which he was not born, Malvolio (perhaps, surprisingly, like Othello[5]) profoundly respects the superficial accountrements of rank, the display of decorum. Before he discovers Maria's forged letter Malvolio violates decorum only in that, while still a steward, he indulges aloud in his fantasies of aspiration. The enactment of fantasy must remain the aristocratic prerogative.

[. . .] The conclusion of *Twelfth Night* [. . .] confirms the aristocratic fantasy [. . .] that clarification is achieved when people are released from indulgence and restored to the degree of greatness with which they were born.

From **Michael Bristol, *Carnival and Theater: Plebeian Culture and the Structure of Authority in Renaissance England*** (New York and London: Methuen, 1985), pp. 202–4

Michael Bristol, like Barber and Krieger (see Modern Criticism, **pp. 64–70**), explores the interrelation between drama and its social and cultural milieu. However, Bristol's approach departs in significant ways from the work of his predecessors. In the book from which the following extract is drawn, Bristol questions Barber's 'stress on the reconciliatory power of festive experience',[1] according to which 'conflict is always seen as deviant, a misunderstanding or delusion to be corrected by a clarification and reinterpretation of social rules rather than through struggle, negotiation and strategic action leading to social change'.[2] Bristol's views were affected by the work of Russian theorist Mikhail Bakhtin, who used the term 'Carnival' to refer to 'a "second life" or "second culture" sustained by the common people or plebeian community throughout the Middle Ages and well into the early modern period'.[3] According to Bakhtin,

> this culture engages with and directly opposes the 'official' culture, . . . [by] represent[ing] everything socially and spiritually exalted on the material, bodily level. This includes cursing, abusive and irreverent speech, symbolic and actual thrashing, and images of inversion and downward movement, both

---

4   See Modern Criticism, **p. 66**.
5   The protagonist of Shakespeare's homonymous tragedy. Othello, a Moorish general in Venice, marries Desdemona, daughter to Brabantio, a powerful senator. Othello and Desdemona's interracial marriage challenges the very structure of Venetian society, which Othello is ironically meant to defend against the threat of a Turkish invasion.

---

1   Bristol, *Carnival and Theater*, p. 31.
2   Bristol, *Carnival and Theatre*, p. 32.
3   Bristol, *Carnival and Theater*, p. 22.

cosmological (the underworld, hell, devils) and anatomical (the buttocks, genitalia, visceral functions).[4]

Hence the attention paid by Bristol to Sir Toby's gastronomic excesses, to the digestive tract – (*He belches*) 'A plague o' these pickled herring!' (1.5.116–7) – and his irreverent disregard for Malvolio's appeal to orderly modesty in Act 2, Scene 3. Unlike Barber, and in line with Bakhtin, Bristol believes that 'Carnival [may] not [be] anti-authoritarian [but it] is a general refusal to understand any fixed and final allocation of authority.'[5]

Bristol's approach is also substantially different from Krieger's. Although, like Krieger, Bristol explores dramatic literature in relation to the historical context within which it was produced, he does not regard it as a mere reflection of the material conditions of its production and of the ideological apparatus that those conditions uphold. Bristol, in fact, believes that literature, in general, and carniva-lesque literature, in particular, actively intervene in the production of ideology, which, in turn, leads to social change.

The festive agon[6] is fully played out in *Twelfth Night*, as Carnival misrule in the persons of Toby and his companions – the gull, the clown and the mischievous servant[7] – contends with Lent in the person of Malvolio. This is often referred to as the 'comic sub-plot' – a series of episodes that constitute a marginal, non-serious commentary on the main action. The position taken here, however, is that the festive agon *is* the 'main action,' continuous with the wider world indicated in the clown's 'return from the outside' and in Malvolio's Parthian[8] shot – 'I'll be revenged on the whole pack of you'. The confrontation between the Carnivalesque and the Lenten principles is represented in the long drinking scene, where Toby, Andrew, Feste and Maria gather to enjoy hospitality with drink, laughter and singing. The scene begins by transgressive rescheduling of the normal order of day and night typical of Carnival and other forms of misrule.

> SIR TO. Approach, Sir Andrew. Not to be abed after midnight is to be up betimes; and 'diluculo surgere', thou knowst——
>
> SIR AND. Nay by my troth, I know not. But I know to be up late is to be up late.
>
> SIR TO. A false conclusion. I hate it as an unfilled can. To be up after midnight, and to go to bed then, is early, so that to go to bed after midnight is to go to bed betimes. Does not our life consist of four elements?

4 Bristol, *Carnival and Theater*, pp. 22–3.
5 Bristol, *Carnival and Theater*, p. 125.
6 Struggle.
7 Sir Andrew Aguecheek, Feste and Fabian.
8 Parting shot, from 'Parthia', a region in south-west Asia, corresponding to modern-day north-east Iran, whose inhabitants were renowned for shooting arrows at their enemies as they were retreating from battle.

SIR AND.   Faith, so they say, but I think it rather consists of eating and
    drinking.
SIR TO.   Thou'rt a scholar. Let us therefore eat and drink.
(see Key Passages, **p. 157**)

This symposium combines bodily satisfaction with philosophical debate and dialogue. The Carnivalesque principle of knowledge operates here, as both crudely
material, literal description and ingeniously transgressive redescriptions are
equally necessary to an adequate account of 'our life'. The simple-minded, tauto-
logical view that 'late is late' is a 'false conclusion' that is none the less compatible
with the abusive casuistry[9] that maintains that 'late is early'. The hateful 'unfilled'
tautology of the simple-minded Andrew that seems to require habits more abste-
mious than Toby likes is 'filled up' by the same simple-minded character's view
that man's life is 'eating and drinking', rather than the four elements. Harmoniz-
able disagreement and the 'abundance of the material principle' are celebrated in
jokes and song until the intervention of Malvolio, whose Lenten severity is man-
dated by his perfectly cogent understanding of precedence and due order.

MAL.   My masters, are you mad? Or what are you? Have you no wit,
    manners, nor honesty, but to gabble like tinkers at this time of
    night? Do ye make an alehouse of my lady's house that ye squeake
    out your coziers catches without any mitigation or remorse of
    voice. Is there no respect of place, persons, nor time in you?
(see Key Passages, **pp. 159–60**)

Irrespective of person, place or time, the rejoinder offered by Carnival is, as
always, a celebration of food and drink.

SIR TO.   ... Art any more than a steward? Dost thou think because
    thou art virtuous, there shall be no more cakes and ale?
(see Key Passages, **p. 160**)

As the festive agon unfolds, this acrimonious feeling gives rise to the active
persecution, humiliation and confinement of Malvolio. But the pattern of festive
agon is not compatible with asymmetrical, one-sided and conclusive outcomes.
The combatants, Carnival and Lent, each have certain obligations, in particular
the obligation to be thrashed.[10] Toby organizes the persecution of Malvolio and
then in a more improvisatory entertainment orchestrates the farcical duel between
Andrew and Viola, the boy-woman. The compensatory thrashing of Toby is given
by Sebastian near the end of the play. Toby, escorted by the clown, appears briefly
to display his bloody coxcomb[11] and is then escorted to his bed. This brief

---

9 A branch of moral philosophy, which involves the application of ethical principles to resolve moral
   dilemmas. Hence, the use of sophisticated reasoning, but, more commonly, of unnecessarily com-
   plicated and specious logic to explain a problem or conundrum.
10 According to Bakhtin, the festive battle between Carnival and Lent ensures a cyclical renewal and
   regeneration of the people who take part in it and their world.
11 A fool's cap or head.

appearance is important, as it visibly and materially confirms the fact of Toby's thrashing and also the importance of that wider world offstage where significant events that have the potential to upset the plots and the intentions enacted on the stage continually occur. Malvolio also has some scores to settle which he will attend to offstage. 'And thus the whirligig of time brings in his revenges.' The battle of angry Carnival and sullen, vindictive Lent is not concluded in the represented world of Illyria, nor is it ever concluded in the world offstage.

From **Karin Coddon, '"Slander in an Allow'd Fool": *Twelfth Night*'s Crisis of the Aristocracy'**, *Studies in English Literature* 33 (1993), pp. 314–15, 316 and 322–3

Like Bristol, Karin Coddon believes that 'far from being merely a temporary and cathartic release from social order, festivity intervenes to alter that order'. However, unlike Bristol, Coddon regards Malvolio and, most of all, Feste (rather than Sir Toby) as the main sources of social disruption in the play. Malvolio may preach respect for 'place, persons [and] time' (see Key Passages, **p. 160**), but his ambition represents a threat against the hierarchical organisation of Elizabethan society, which was becoming increasingly vulnerable to the upward mobility of the 'middling sort', the social group to which Malvolio belongs (see Contextual Overview, **pp. 8–10**). However, as Coddon points out, Malvolio is no social revolutionary: he may wish to curb Sir Toby's excesses, but he ultimately wants to become 'Count Malvolio'. Feste, as the following extract shows, is the only genuine source of resistance to the Elizabethan class system. By drawing on the notion of *interpellation*, formulated by French Marxist theorist Louis Althusser to define the way in which ideology summons individuals to occupy specific subject positions, Coddon interprets Feste's refusal to justify his absence at the beginning of Act 1, Scene 5 as a successful attempt to resist identification with the traditional role of the licensed fool. Interestingly, the progressive decline of the feudal aristocratic household releases Feste from the confines of harmless fooling. Several critics, including Coddon, have remarked on the fact that Feste demands to be paid, and by doing so, he draws our attention to his status as professional entertainer. Feste, therefore, resembles the fluid social role of the Elizabethan actor, who earned a living partly through the protection of powerful aristocratic patrons and partly through the income generated by the paying audiences who visited London's recently established commercial playhouses.

Orsino's opening trope, [. . .]–

> If music be the food of love, play on,
> Give me excess of it, that, surfeiting,
> The appetite may sicken, and so die
>
> (see Key Passages, **p. 141**)

–lends to his lyric self-indulgence a material marker of social privilege and its excesses. It serves to yoke together the amorous appetites of the relatively decorous Orsino and the more grotesque, "carnivalesque" appetites of Sir Toby Belch.[1] For Sir Toby is, of course, the play's most comical – and most pointed – travesty of aristocratic self-indulgence. His revels are informed by the popular tradition of "seasonal misrule," a tradition already suspect for its violations of class and gender boundaries.[2] Sir Toby cavorts not only with his fellow titled tosspot Sir Andrew Aguecheek, but also with his social inferiors – Feste, Fabian, and Maria, the last of whom he marries.[3] The deflation of Malvolio's ambition to wed into the aristocracy is countered by the marriage of Olivia's uncle to her serving-woman. The play's fantasy transgressions typical of festive misrule – Olivia's infatuation with a disguised woman, "Cesario's" with Orsino – are ostensibly contained as gender stability is restored. Like Malvolio's vow of revenge, however, Sir Toby's offstage marriage to Maria is a reminder of the instability of rank and order that persists outside the world of the play. Far from being merely a temporary and cathartic release from social order, festivity intervenes to alter that order. Sir Toby's marriage to Maria makes explicit the identification of festivity with social fluidity, despite the play's apparent recuperation of transvestism and homoerotic desire.

But Sir Toby's marriage is not the play's sole – or most significant – offstage social transgression. Feste's first appearance in I.v. aligns the clown with insubordination, with the equivocal boundaries between licensed and unlicensed foolery.

> MARIA.   Nay, either tell me where thou hast been, or I will open my lips so wide as a bristle may enter, in way of thy excuse: my lady will hang thee for thy absence.
> CLOWN.   Let her hang me: he that is well hanged in this world needs to fear no colours.
>
> (1.5.1–5)

As has been frequently noted, Feste's entrance is marked by an emphatic lacuna; his introduction is colored not only by the unauthorized absence from Olivia's household, but also by his defiant resistance ("Let her hang me") to Maria's interrogations about his whereabouts, even under the threat of hanging or unemployment. The clown's unlicensed insubordination lies less in the nature of his absence than in his refusal to represent a "subjectivity" to his interrogator. [. . .]

Upon Olivia's appearance, the clown launches into what is ostensibly the licensed insubordination allowed his function by his patroness and superior. Feste's witty impertinence reestablishes his "allow'd," public role as jester. Though

---

1   [Coddon's note.] Cf. Terry Eagleton: "Like Falstaff [Sir Toby] . . . is a rampant hedonist, complacently anchored in his body, falling at once 'beyond' the symbolic order of society in his verbal anarchy, and 'below' it in his carnivalesque refusal to submit his body to social control" (*William Shakespeare* [Oxford: Basil Blackwell, 1986], p. 32).

2   [Coddon's note.] On "seasonal misrule," see Stuart Clark, "Inversion, Misrule, and the Meaning of Witchcraft," *Past and Present* 87 (May 1980): 98–127.

3   [Coddon's note.] Ralph Berry remarks that Maria's exact social status is somewhat unclear, thought he observes that other characters frequently address her as a menial servant (*Shakespeare and Social Class* [Atlantic Heights, NJ: Humanities Press International, 1988], pp. 70–1).

he effectively proves her a fool, Olivia concedes, "There is no slander in an allow'd fool" (I.v.94). Yet because Feste's cheeky demonstration of his mistress's foolishness has been preceded by his *un*licensed absence, Olivia's authority here seems superfluous, even specious, as though Feste is but humoring her by playing the prescribed role of servant. [. . .]

Significantly, the clown's closing song seems to take its uncertain, melancholy tone not from the promised (though deferred) wedding and "golden time" of Orsino's last speech, but from the bitter note of Malvolio's final words. Far from heralding a "golden time," a term that itself evokes the pastoral myths of idyllic, benevolent relations between masters and servants,[4] the haunting song marks the end of holiday time and takes the play back into history, into materiality. Not just the wind and rain, but their inexorability against the festive vices of lust and drunkenness, the harshness of "man's estate" wherein gates are shut against foolery, call attention to the illusory nature of comic resolution and to the uncertain world to which actor and spectator alike must return. The final line, "And we'll strive to please you every day" (line 407), is a reminder that playing itself, while trafficking in illusion, is historically embedded, materially reproducible in time and space, and thus vulnerable as well to "wind and rain," to the threats that escape narrative closure. But like Malvolio's threat, Feste too is outside the narrative here, his song not mediated by the now-vanished illusory world of Illyria. [. . .] If Malvolio's evasion of closure deflates the ideal of a "golden time," Feste's signifies a resonant deconstruction of the boundaries between festivity and history. He stands as an emblem of the theater's capacity to intervene in lived experience.

From **Keir Elam, "'In What Chapter of His Bosom?'": Reading Shakespeare's Bodies'**, in Terence Hawkes (ed.), *Alternative Shakespeares 2* (London and New York: Routledge, 1996), pp. 145–8, 155–7

Keir Elam, like Coddon, qualifies Bristol's Bakhtinian approach to *Twelfth Night* by stressing that early modern culture, in general, and theatrical culture, in particular, successfully negotiated viable modes of social resistance at a time when the disruptive energy associated with medieval carnivals and the carnivalesque body started to clash with the emergence of a new model of subjectivity, which privileged balance and self-restraint over bodily excess. If the degradation of Orsino's and Olivia's bodies, which Elam discusses in the first half of the following extract, suggests that the grotesque body did start to be seen as abhorrent and offensive and in need to be disciplined and contained, the carnivalesque energy associated with Sir Toby continues to ensure resistance and regeneration. Even more crucially, Elam helps us realise that if the *private* body started to be trained to aspire to an ideal of orderly containment,

---

4   [Coddon's note.] On the pastoral and its mythologizing of master–servant relations, see Louis A. Montrose, "'Eliza, Queene of shepheardes' and the Pastoral of Power," *English Literary Renaissance* 10 (1980): 153–82 (see especially pp. 157–59).

the *public* body of the Elizabethan actor resisted social categorisation (or *class*-ification).

Elam's essay provides a corrective to another influential approach, which privileges gender and medical discourse over other aspects of early modern culture. More specifically, Elam criticises Stephen Greenblatt (see Modern Criticism, **pp. 82–90**) for reading *Twelfth Night* alongside contemporary Galenic medical tracts (see Contextual Overview, **pp. 10–11**), as if dramatic and medical early modern cultures were perfectly homogeneous. Elam wittily argues that Greenblatt extends the Galenic homology between the sexes to an assumed homology between dramatic and medical texts.[1] By establishing this connection, Greenblatt endorses the anti-theatrical views expressed by contemporary pamphleteers like Philip Stubbes (see Contemporary Documents, **pp. 25–6**) who warned their readers against the power of the *dramatic* body of the character to infect and corrupt the *physical* body of the actor. Conversely, Elam believes that *Twelfth Night* refutes those views, which Greenblatt's comparison between medical and dramatic texts paradoxically re-enacts.

To see what is going on in the Shakespeare Corp,[2] let us take an exemplary and indeed aristocratic early modern body: Duke Orsino's in *Twelfth Night*. Orsino's body is both subject and object of the comedy's opening speech, in which the Duke appears to be musing on his unrequited desire for Olivia, but is in fact thinking about himself: 'If music be the food of love, play on, / Give me excess of it, that, surfeiting, / The appetite may sicken, and so die' (see Key Passages, **p. 141**). Orsino is caught up in a narcissistic preoccupation with his own sexual and physiological processes: his call for an excess of 'it' – music, but also the 'food' of love – evokes a vision in which his 'appetite', alimentary and sexual, will be overfed to the point of nausea and death: death of appetite itself, death of desire in the form of orgasm ('die' in its Elizabethan erotic sense) and perhaps even death of the body in an intestinal/seminal explosion. The narcissism of Orsino's sexual drives is confirmed in his later fantasy of being turned into a hart/heart: 'And my desires, like fell and cruell hounds, / E'er since pursue me' (see Key Passages, **p. 142**). His desires pursue not Olivia but himself. Olivia's reprimand to Malvolio might well be directed towards Orsino: 'O you are sick of self-love' (1.5.86).
[. . .]

Orsino returns later to the alimentary tract and other obscure interiorities in his misogynistic discourse on female desire, addressed to the disguised Viola–Cesario:

> they lack retention,
> Alas, their love may be call'd appetite,
> No motion of the liver, but the palate,
> That suffers [sic] cloyment, and revolt;

---

1   Elam, 'In What Chapter of His Bosom?', p. 151.
2   Scholars who study Shakespeare's representation of the body in relation to dramatic conventions and extra-dramatic discourses and social practices.

But mine is all as hungry as the sea,
And can digest as much.

(see Key Passages, pp. 163–4)

In contrasting his own passion with mere female 'appetite', Orsino conducts a comparative physiological anatomy of the organs of love (the liver) and of sexual desire (the palate), and finds women to be in possession only of the latter. There are various ironies in this discourse, all at Orsino's own expense. First, he is reducing the idolatrized object of his own noble passion, Olivia, to animal-like libidinous flesh, incapable of love. Second, he rightly supposes his interlocutor Cesario to be capable of 'male' love, but is blind to the fact that 'he' is a woman and he, Orsino, 'his' beloved object. And third, his talk of female 'appetite' and 'cloyment' recalls his earlier self-description, and his own rapidly surfeited desire ('Enough, no more; / 'Tis not so sweet now as it was before', see Key Passages, p. 141) suggesting an implicit confession of effeminacy that undermines his present claims to masculine passion.

But there may be still darker organic things going on in Orsino's unpleasant speech. His claim that women 'lack retention' has as its immediate meaning their incapacity for love. But the accusation also raises the spectre of female incontinence: the sexual incontinence already implicit in the 'appetite' charge – and which was an essential ingredient of early modern misogyny and of the privatizing discourses regarding the (female) body[3] – but also, perhaps, menstrual and urinary incontinence. Gail Kern Paster has suggested, in her important study of early modern 'disciplines of shame' ('influenced', as she admits, 'by Michel Foucault'), that Shakespearean and Renaissance drama frequently represents women as 'leaky vessels', incapable of bladder control,[4] and that such bladder incontinence is a source of embarrassment and, consequently, of comicity. For Orsino and others, women – in this case Olivia – wet themselves. This may in part explain the liquid terminology – what Thomas Laqueur[5] and Alphonso Lingis[6] term the 'fluid economy' – of Orsino's discourse: 'hungry as the sea' (compare his earlier 'Receiveth as the sea', [see Key Passages, p. 141]. Although this again implicates Orsino in the accusation, since the 'sea' in question is his own.

The 'joke about the spectacle of women urinating', as Paster puts it,[7] recurs in Malvolio's letter scene, and the micturating lady is once again Olivia. On finding 'Olivia's' billet doux, Malvolio thinks he recognizes her handwriting: "By my life, this is my lady's hand these be her very C's, her U's, and her T's, and thus makes she her great P's" (see Key Passages, p. 169)'. The obscene pun in Malvolio's CUT is evident enough, as is Malvolio's 'unconscious' reference to urination in 'her great P's', although how one interprets Olivia's CUT and P's is another

---

3   [Elam's note.] See, for example, Gaspare Pallavicino's condemnation of female promiscuity in Castiglione's *The Book of the Courtier*: 'believe not that men are so incontinent as women be . . . For of the incontinencie of woman arise infinite inconveniences, that doe not of mens' (trans. Sir Thomas Hoby (1561), London: Dent (1975), p. 219).

4   Gail Kern Paster, *The Body Embarrassed: Drama and the Disciplines of Shame in Early Modern England* (Ithaca, NY: Cornell University Press, 1993), pp. 1, 23–63.

5   Thomas Laqueur, *Making Sex: Body and Gender from the Greeks to Freud* (Cambridge, Mass.: Harvard University Press, 1990), p. 43.

6   Alphonso Lingis, *Foreign Bodies* (New York and London: Routledge, 1994), p. 133.

7   Paster, *The Body Embarrassed*, p. 30.

matter. For Jonathan Goldberg, for example, they are castrating letters that point to 'a desire unattainable on a stage that can only impersonate sexual difference', due to the use of boy-actors in the Elizabethan theatre.[8] The cut is not so much Olivia's as Malvolio's and the actor's. For Dympna Callaghan, somewhat similarly, Malvolio has been 'feminized, ridiculed, castrated' and his body has been 'reduced to the most denigrated bodily part – a "cut"'.[9] Paster, instead, sees a trajectory in Malvolio's voyeuristic desire 'from the genital to the excretory', which simultaneously degrades Olivia's body, reduced to 'the lowly status of generic female by that specifically shameful female signifier – the "cut"'.[10]

From bowel movements to bladder evacuation: in any case 'what is at stake here', asserts Paster, 'is a semiology of excretion'.[11] What may really be at stake here is a semiology of social aspiration. The joke is not so much on Olivia's body as on Malvolio's secret hope to reach Olivia's social level. Watching Olivia pee is a sign not so much of sexual pleasure as of social equality: only her husband (C[o]unt Malvolio?) has the right to do so. Like Orsino, Malvolio, sick of self-love, does not desire Olivia but, in his case, his own social advancement.

[. . .]

[. . .] At the end of her encounter with Cesario, Olivia soliloquizes on the effects of his charms:

> OLIVIA   How now?
> Even so quickly may one catch the plague?
> Methinks I feel this youth's perfections
> With an invisible and subtle stealth
> To creep in at mine eyes. Well, let it be.
>
> (see Key Passages, **pp. 151–2**)

Olivia's 'catch the plague' is of course metaphorical, since she has been struck by an infection of the amorous kind that the moralists warned audiences about (and from a doubly cross-dressed boy-girl-boy to boot). But the 'plague' recurs other times in the play's opening scenes, forming what Shakespearean critics used to call an 'image group'.[12] Earlier in the same scene Olivia's kinsman Sir Toby presents his corporeal credentials:

> SIR TOBY   [*Belches.*] A plague o' these pickle-herring!
>
> (1.5.116–17)

Sir Toby – like his drinking companion Sir Andrew, an Ague-cheeked or thin-buttocked sign of fever and cowardice – is himself a humoral symptom, a Belch,

---

8 Jonathan Goldberg, 'Textual Properties', *Shakespeare Quarterly* 37 (1986), p. 217.
9 Dympna Callaghan, '"And All is Semblative a Woman's Part": Body Politics and *Twelfth Night*', *Textual Practice* (1993), p. 436.
10 Paster, *The Body Embarrassed*, p. 33.
11 Paster, *The Body Embarrassed*, p. 34.
12 [Elam's note.] See Caroline E. Spurgeon, *Shakespeare Imagery and What It Tells Us* (Cambridge: Cambridge University Press, 1935), on the recurring plague image in Shakespeare, see in particular pp. 130–2. [Outbreaks of the plague were a dreaded and recurrent event in Shakespeare's London (see Chronology, **pp. 16–17**)].

of the 'sharp belchings, fulsome crudities, wind and rumbling in the guts' class that Robert Burton attributed to 'windy hypochondriacal melancholy',[13] but which in his case indicates, on the contrary, windy, sanguine and dyspeptic *joie de vivre*. And the redundantly belching Belch's 'A plague . . .' appears to be simply an imprecation against his own troubled intestine. Just as his opening lines in the play –

> SIR TOBY What a plague means my niece to take the death of her
> brother thus? I am sure care's an enemy to life.
>
> (see Key Passages, **p. 143**)

– are an imprecation against windy or tearful melancholy itself: still more, against melancholy death.[14]

Against death: here is the 'point' of Belch's pestilential image group, of his recurring 'plagues': they are part of his steadfast stand against the mortality of his abundant flesh. Like Falstaff,[15] with his 'What a plague have I to do with a buff jerkin? (*1 King Henry IV* 1.2.45–6), Belch opposes his eructating sub-Rabelaisian[16] carnivalesque body[17] [. . .] to the world and its reality principle, which is to say to its death principle. Like Falstaff, he refuses to dress up or thin down, since thinness is a symptom of the Ague, perhaps of the Plague, and so of death: 'Confine? I'll confine myself no finer than I am', he shouts, when Maria enjoins him on behalf of her mourning mistress to confine or contain his body within decorous limits (see Key Passages, **p. 143**). Confinement is the privilege of the grave.

Belch's corporeal campaign against the mortal reality principle is no mere 'comic' detail in a play which begins with two male deaths – the 'real' death of Olivia's brother and the 'false' death of Viola's brother – and ends with belated news of a third male death, that of Viola's and Sebastian's father (see Key Passages, **p. 182**). What if we were to take Belch's talismanic 'plagues' literally? What if the unnamed cause of death of Olivia's unnamed brother were indeed the pestilence?

Belch's swearing is not the only trace or shadow of the plague in *Twelfth Night*. And it is not the only link between Olivia and the disease. In the play's opening scene, Orsino's one memorable compliment to Olivia explicitly opposes her to the epidemic:

> ORSINO O, when mine eyes did see Olivia first,
> Methought she purg'd the air of pestilence;
>
> (see Key Passages, **p. 142**)

---

13 [Elam's note.] Quoted in Gail Kern Paster, *The Body Embarrassed: Drama and the Disciplines of Shame in Early Modern England* (Ithaca: Cornell University Press, 1993), 12–3.
14 [Elam's note.] On 'plague' as Elizabethan swearword, see Geoffrey Hughes, *Swearing: A Social History of Foul Language, Oaths and Profamity in England* (Oxford: Blackwell, 1986), p. 190.
15 See Footnote 2 on **p. 64**.
16 See Footnote 1 on **p. 54**.
17 See Mikhail Bakhtin, *Rabelais and His World*, trans. Helene Iswolsky (Bloomington: Indiana University Press, 1984) and Michael D. Bristol, *Carnival and Theater: Plebeian Culture and the Structure of Authority in Renaissance England* (New York and London: Methuen, 1985).

Orsino's encomium[18] may be a conceit ('Methought'), but it is rooted in early modern medical lore. The pestilence was believed – not only by the Puritans – to be transmitted through the air by infected breath, for example from spectator to spectator. Apostrophizing London three years after the devastating epidemic of 1603, Thomas Dekker tells the city that 'Sicknes was sent to breathe her unholsome ayres into thy nostrils'.[19] And Jehan Goeruot warns in his *Regiment of Life* (1546) that 'the venomous air itself is not half so vehement to infect as is the conversation or breath of them that are infected already'.[20] 'Conversation', or social intercourse: the plague is a communicational disease. Olivia instead – like the air sweeteners used by Shakespeare's contemporaries to disperse the noxiousness of the atmosphere[21] – purges the unwholesome air for Orsino, even if she has lost her own brother.

What may well be at stake in this dialectic of plague and purgation is a claim concerning the comedy itself and theatrical representation in general. *Twelfth Night*, like Olivia – and indeed 'through' Olivia and the women, given the mortality rate among the males – does not transmit unwholesome airs into the nostrils of London but on the contrary 'purges' the air of pathology by taking on and exorcizing death. This is no Aristotelian catharsis[22] but an anti-epidemiological act of resistance, pitching the life of the comedy, of the playhouse, of the actor and his performance against the mortal enemies of the theatre, whether they be virological or ideological. Rather than confirm the moralists' charge of contagious dalliance, *Twelfth Night* refuses the deadly culture of the symptom: not by chance the play's own 'Puritan', Malvolio, is subjected to a ritual purging, even if he does promise post-dramatic revenge (the epidemic of 1603? the closing of the theatres in 1642?).

The (Wo)man's Part: (De)constructing Gender and Sexual Identity

From **Juliet Dusinberre,** *Shakespeare and the Nature of Women,* (London: Macmillan, 1975), pp. 243, 266–7

Juliet Dusinberre's work was ground-breaking in the mid-1970s, when feminist approaches to Shakespeare were yet to be officially acknowledged as a legitimate area of enquiry in their own right. Her book *Shakespeare and the Nature of Women* was written as a polemical response to Theodore Spencer's 1942 *Shakespeare and the Nature of Man*, which focused almost exclusively on male

---

18 Praise.
19 Thomas Dekker, *The Seven Deadly Sinnes of London (1606),* in A. B. Grosart (ed.), *The Non-Dramatic Works of Thomas Dekker,* Vol. II (London: The Huth Library, 1884–6), p. 10.
20 Quoted in Leeds Barroll, *Politics, Plague, and Shakespeare's Theater: The Stuart Years* (Ithaca, NY: Cornell University Press, 1991), p. 94.
21 See Barroll, *Politics, Plague, and Shakespeare's Theater: The Stuart Years,* p. 94.
22 A process whereby tragedy was supposed to cleanse the audience of the detrimental passions explored in the fictive world of the play.

characters. In Spencer, female identity was almost seamlessly subsumed within the generic category of 'mankind'. By analysing Shakespeare's female characters in relation to contemporary social and political changes, theatrical culture and staging conventions, Dusinberre argued that Shakespeare was sympathetic towards women and their changing roles in Elizabethan and Jacobean England.

[. . .] Breeches of themselves bestow no bravery on either the natural inmate or the usurper. Viola discovers when she puts on a sword a diffidence no greater than that of her male adversary to whom Nature had not given a sheath: but rather the way in which the world finds difference in similarity. Pacifism in women is cowardice in men. While Viola, pressed into a duel at the point of Sir Toby's sword, gasps: 'Pray God defend me! A little thing would make me tell them how much I lack of a man,' (3.4.293–4). Sir Andrew hears in trembling that 'a terrible oath, with a swaggering accent sharply twanged off, gives manhood more approbation than ever proof itself would have earned him' (3.4.176–9). Both 'men' need instruction in manhood – the man terrified as a girl, and the girl terrified because taken for a man. If there is to be any killing between these two it will be 'by the look, like cockatrices' (3.4.192). Custom gives a man a sword and teaches him how to use it, so that when Sebastian strides across the stage strewing it with broken pates Shakespeare establishes that this is the male twin and Cesario's masculinity a pastiche. [. . .]

To be queen of a fancy so opal as Orsino's seems an unenviable bliss and Orsino, having squandered his treasury of love, is himself loth to lose his page: 'Cesario, come! / For so you shall be, while you are a man.' (see Key Passages, **p. 184**) Outfaced by his own eloquence, he can find – like Cordelia[1] – no genuine currency in which to court Viola except

> Give me thy hand,
> And let me see thee in thy woman's weeds.
>
> (see Key Passages, **p. 183**)

This is exactly what the audience does not want to do; Viola is Viola in her breeches. Constant where Orsino is changeable, possessing a moral sensitivity which places Olivia in the same hemisphere as Cressida,[2] Viola's other self is not the man she loves, but her brother:

> One face, one voice, one habit, and two persons,
> A natural perspective, that is and is not.
>
> (see Key Passages, **p. 181**)

Viola sees herself in his mirror:

---

1 The king's youngest daughter in *King Lear*.
2 Shakespeare reworked the well-known story of Troilus and Cressida in his homonymous play, where Cressida, who is parted from her lover Troilus to rejoin her father, soon seems to forget her feelings for him.

> If spirits can assume both form and suit
> You come to fright us.
>
> (see Key Passages, **p. 182**)

Sebastian's presence exorcises the wickedness of disguise; Nature has clothed his spirit in a shape to question Viola's 'masculine usurp'd attire:'

> A spirit I am indeed,
> But am in that dimension grossly clad,
> Which from the womb I did participate.
>
> (see Key Passages, **p. 182**)

In the magical reunion of the twins, man and woman, Shakespeare soothes the mind with an illusion of concord between the masculine and feminine only to dispel the illusion by separating Viola from the second self with whom she has learnt to live. She is diminished by a return to a world where she must be Orsino's lady after the momentary freedom of a Twelfth Night masculinity which restored Nature's wholeness.

From **Stephen Greenblatt, 'Fiction and Friction',** in *Shakespearean Negotiations: The Circulation of Social Energy in Renaissance England* (Berkeley, Calif.: University of California Press, 1988), pp. 66–8, 69–73, 75–6, 78, 91–3

Stephen Greenblatt is one of the founders of an influential approach to early modern literature and culture called new historicism. Deeply affected by French theorist Michel Foucault (1926–84), Greenblatt's approach rests on the assumption that subjectivity (that is, our own sense of personal identity) is the product of historical and cultural contexts and, therefore, change across time and across cultures (see also Critical History, **p. 46**). Greenblatt, therefore, departs from Barber's theory according to which 'the most fundamental distinction [*Twelfth Night*] brings home to us is the difference between men and women' (see Modern Criticism, **p. 65**), by polemically pointing out that 'not only may [that] distinction be blurred, but the home to which it is supposed to be brought may seem less securely ours, less cosy and familiar, than we have come to expect'.

The type of historical criticism practised by Greenblatt is generally described as *new* in order to distinguish it from other historical approaches that understand literature as a mere reflection of the social context within which it was produced. *New* historicism regards literature as one of the multiple and interrelated discursive practices which contributed to fashioning the early modern subject. Instead of regarding *Twelfth Night* as a mere reflection of the Elizabethan context within which it was first written and performed, as Krieger had done in 1979 (see Modern Criticism, **pp. 67–70**), Greenblatt highlights a dynamic exchange between Shakespeare's representation of twinned gender identity in *Twelfth Night* and contemporary views on the differential homology between the sexes derived from Galenic physiology (see Contextual Overview, pp. 10–11). Greenblatt argues that the Galenic model threatened to expose the biological instability of sex distinctions but never challenged the belief in the physiological superiority of the male body. Similarly, the deferment of Cesario's transformation into Viola beyond the end of the play challenges normative heterosexuality, while confirming the early modern cultural assumption that 'a passage from male to female was coded ideologically as a descent'.

In September 1580, as he passed through a small French town on his way to Switzerland and Italy, Montaigne was told an unusual story that he duly recorded in his travel journal. It seems that seven or eight girls from a place called Chaumont-en-Bassigni plotted together "to dress up as males and thus continue their life in the world". One of them set up as a weaver, "a well-disposed young man who made friends with everybody," and moved to a village called Montier-en-Der. There the weaver fell in love with a woman, courted her, and married. The couple lived together for four or five months, to the wife's satisfaction, "so they say". But then, Montaigne reports, the transvestite was recognized by someone form Chaumont; "the matter was brought to justice, and she was condemned to be hanged, which she said she would rather undergo than return to a girl's status; and she was hanged for using illicit devices to supply her defect in sex." The execution, Montaigne was told, had taken place only a few days before.

I begin with this story because in *Twelfth Night* Shakespeare almost, but not quite, retells it. It is one of those shadow stories that haunt the plays, rising to view whenever the plot edges toward a potential dilemma or resolution that it in fact eschews. If we dwell on these shadow stories, we shall be accused of daydreaming (a serious charge, for some reason, against literary critics); the plays insist only that we register them in passing as we take in (or are taken in by) the events that "actually" happen. What if Olivia had succeeded in marrying Orsino's page Cesario? And what if the scandal of a marriage contracted so far beneath a countess's station were topped by a still greater scandal: the revelation that the young groom was in fact a disguised girl? Such a marriage—if we could still call it one—would make some sense in a play that had continually tantalized its audience with the spectacle of homoerotic desire: Cesario in love with 'his' master Orsino, Orsino evidently drawn toward Cesario, Antonio passionately in love with Sebastian, Olivia aroused by a page whose effeminacy everyone remarks. But how could the play account for such desire, or rather, since an account is neither called for nor tendered, how could the play extricate itself from the objectification of illicit desire in a legal marriage?

The case recorded by Montaigne, let us recall, did not set off a psychological examination—the "scientia sexualis" that Foucault finds at the heart of the modern history of sexuality—but a legal proceeding, a trial issuing in a condemnation not, it seems, for deception but for the use of prohibited sexual devices, devices that enable a woman to take the part of a man. So too at the critical moment of misunderstanding in *Twelfth Night*, when Olivia urges the apparently timorous Cesario to take up his new status as her husband, the issue is defined not in psychological but in legal terms. A priest is brought in to testify to the procedural impeccability of the ceremony he has performed:

> A contract of eternal bond of love,
> Confirm'd by mutual joinder of your hands,
> Attested by the holy close of lips,
> Strength'ned by interchangement of your rings,
> And all the ceremony of this compact
> Seal'd in my function, by my testimony.
>
> (5.1.154–59)

This legal validity would clash violently with the gross impropriety of a homo-sexual coupling; presumably, there would have to be a ceremony of undoing to resolve the scandal. But then, of course, Olivia does not succeed; she actually marries Viola's twin who is, as it happens, a male. At the moment that Cesario discloses what lies beneath the "masculine usurp'd attire"—"I am Viola"—her twin Sebastian frees Olivia from the scandalous shadow story:

> So comes it, lady, you have been mistook;
> But Nature to her bias drew in that.
>
> (see Key Passages, **pp. 182–3**)

What happened in Montier-en-Der was against nature; in *Twelfth Night* events pursue their natural curve, the curve that assures the proper mating of man and woman. To be matched with someone of one's own sex is to follow an unnatur-ally straight line; heterosexuality, as the image of nature drawing to her bias implies, is bent. Shakespeare's metaphor is from the game of bowls; the "bias" refers not only to the curve described by the bowl as it rolls along the pitch but also to the weight implanted in the bowl to cause it to swerve. Something off-center, then, is implanted in nature—in Olivia's nature, in the nature that more generally governs the plot of the comedy—that deflects men and women from their ostensible desires and toward the pairings for which they are destined.

This deflection can be revealed only in movement. As befits a play intended for performance, the metaphor for nature invokes not simply internal structure but a structure whose realization depends upon temporal unfolding, or *rolling*. An enacted imbalance or deviation is providential, for a perfect sphere would roll straight to social, theological, legal disaster: success lies in a strategic, happy swerving. The swerving is not totally predictable because the bowl will encounter obstacles, or "rubs", that will make its course erratic; if sometimes frustrating, these rubs are also part of the pleasure and excitement of the game. Licit sexuality in *Twelfth Night*—the only craving that the play can represent as capable of finding satisfaction—depends upon a movement that deviates from the desired object straight in one's path toward a marginal object, a body one scarcely knows. Nature is an *unbalancing* act.

Swerving is not a random image in the play, it is one of the central structural principles of *Twelfth Night*, a principle that links individual characters endowed with their own private motivations to the larger social order glimpsed in the ducal court and the aristocratic household. The play's initiatory design invites the

audience to envisage the unification of court and household through the marriage
of their symbolic heads, Orsino and Olivia. [. . .] All that stands in the way, the
play makes clear in its opening moments, is the extravagant irrationality of
her vow:

> The element itself, till seven years' heat,
> Shall not behold her face at ample view;
> But like a cloistress she will veiled walk,
> And water once a day her chamber round
> With eye-offending brine; all this to season
> A brother's dead love, which she would keep fresh
> And lasting in her sad remembrance.
>
> (see Key Passages, **p. 142**)

Olivia's swerving from this vow—absurdly ambitious in its projected dura-
tion, comically ritualized, perversely wedded to misery—is entirely predictable.[1]
Indeed, in lines that play on the standard theological term for marital intercourse—"to pay the debt"—Orsino takes her mourning less as an impediment
to his love than as an erotic promissory note:

> O, she that hath a heart of that fine frame
> To pay this debt of love but to a brother,
> How will she love when the rich golden shaft
> Hath kill'd the flock of all affections else
> That live in her.
>
> (see Key Passages, **p. 142**)

The surprise for Orsino is that the swerving, when it comes, is not in his direction. That it is not depends upon a series of events that the play also represents as
swervings: a shipwreck that keeps Viola and Sebastian from reaching their destination, the blocking of Viola's initial intention to serve Olivia, Viola's relatively
unmotivated decision to disguise herself in men's clothing, the mistaking of Sebastian for the disguised Viola, and so forth. These apparently random accidents are
at once zany deflections of direction, intention, and identity and comically predictable drives toward a resolution no less conventional that the one for which
Orsino had longed. The plot initially invoked by Shakespeare's play is displaced
by another, equally familiar, plot—the plot of cross-dressing and cross-coupling
that had become a heavily overworked convention of Italian and Spanish comedy.

Swerving in *Twelfth Night*, then, is at once a source of festive surprise and a
time-honored theatrical method of achieving a conventional, reassuring resolution. No one but Viola gets quite what she or he consciously sets out to get in
the play, and Viola gets what she wants only because she is willing to submit
herself to the very principle of deflection: "I am not that I play" (see Key Passages,
p. 148). She embraces a strategy that the play suggests is not simply an accident of

---

1 [Greenblatt's note.] In the image of the cloistress, Olivia's vow picks up for Shakespeare's Protestant audience associations with life-denying monastic vows, which must be broken to honour the
legitimate claims of the flesh by entering into holy matrimony [see Contextual Overview, **pp. 8–9**].

circumstance but an essential life-truth: you reach a desired or at least, desirable destination not by pursuing a straight line but by following a curved path. This principle underlies Sebastian's explanation of Olivia's mistake: "Nature to her bias drew in that."

Sebastian glosses his own image with the comment, "You would have been contracted to a maid" (see Key Passages, **p. 183**); that is, he invites Olivia to contemplate what would have happened had nature *not* drawn to her bias. The line seems to call forth its complement—"But now you are contracted to a man"—yet characteristically *Twelfth Night* does not give us such a sensible and perfectly predictable turn. Instead Sebastian concludes by renewing the paradox after it had seemed resolved:

> Nor are you therein, by my life, deceived,
> You are betroth'd both to a maid and man.
>
> (see Key Passages, **p. 183**)

A man because Sebastian has beneath his apparel what Cesario lacks – "Pray God defend me!" cries Cesario before the duel with Sir Andrew, "A little thing would make me tell them how much I lack of a man" (3.4.293–4); a maid because the term, by a quibble whose several sixteenth-century examples the OED records, could be applied to a male virgin. Its use here refers wittily not only to Sebastian's virginity but to the homosexual coupling that Olivia has narrowly escaped. Only by not getting what she wants has Olivia been able to get what she wants and, more important, to want what she gets.

Nature has triumphed. The sexes are sorted out, correctly paired, and dismissed to bliss—or will be as soon as Viola changes her clothes. And nature's triumph is society's triumph, for the same clarification that keeps marriage from being scandalized by gender confusion keeps it from being scandalized by status confusion: no sooner has Sebastian explained to Olivia that he is both a maid and man than Orsino adds, as if he were in no way changing the subject, "Be not amaz'd, right noble is his blood." This is the first mention of the twins' nobility—previously we had only heard Cesario's declaration, "I am a gentleman"—and Orsino's knowledge must stem from the same source that settled the question of identity: the name of the father.[2] Throughout the play we have been allowed to think that Viola and Sebastian are beneath Olivia's station—hence the spectral doubling of Malvolio's dream of social climbing—and consequently that the play's festive inversions have been purchased at the cost of the more perfect social alliance between the duke and the countess. Now, through the magical power of

---

2 [Greenblatt's note.] To Sebastian's question, 'What name? What Parentage?' Viola answers with the father's name (the mother in effect having no bearing on the question of parentage): 'Sebastain was my father' [see Key Passages, **p. 182**]. At the first mention of Orsino's name, Viola had remarked, 'Orsino! I have heard my father name him' (1.2.24). At the play's close, when we learn that this naming must have betokened a measure of social equality, the dialogue swerves from the natural back to the social. That is, in the face of the gender confusion, attention to social conflict had apparently been deflected by a concern for the natural; now the social returns the favour by deflecting attention from the natural. The play hastens to its conclusion by matching Orsino to Viola while gesturing towards Malvolio's grievance [. . .].

the name of the father, we learn that the threat to the social order and the threat to the sexual order were equally illusory. All's well that ends well.

"The most fundamental distinction the play brings home to us," remarks C. L. Barber in his well-known essay on *Twelfth Night*,[3]

> is the difference between men and women. . . . Just as the saturnalian reversal of social roles need not threaten the social structure, but can serve instead to consolidate it, so a temporary, playful reversal of sexual roles can renew the meaning of the normal relation. One can add that with sexual as with other relations, it is when the normal is secure that playful aberration is benign. This basic security explains why there is so little that is queazy in all Shakespeare's handling of boy actors playing women, and playing women pretending to be men.[4]

Perhaps. Yet however acute these remarks may be as a humane vision of life, we must question them as a summary judgment of Shakespearean comedy in general and of *Twelfth Night* in particular. At that play's end, Viola is still Cesario—"For so you shall be," says Orsino, "while you are a man" (see Key Passages, **p. 184**)— and Olivia, strong-willed as ever, is betrothed to one who is, by his own account, both "a maid and man". At the risk of intensifying our sense of the "queazy" (a category that might reward some inquiry), I would suggest that *Twelfth Night* may not finally bring home to us the fundamental distinction between men and women; not only may the distinction be blurred, but the home to which it is supposed to be brought may seem less securely ours, less cozy and familiar, than we have come to expect.

But how can we unsettle the secure relation between the normal and the aberrant? How can we question the nature that like a weighted bowl so providentially draws to her bias and resolves the comic predicaments? I propose that we examine the bowl more carefully, search out the off-center weight implanted in it, analyze why it follows the curve of gender. To do so we must historicize Shakespearean sexual nature, restoring it to its relation of negotiation and exchange with other social discourses of the body. For this task it is essential to break away from the textual isolation that is the primary principle of formalism and to move outside the charmed circle of a particular story and its variants. How can we do this? How but by swerving?

[. . .]

[A] culture's sexual discourse plays a critical role in the shaping of identity. It does so by helping to implant in each person a system of dispositions and orientations that governs individual improvisations, to implant, in other words, the defining off-center weight: "But nature to her bias drew in that."

The concrete individual exists only in relation to forces that pull against spontaneous singularity and that draw any given life, however peculiarly formed, toward communal norms. [. . .] It has been traditional, since Jakob Burckhardt, to trace the origins of autonomous individuality to the Renaissance, but the material

3   See Modern Criticism, **pp. 64–7.**
4   See Modern Criticism, **p. 65.**

under consideration here suggests that individual identity in the early modern period served less as a final goal than as a way station on the road to a firm and decisive identification with normative structures.

Of these structures, the most powerful appear to have been those governing sexual identity. Male writers of the period regarded gender as an enduring sign of distinction, both in the sense of privilege and in the sense of differentiation. A man in Renaissance society had symbolic and material advantages that no woman could hope to attain, and he had them by virtue of separating himself, first as a child and then as an adult, from women. All other significant differential indices of individual existence—social class, religion, language, nation—could, at least, in imagination, be stripped away, only to reveal the underlying natural fact of sexual difference. The Renaissance delighted in stories of transformation of individuals out of all recognition—the king confused with the beggar, the great prince reduced to the condition of a wild man, the pauper changed into a rich lord. Only the primary differentiation given by God himself—"male and female he made them"—would seem to have been exempt from this swirling indeterminacy. Even here, of course, confusion was possible, for as the many stories of cross-dressing suggest, apparel may deceive the eyes of the most skilled observer. But beneath the apparel the body itself cannot lie—or so we might expect.

Yet in Renaissance stories, paradoxically, the apparently fragile and mutable social codes are almost always reinscribed—despite his savage upbringing, the true prince reveals his noble nature—while sexual difference, the foundation of all individuation, turns out to be unstable and artificial at its origin. [. . .] At least since the time of Galen it had been widely thought that both males and females contained both male and female elements (Duval goes so far as to posit male and female seed[5]); the predominance, rather than the exclusion, of one or the other helped, along with the original position of the seed in the womb and other factors, to determine sexual identity and to make possible a harmonious accord between sex and gender. Predominance was never—or at least rarely—absolute, nor, in the opinion of most, was it established in final and definitive form in the womb. On the contrary, virtually all males experienced a transition during childhood from a state close to that of females—indeed often called "effeminate"—to one befitting an adult man. Conversely, if less frequently, the predominance of the appropriate female characteristics could take some time to establish itself. Where the female elements were dominant but still insufficiently strong, the woman would be a virago; similarly, a man in whom male seed was weaker than it should be was likely to remain effeminate. And in those rare cases, as Duval notes, where the competition between male and female elements was absolutely undecided, a hermaphrodite could be formed.

All of this implies, as I have suggested, the persistent doubleness, the inherent twinship, of all individuals.

[. . .]

Shakespeare's most ingenious representation of this twinned gender identity, which must have empowered the transvestite performances of his company's boy actors, is in *Twelfth Night*, with its fiction of male and female identical twins who

---

5 Jacques Duval, *On Hermaphrodites* (1603).

are at the border of adulthood: "Not yet old enough for a man, nor young enough for a boy" (see Key Passages, **p. 147**). With a change of a few conventional signals, the exquisitely feminine Viola and the manly Sebastian are indistinguishable: hence, perhaps, the disquieting intensity of Antonio's passion for Sebastian and the ease with which the confused Olivia is "betroth'd both to a maid and man" (see Key Passages, **p. 183**). Near the play's opening, Orsino nicely captures the gender confusion in an unintentionally ironic description of his young page Cesario—actually Viola in disguise:

> thy small pipe
> Is as the maiden's organ, shrill and sound,
> And all is semblative a woman's part.
>
> (see Key Passages, **p. 145**)

At the play's close, Orsino has not yet seen Viola—whom he intends to marry—in woman's clothes; she remains in appearance Cesario and therefore still the mirror image of her brother:

> One face, one voice, one habit, and two persons,
> A natural perspective, that is and is not!
>
> (see Key Passages, **p. 181**)

To be sure, the play suggests that beneath her "masculine usurp'd attire" is a body in which the feminine elements are dominant, and the "true" mettle of her sex resolves the play's ambiguities by attaching Orsino's desire to an appropriate and "natural" object. Viola will in the end—that is, when the play is done—put off her assumed male role and become "Orsino's mistress, and his fancy's queen" (see Key Passages, **p. 184**). But this transformation is not enacted—it remains "high fantastical"—and the only authentic transformation that the Elizabethan audience could anticipate when the play was done was the metamorphosis of Viola back into a boy.

Though Shakespeare characteristically represents his women characters—Rosalind[6], Portia[7], Viola—as realizing their identities through cross-dressing, this whole conception of individuation seems to me bound up with Renaissance conceptions of the emergence of male identity. Viola in disguise is said to look like one whose "mother's milk were scarce out of him" (see Key Passages, **p. 147**); in effect a boy is still close to the state of a girl and passes into manhood only when he has put enough distance between himself and his mother's milk. If a crucial step in male individuation is separation from the female, this separation is enacted inversely in the rites of cross-dressing; characters like Rosalind and Viola pass through the state of being men in order to become women. Shakespearean women are in this sense the representation of Shakespearean men, the projected mirror images of masculine self-differentiation.

Why should the comedies traffic in mirror images? Why don't they represent

---

6   Main female character in *As You Like It*.
7   Main female character in *The Merchant of Venice*.

this male trajectory of identity through male characters dressing up as women? In part because women had less freedom of movement, real or imaginary, than men, and hence donning women's clothes would entail not the rolling on which the course of nature depends but rather a stilling of momentum. In part because a passage from male to female was coded ideologically as a descent from superior to inferior and hence as an unnatural act or a social disgrace. And in part because women were, as we have seen, already understood to be inverted mirror images of men in their very genital structure. One consequence of this conceptual scheme— "For that which man hath apparent without, that women have hid within"—is an apparent homoeroticism in all sexuality. Though by divine and human decree the consummation of desire could be licitly figured only in the love of a man and a woman, it did not follow that desire was inherently heterosexual. The delicious confusions of *Twelfth Night* depend upon the mobility of desire. And if poor Antonio is left out in the cold, Orsino does in a sense get his Cesario.

From **Catherine Belsey, 'Disrupting Sexual Difference: Meaning and Gender in the Comedies'**, in J. Drakakis (ed.), *Alternative Shakespeares* (London and New York: Routledge, 1985), pp. 185, 187–8 and 190

In this essay, Catherine Belsey argues that Shakespearean comedy disrupts sexual difference. Inspired by Swiss linguist Ferdinand de Saussure and French philosopher Jacques Derrida, Belsey believes that the meaning that we attach to the terms 'masculine' and 'feminine', like meaning in general, bears no relation to an objective mode of being (the referent). The meaning of verbal categories like 'masculine' and 'feminine' depends on the historically determined relation of difference between them. Attempting to fix these terms means, as Belsey puts it, 'to confine what is possible to what *is*. Conversely', as Belsey continues, 'to disrupt this fixity is to glimpse alternative possibilities'.[1] In disrupting sexual difference, *Twelfth Night* reveals the artificial and unstable quality of gender roles. More specifically, by focusing on Viola and Orsino's exchange in the second half of Act 2, Scene 4, Belsey shows how 'Viola's father's pining daughter [see Key Passages, **p. 164**] . . . is neither Viola nor Cesario, but a speaker who at this moment occupies a place which is not precisely masculine or feminine'.

Like Greenblatt, Belsey reads literature *historically*, that is, in relation to other aspects of early modern culture, which affected to the construction of masculine and feminine identities. While Greenblatt focuses on medical discourse to explain why Shakespeare and his contemporaries would regard gender distinctions as inherently unstable, Belsey associates the disruption of sexual difference with the shift from a medieval and strictly patriarchal understanding of the nuclear family to a new, humanist ideal of affective marriage, based on elective affinities, reciprocal respect and domestic harmony (see also Contextual Overview, **pp. 8–10**).

---

1   Belsey, 'Disrupting Sexual Difference', pp. 166–7.

In *Twelfth Night* these dangers,[2] here romantic rather than erotic, constitute the plot itself – which means for the spectators a certain suspense and the promise of resolution. Viola, addressing the audience, formulates both the enigma and the promise of closure:

> What will become of this? As I am man,
> My state is desperate for my master's love:
> As I am woman (now alas the day!)
> What thriftless sighs shall poor Olivia breathe?
> O time, thou must untangle this, not I,
> It is too hard a knot for me t' untie.
>
> (see Key Passages, **p. 155**)

Of all Shakespeare's comedies it is perhaps *Twelfth Night* which takes the most remarkable risks with the identity of its central figure. Viola is just as feminine as Rosalind,[3] as the text constantly insists (see Key Passages, **p. 145**), and Cesario is as witty a saucy lackey as Ganymede.[4] But it is only in *Twelfth Night* that the protagonist specifically says, 'I am not what I am' (3.1.139) where 'seem' would have scanned just as well and preserved the unity of the subject.

The standard criticism has had few difficulties with the 'Patience on a monument' speech, identifying the pining figure it defines as Viola herself, and so *in a sense* she is.[5] But it is by no means an unproblematic sense. [. . .]

How do the identifications work in this instance? Cesario is Viola and Cesario's father's daughter is Patience who is also Viola. But the equations break down almost at once with, 'what's her history?' 'A blank'. Viola's history is the play we are watching, which is certainly not a blank but packed with events. Nor is it true that she never told her love. She has already told it once in this scene (see Key Passages, **p. 162**), and she is here telling it again in hints so broad that even Orsino is able to pick them up once he has one more clue (see Key Passages, **p. 183**). In the play as a whole Viola is neither pining nor sitting, but is to be seen busily composing speeches to Olivia and exchanging jokes with Feste; and far from smiling at grief, she is here lamenting the melancholy which is the effect of unrequited love.

How then do we understand these fictions as telling a kind of truth? By recognizing that the Viola who speaks is not identical to the Viola she speaks of. If

---

2 Belsey is here referring to the 'dangers which follow from the disruption of sexual difference' ('Disrupting Sexual Difference', p. 185).
3 The main female character in Shakespeare's *As You Like It*.
4 Rosalind in disguise.
5 [Belsey's note.] There are exceptions. C. L Barber identifies the Patience figure as 'a sort of polarity within Viola' (C. L. Barber, *Shakespeare's Festive Comedy* [Princeton, NJ: Princeton University Press, 1959], 247). In other cases a certain unease is evident in the identifications. Viola is describing 'her sister', but the image 'is drawn from her own experience' (Alexander Leggatt, *Shakespeare's Comedy of Love* [London: Methuen, 1974], pp. 236–7). According to the Arden editor(s), the speech describes 'Cesario's sister's love for a man to whom she never told it'. A footnote adds, 'I express it thus for brevity's sake. This is how it appears to Orsino: but everything Viola says is directly applicable to herself in her real person' (J. M. Lothian and T. W. Craik (eds.), *Twelfth Night*, The Arden Shakespeare [London: Methuen, 1975], p. lxviii). Kenneth Muir succeeds in evading any very specific identification of the speaker: 'Cesario tells the story of her imaginary sister ... But we know that Viola is too intelligent and too well-balanced to go the way of her "sister"' (Kenneth Muir, *Shakespeare's Comic Sequence* [Liverpool: Liverpool University Press, 1977], p. 98).

Viola is Patience, silent like Patient Griselda,[6] it is not Viola who speaks here. Viola-as-Cesario repudiates the dynastic meaning of the feminine as patience, and yet that meaning is as present in Cesario's speech as the other, the difference which simultaneously defines Cesario as Orsino's companion and partner in suffering, and Viola as a woman.

In reply to Orsino's question, 'But died thy sister of her love?', the exchange ends with a riddle. 'I am all the daughters of my father's house, / And all the brothers too: and yet I know not' (see Key Passages, **p. 164**). At the level of the plot the answer to the riddle is deferred to the end of the play: Viola doesn't die; she marries Orsino. But to an attentive audience another riddle presents itself: who tells the blank history of Viola's father's pining daughter? The answer is neither Viola nor Cesario, but a speaker who at this moment occupies a place which is not precisely masculine or feminine, where the notion of identity itself is disrupted to display a difference within subjectivity, and the singularity which resides in *this* difference.

It cannot, of course, be sustained. At the end of each story the heroine abandons her disguise and dwindles into a wife. Closure depends on closing off the glimpsed transgression and reinstating a clearly defined sexual difference. But the plays are more than their endings, and the heroines become wives only after they have been shown to be something altogether more singular – because more plural. [. . .]

It is not obvious from a feminist point of view that, in so far as they seem finally to re-affirm sexual polarity, Shakespeare's comedies have happy endings. It is certain from the same point of view that the contest for the meaning of the family in the sixteenth and seventeenth centuries did not, though on this there is a good deal more to be said.[7] What I have been arguing is that that contest momentarily unfixed the existing system of differences, and in the gap thus produced we are able to glimpse a possible meaning, an image of a mode of being, which is not a-sexual, nor bisexual, but which disrupts the system of differences on which sexual stereotyping depends.

From **William Dodd, '"So Full of Shape is Fancy": Gender and Point of View in *Twelfth Night*'**, in Robert Clark and Piero Boitani (eds), *English Studies in Transition* (London and New York: Routledge, 1993), pp. 156, 158–60 and 163–4

Unlike Catherine Belsey, who regrets that 'closure depends on closing off the glimpsed transgression and reinstating a clearly defined sexual difference',

---

6   A popular story based on the last tale in *The Decameron*, a collection of short stories, or *novellas*, by Italian writer Giovanni Boccaccio (1313–75). This story was reworked into 'The Clerk's Tale' by English poet, Geoffrey Chaucer (1343–1400) and included in the most famous of his work, *The Canterbury Tales*. Griselda, the daughter of a poor peasant whose patience is repeatedly tested by her cruel aristocratic husband, became associated with patience and endurance.
7   Belsey did write more extensively about the early modern family after this article was published in 1985. For more details, see *The Loss of Eden: the Construction of Family Values in Early Modern Culture* (Basingstoke: Macmillan, 1999).

William Dodd believes that *Twelfth Night* 'defer[s] the formal solution of the identity game beyond the end of the play'. As a result, rather than moving towards 'individuation and maturity', *Twelfth Night* points '"backward" towards a merger with the narcissistic object'. The ending of *Twelfth Night*, in other words, can be understood as a dramatic re-enactment of what French psycho-analyst Jacques Lacan (1901–81) calls the 'mirror-stage'. While according to Sigmund Freud (1856–1939), the founder of psychoanalysis, personal identity starts to emerge during infancy, when the baby identifies with one parent and vies for the love and attention of the other (a psychological mechanism which Freud famously called the 'Oedipus Complex'), Lacan argued that personal identity is an effect of language acquisition. When the baby starts to speak, he or she is forced to identify with the necessarily partial and limited subject position defined by the pronoun 'I'. The potential for self-expression offered by the pronoun 'I', as much as by language itself, is comparable to the image an obser-ver projects onto a mirror: while allowing recognition, identification is necessar-ily partial. As a result, Lacan understands desire as a tension towards the sense of unity between the self and the other, the self and the world, which the baby relinquishes as he or she enters the world of language, which rests on difference (linguistic and social) and deferral (of meaning and of complete identification). *Twelfth Night* seems to tap on a regressive desire to recover the sense of unity that precedes linguistic and social individuation, which is also one of the pos-sible readings of the myth of Narcissus (see Modern Criticism, **pp. 60–3**). According to Dodd, the ending of *Twelfth Night* dwells on the androgynous brother and the androgynous sister, who has altered her appearance to look exactly like her brother, in order to reimagine the 'mirror-stage' as a formative moment of recognition and identification, which does not preclude but recovers unity *and* alterity. Dodd, therefore, takes his distance both from critics like Greenblatt, who regard the final scene as a celebration of (male) homoeroticism in all sexuality (see Modern Criticism, **p. 90**), and from other psychoanalytic critics, like Coppélia Kahn, who regard homoerotic desires as a prelude to the establishment of normative heterosexual bonds.[1]

Oddly enough, the reunion of Viola and Sebastian is often passed over rather rapidly by critics of *Twelfth Night* [. . .]. It looks as though, in pursuing their various interpretations, they were bent on following out the entangled desires of Olivia, Orsino and Viola. This is perhaps natural if we consider that these three vectors have vied for our attention for most of the main plot so far. [. . .]

Perhaps the clearest internal clue to Shakespeare's new strategy is to be found in Sebastian's amazing short-sightedness after he walks on to the stage in the closing scene. It takes him all of eighteen lines – at least forty or fifty seconds of perform-ance time – to notice Cesario. It is only when Antonio exclaims, 'How have you made division of yourself? / An apple cleft in two is not more twin / Than these

1   Coppélia Kahn, *Man's Estate: Masculine Identity in Shakespeare* (Berkeley, Calif. and London: University of California Press, 1981).

two creatures. Which is Sebastian?' (see Key Passages, **p. 181**), that Sebastian's gaze finally falls on his double. His attention is first riveted by his just-wed Olivia, and then by his friend Antonio ('O my dear Antonio, / How have the hours rack'd and tortur'd me, / Since I have lost thee!' (see Key Passages, **p. 181**). When his eyes do finally meet those of Viola, she thus eclipses the other two as the privileged focus of Sebastian's, and the audience's, attention.[2] Not only is our expectation kindled to urgency by this delay-sequence, it is also specifically directed toward the reunion of the twins as the climactic, and hence psychologically most significant, relationship. That our experience of the crucial meeting should here find its dynamic vehicle in Sebastian is perhaps the most eloquent hint of the polymorphic fantasy[3] which the finale of this play has brought to fruition as we are aligned with a figure whose gaze is shown embracing, with growing intensity, first a heterosexual object, then a homoerotic object,[4] and lastly an androgynous self-image.[5] And what more fitting vehicle for an audience's involvement than this Serendip who wanders into the world of Illyria and finds more desires satisfied than he had even begun to formulate?

Yet the meeting of Sebastian's and Cesario's gaze does not dissolve the enigma. For thirty-three lines – over a minute and a half of acting time – Shakespeare manages to hold his twins on this side of the brink of explicit mutual identification. Viola is committed to riddling to the end, promising further proofs when none is needed:

> If nothing lets to make us happy both,
> But this my masculine usurp'd attire,
> Do not embrace me, till each circumstance
> Of place, time, fortune, do cohere and jump
> That I am Viola
>
> (see Key Passages, **p. 182**)

---

2   [Dodd's note.] This effect will be reinforced if Viola's stage position at this point fits Hasler's hypothesis: 'As "Cesario" walks away from her once again, even the doting Olivia loses patience with him: she interrupts him immediately. The incident causes the three figures to be spaced out more widely across the stage' (J. Hasler, 'The dramaturgy of the ending of *Twelfth Night*', in S. Wells (ed.), *Twelfth Night: Critical Essays* (New York and London: Garland, 1986), p.284.

3   A fantasy which, as Dodd specifies later on in the same sentence, embraces many different desired objects: 'a heterosexual object, then a homoerotic object, and lastly an androgynous self-image'.

4   [Dodd's note.] The kind of Renaissance male relationship I assume as a model for that of Antonio-Sebastian is lucidly described in [Alan] Bray, *Homosexuality in Renaissance England*, 2nd edn, (London: Gay Men's Press, 1988)].

5   [Dodd's note.] Marianne Novy among others has drawn attention to the 'Neoplatonic iconology' of Antonio's 'An apple cleft in two is not more twin / Than these creatures', remarking how 'the language surrounding the recognition of Sebastian and Viola emphasizes its analogy to the mutual recognition of lovers' (Marianne Novy, *Love's Argument: Gender Relations in Shakespeare* [Chapel Hill, NC and London: University of North Carolina, 1984], pp. 38–9). It needs to be added that the application of the Neoplatonic myth to *twins* instead of lovers is, though justified by their identical appearance, not without consequences, connoting their relationship as one of consuming mutual desire. [Editor's note] Dodd is here referring to the cultural currency of ideas associated with Greek philosopher Plato (428 BC?–348BC?) during the early modern period. In *The Symposium*, Plato memorably argued that some men and women were originally part of a single being, whose perfection made even the gods jealous. Zeus, the most powerful of the gods, decided to split this ancestral androgynous creature into two halves, who have since craved to be rejoined. Hence Plato's theory about the origin of love.

'When thou hast done, thou hast not done, For I have more . . .' she seems to be saying. For Viola and Sebastian to identify each other explicitly would mean acquiescing in their separateness, giving up their single mirrored self.[6] Instead, their encounter is orchestrated so as to maintain them in a trance of wonder, holding desire focused on its fantasized object and ultimately deferring the formal solution of the identity game beyond the end of the play. Shakespeare, like Lacan, was well aware that desire endlessly outstrips the satisfaction of need.

Left outside the spotlight of this reunion, Orsino and Olivia are now assigned choral roles: 'One face, one voice, one habit, and two persons! / A natural perspective, that is, and is not!' (see Key Passages, **p. 181**) exclaims the count. 'Most wonderful!' cries the lady.

The winding-up procedures now get under way and assign count and countess to the twin of the appropriate sex. But even now Viola doesn't actually hurry offstage to change. As critics have often remarked, she remains cross-dressed to the end,[7] so that Orsino can say in the concluding speech of the play:

> Cesario, come;
> For so you shall be while you are a man;
> But when in other habits you are seen,
> Orsino's mistress, and his fancy's queen.

(see Key Passages, **p. 184**)

The words of Shakespeare's sonnet 20 – 'the master mistress of my passion' come readily to mind[8] – and the lines appear further to confirm Janet Adelman's reading of *As You Like It* and *Twelfth Night* as enabling a fantasy of simultaneity of homosexual and heterosexual love. Yet this fantasy seems to me to find its fullest expression less in Orsino's desire for an androgynous creature than in the reciprocal enthralment of an androgynous sister and an androgynous brother, which gathers up the emotional focus of this scene.[9] For we must not

---

6   [Dodd's note.] As Stevie Davies reminds us: 'Boy-and-girl twins are the *coincidentia oppositorum* in person, simultaneous selves of opposed gender, attached to a source at a fused root of being' (S. Davies, *The Idea of Woman in Renaissance Literature: The Feminine Reclaimed* [Brighton: Harvester, 1986], p. 105).

7   [Dodd's note.] Arguing that the constant association of boys with women 'tends to point towards an image of youth as a blessed period of sexual indeterminacy', Janet Adelman notes that comedy endings depend on the resolution of this indeterminacy: '[. . .] If *Twelfth Night* celebrates marriage and the necessary sorting out into male and female that enables marriage, it also mourns the loss of sexual indeterminacy and works to repair that loss through fantasy. [. . .] *Twelfth Night* leaves its delicately androgynous image unresolved' (Janet Adelman, 'Male Bonding in Shakespeare's Comedies', in P. Erickson and C. Kahn (eds), *Shakespeare's Rough Magic: Renaissance Essays in Honor of C. L. Barber* [Newark, Del.: University of Delaware Press, 1985], 89–90, 87).

8   [Dodd's note.] McLuskie cites this sonnet as showing 'an awareness that men and women might be created out of an overlapping system of differences and, more dangerously, that these physical attributes might inspire love regardless of their ascription to a particular gender' (Kate McLuskie, *Renaissance Dramatists* [New York: Harvester Wheatsheaf, 1989], p. 116).

9   [Dodd's note.] Phyllis Rackin suggests that : '*Twelfth Night* incorporates the reality principle in its conclusion by splitting the unitary figure of the androgyne into the marvellously identical boy-girl twins who are needed to make the resolution possible' (P. Rackin, 'Androgyny, mimesis, and the marriage of the boy heroine on the Ranaissance stage', in *PMLA* 102 [1987], p. 38). It seems to me that Shakespeare actually *avoids* doing this by having Viola remain cross-dressed to the end: we are left with *two* androgynous figures rather than one.

forget that if the actor of Cesario is a boy who resembles a young woman, the actor of Sebastian must appear equally ambivalent if he is to be perceived as identical with his sister. It is, moreover, an enthralment that remains suspended and unresolved, projecting the audience's desires beyond the confines of the play.

[. . .]

This kind of reading of *Twelfth Night* thus seems to provide support for the kind of claims made by Belsey (see Modern Criticism, **pp. 90–3**) and Adelman.[10] Attention to dramatic focus and to the way the audience's emotions are orchestrated suggests how frequently the play brings fantasies of sexual indeterminacy and merging close to the surface of our awareness and how it nurtures them by deferring their resolution beyond the formal closure of the play.[11] On the other hand, I find less evidence in *Twelfth Night* to support such claims as Coppélia Kahn's that 'The dramatic device of identical opposite-sex twins allows Orsino and Olivia to navigate the crucial passage from identification to object choice, from adolescent sexual experimentation to adult intimacy'[12] [. . .] The dramatic focus, as I hope to have shown, does not point forward to individuation and maturity, but rather 'backward' towards a merger with the narcissistic object.

From **Lorna Hutson, 'On Not Being Deceived: Rhetoric and the Body in *Twelfth Night*'**, *Texas Studies in Literature and Language* 38 (1996), pp. 146–7, 158–9, 160–1, 164–5, 166, 167–8 and 174

Lorna Hutson offers a fascinating critique of recent approaches that privilege early modern conceptions of the body over other relevant cultural contexts. Hutson believes that critics like Stephen Greenblatt, who have related Shakespeare's representation of gender instability in *Twelfth Night* to Galenic physiology in order to *historicise* our approach to the play, have, in fact, perpetuated the misogynist views intrinsic to the Galenic model by suggesting that the play celebrates the fantasy of (male) homoeroticism in all sexuality (see Modern Criticism, **p. 90**). According to Hutson, Viola's appeal stems from her 'ability to improvise social credit, or credibility'. By comparing Olivia and Viola's exchange in Act 1, Scene 5 with its counterpart in *Gl'Ingannati* (see Contemporary Documents, **pp. 26–8**), Hutson shows the extent to which Shakespeare downplayed the erotic potential of this encounter by emphasising Viola's rhetorical ability to generate emotional credibility, thus transforming the audience from voyeurs into auditors. According to Hutson, Viola's 'capacity to arouse desire resides less in the androgynous beauty of the body, than in the body conceived

---

10   See Footnote 7, **p. 95**.
11   [Dodd's note.] Cf. Greenblatt (see Modern Criticism, **pp. 82–90**): 'the unrepresented consummations of unrepresented marriages call attention to the unmooring of desire, the generalizing of the libidinal, that is the special pleasure of Shakespearean fiction' ('Fiction and Friction', p. 89).
12   [Dodd's note.] Kahn, *Man's Estate*, p. 210.

as the medium of *elocutio*',[1] while the play as a whole encourages fantasies about the 'opportunity for social advancement and erotic gratification afforded by education'.

What bothers me most about these arguments[2] is that while they seem to be historicizing and de-essentializing our ideas about the relationship of gender to sexuality, the "fantasies" and "anxieties" that they identify in early modern dramatic texts take no account at all of the way in which, in sixteenth-century society, a woman's sexual behavior was perceived to affect the honor and therefore the credit and economic power of her kinsmen. Nor do they consider the way in which such traditional conceptions of sexual honor, credit, and wealth were themselves being rapidly transformed by the technology of persuasion—or "credit"—that such dramatic texts as Shakespeare's represented. None of these critics appear to entertain the possibility that the capacity to plot, write, and *be able to make use* of the erudition and wit of a comedy such as *Twelfth Night* might in itself be more central to sixteenth- and seventeenth-century conceptions of what it meant to "be a man" than any theory derived from Galen. Moreover, for all the emphasis on plurality, the "polymorphous potential" and the "unmooring of desire" released by the comedies, there still seems to be a commitment to the twentieth-century "lit-crit" notion that what the comedies are really all about is individual identity. Traub explores how characters negotiate their individual desires in the plays as if they were real people and not even partly figures in a persuasive discourse or agents of a plot,[3] while Greenblatt celebrates "the emergence of identity through the experience of erotic heat" as "this Shakespearean discovery, perfected over a six- or seven- year period from *Taming* to *Twelfth Night*."[4] It seems that where literary criticism, as it was once conceived, celebrated the saturnalian energies of Shakespeare's comedies for returning us to a "natural" social and sexual order,[5] these theorists of desire want to find a historically specific concept of "nature"—the Galenic one-sex body—that mimics what is actually their essentialized notion of culture as something which is always preoccupied with the theatrical destabilization of "identities"—identity is "always a masquerade, a charade, other." But what if the errors, confusions, and masquerades of comedy were not, in their own time, thought of as dramas of identity? And what if the way in which the plays construct sexual difference in relation to the audience crucially concerned not the sexual object-choice of men or women in

1   Latin term meaning the mastery of style and delivery in written and spoken discourse.
2   Hutson is referring to 'a certain kind of "body" criticism, including Greenblatt's essay on *Twelfth Night* (see Modern Criticism, **pp. 82–90**), and Thomas Laqueur's *Making Sex: Body and Gender from the Greeks to Freud* (Cambridge, Mass.: Harvard University Press, 1987), which gives too much prominence to the Galenic model of human physiology, thus perpetuating the notion that femininity in the early modern period is best described as latent (and therefore inferior) virility'.
3   This is a reference to Valerie Traub's *Desire and Anxiety: Circulation of Sexuality in Shakespearean Drama* (New York and London: Routledge, 1992).
4   Greenblatt, 'Fiction and Friction', p. 80.
5   Hutson is here referring to mid-twentieth-century studies, including C. L. Barber's *Shakespeare's Festive Comedies* (see Modern Criticism, **pp. 64–7**).

the audience, but whether or not they were able to make use of the play as a discourse, an argument, to enhance their own agency? [. . .]

My counter-argument depends on the claim that the kind of comic plot from which Shakespeare never wavered—the five-act plot derived from Terence and Plautus[6]—was perceived in his own time to be concerned, not with the emergence of identity, but with men's discursive ability to improvise social credit, or credibility. [. . .] Reading *Gl'Ingannati*,[7] Shakespeare would have come across a model for a scene between Olivia and Viola/Cesario. The scene in question requires the audience to share the voyeuristic position of Flammineo's servants who stumble across Isabella and Lelia/Fabio during an intimate exchange of words and caresses. [. . .] Without denying the possibility of performing the equivalent scene between Olivia and Viola/Cesario in such a way as to maximize its erotic possibilities, I would want to argue that the rhetorical excess which distinguishes Shakespeare's text from the Italian model insists on a far higher level of engagement from the audience *as auditors*. This, in turn, reorients the dramatic meaning of the scene from pleasure in the spectacle of erotic possibility towards complicity in the act of *interpretation* by means of which a reader or auditor lends credibility to the figures, tropes, and fictions in the discourse of another.

Such audience complicity in the bestowal of credibility through interpretation replicates what the scene offers by way of a narrative of "desire." Olivia's desire for Viola/Cesario must become intelligible (unless we ignore the text altogether) through Viola/Cesario's progression away from formal literary models of courtship towards the affective intimacy of a more familiar mode of address, exemplified in the deservedly famous speech which begins, "Make me a willow cabin at your gate" (see Key Passages, **pp. 150–1**). At this point we have already witnessed Olivia's unenchanted exposure of the economics of the Petrarchan argument (see Contextual Overview, **pp. 13–14**), her parody of its facile and opportunistic movement from the praise of natural beauty to the imperatives of husbandry and reproduction: "O sir, I will not be so hard-hearted, I will give out divers schedules of my beauty" (see Key Passages, **p. 150**). Cesario's subsequent readiness to improvise a first-person fiction of abandonment in love represents an ability to extemporize, to seize "the gifts of moment" and so illustrate the crowning glory of classical rhetorical education. [. . .]

Olivia's desire for Viola/Cesario becomes apparent as a response to this speech and is inseparable, in its articulation, from the material expression of belief ("credit") that would exempt the unknown stranger from providing the heraldic display (the "blazon" [see Contemporary Documents, **pp. 33–5**]) that would put "his" gentility beyond doubt:

> "What is my parentage?"
> "Above my fortunes, yet my state is well,
> I am a gentleman." I'll be sworn thou art;
> Thy tongue, thy face, thy limbs, actions and spirit

---

6   Titus Maccius Plautus (c. 254 BC–c. 184 BC) and Publius Terentius Afer (c. 190 BC–c. 158 BC) were two influential Roman playwrights, who wrote popular comedies, including *Miles Gloriosus* and *The Eunuch*, which were widely imitated by Renaissance dramatists across western Europe.

7   See Contemporary Documents, **pp. 26–8**.

Do give thee five-fold blazon. Not too fast: soft! soft!
Unless the master were the man . . .

(see Key Passages, **p. 151**)

Olivia's desire motivates her affirmation of Cesario's somewhat evasive protest-
ation of gentility on the grounds of "his" exceptional beauty, eloquence, and
presence of mind. What this implies, then, is that the capacity to arouse desire
resides less in the androgynous beauty of the body, than in the body conceived as
the medium of *elocutio*[8] ("tongue . . . face . . . limbs . . . actions . . . spirit"); that
is, the apt delivery of the mind's invention. Viola/Cesario *embodies* the capacity
of timely and well expressed speech to compel for a mere fiction *credit*, that is the
kind of materially consequential belief (in this case, belief in matrimonial eligibility) that is rarely afforded to the "real thing."

The transgressive "glimpse" being offered to a seventeenth-century audience
here, I would suggest, is less that of lesbian desire than that of the opportunity for
social advancement and erotic gratification afforded by education for any servant
of ability entrusted with missions of such intimate familiarity. [. . .]

What was positive for seventeenth-century women about the way in which
Twelfth Night addressed them, then, was due less to the "high cultural investment
in female erotic pleasure . . . because it was thought necessary for conception to
occur" than to its opposite: the extent to which, by refusing to subject Olivia to
the "mal . . . voglio"[9] of an explicitly sexual encounter with Sebastian on the
model of Isabella's with Fabrizio, Shakespeare manages to portray a heroine
whose prudence, good judgment, and ability to govern others remain uncompro-
mised even by her contract with the beautiful youth. For in marrying Sebastian,
Olivia has arguably yielded to no whim, but carried out the strategic plan first
made known to us by Sir Toby Belch: "she'll not match above her degree, neither
in estate, years, nor wit" (1.3.105–106). Olivia never wavers from this purpose,
and in providing the precedent that it elsewhere pretends to deny—marriage
between a noblewoman and one beneath her—the play endorses the real-life
example of the highly intelligent Katherine Brandon, Duchess of Suffolk, who,
after having been married at fourteen to her forty-nine-year-old noble guardian,
later decided to marry none other then her gentleman usher, who was "an accomplished gentleman, well versed in the study of the languages . . . bold in discourse,
quick in repartee." There were, as Katherine Brandon's biographer commented,
"many reasons why the clever and serviceable gentleman usher who conducted
her business . . . should seem to the Duchess a more desirable husband than an
ambitious noble."[10] Shakespeare's play, around 1602, contributed to the undoing
of the social and sexual stereotyping that would make of that last statement
nothing but a dirty joke.

---

8 See Footnote 1, **p. 97**.
9 From the Italian 'malvolere', meaning 'ill-will', or 'to have a dislike for somebody'; also a pun on
   Malvolio's name and the 'ill-will' he bears to the other members of Olivia's household. Hutson is
   here referring to the fact that the authors of earlier versions of the main plot subject Olivia's
   predecessors to a sexual encounter with the wrong twin.
10 The source of these quotations is Lady Cecilie Goff, *A Woman of the Tudor Age* (London: John
   Murray, 1930), p. 213.

The Work in Performance

Introduction

Twelfth Night on the Seventeenth- and Eighteenth-Century Stage

> If this were played upon a stage now,
> I could condemn it as an improbable fiction.

When Fabian speaks these lines in Act 3, Scene 4 he is referring to the fact that Malvolio, undeterred by Olivia's horrified response to his yellow stockings, is behaving as if he was indeed 'Count Malvolio'. Early modern dramatists often attracted their audiences' attention to the artificial and constructed quality of theatrical illusion, and Fabian's remark may therefore suggest how Shakespeare expected his audience to regard the play as a whole. As mentioned above (see Introduction, p. 3), *Twelfth Night*, or the Feast of the Epiphany, celebrates the Wise Men's arrival in Bethlehem, where they worshipped the Baby Jesus and witnessed the 'improbable' spectacle of the word of God turned into flesh and blood. Fabian's remark may, therefore, apply both to Malvolio's 'improbable' (and farcical) transformation into a smiling fool *and* to Cesario's 'improbable' (and quasi-mystical) metamorphosis into two creatures, Viola and Sebastian. However, John Manningham's diary entry (see Contextual Overview, p. 7) suggests that at least one member of the elite audience who watched *Twelfth Night* in the great hall at the Middle Temple on 2 February 1602 found the farcical improbabilities associated with the gulling of Malvolio more diverting and entertaining than the romantic improbabilities generated by the staggered arrival of Viola and Sebastian in Illyria. Manningham's response may have been affected by the fact that *Twelfth Night* was performed at the Middle Temple to celebrate a special holiday called Candlemas. Bruce Smith has usefully evoked its significance as follows:

> The *candle* in Candlemas refers to the candles that once had been brought to church to be blessed on this day, just as the Virgin Mary had been brought to the temple to be purified forty days after giving birth to Christ. Protestant theologians may have put an end to what they considered the superstitious practice of blessing candles, but Candlemas in 1602 remained a welcome island of light amid the gloom of early

February. Candles were a relatively expensive commodity in Shakespeare's England: a single wax candle cost as much as three pence – three times the price of a standing place at the Globe. A hall full of candlelight against the dark night outside was a rare and luxurious sight. What *Twelfth Night* offered John Manningham and his friends was a perfect entertainment for such a splendid occasion: a few golden hours of respite from the grey world of winter.[1]

The holiday spirit may, therefore, account for Manningham's response to the gulling of Malvolio as a 'good practice', as a source of lighthearted entertainment.

Twelfth Night was also staged at court, possibly during the last years of Elizabeth's reign and certainly twice under James I, once in 1618 and then again in 1623, and at the Globe, the permanent playhouse used by Shakespeare's company since its opening on 12 June 1599. Unfortunately, we have no eyewitness accounts of these performances, but Laura Levine, Paul Yachnin and Jason Scott-Warren offer interesting theories about how Shakespeare's elite audience at court and his paying audiences at the Globe may have responded to *Twelfth Night*. Levine, for example, reflects on how Shakespeare's contemporaries would have reacted to a boy actor playing Viola disguised as Cesario, while Yachnin coins a new phrase, 'populuxe drama', to describe the appeal of *popular* entertainment intent on providing a glimpse of *courtly* culture. According to Yachnin *Twelfth Night* offers Shakespeare's paying audience 'an experience of virtual courtliness'. Jason Scott-Warren focuses instead on the link between Malvolio's gulling and bearbaiting, which often took place alongside dramatic performances in commercial playhouses. The extracts by Paul Yachnin and Jason Scott-Warren therefore complement each other in showing how *Twelfth Night* would satisfy both fantasies of upward mobility through its 'retailing of courtliness' and the growing demand for popular forms of entertainment, associated with commercial drama and bearbaiting.

Shakespeare's extensive use of music in *Twelfth Night* may also suggest that he was consciously appealing to richer and more sophisticated audiences, who may not have had access to the court but who could afford to pay more than the groundlings (the standing audience in the public playhouses) for a visit to the theatre. Before Shakespeare's company began to use the indoor theatre at Blackfriars in 1609, indoor venues were used by children's companies, who were renowned for the musical skills of their young members. Lois Potter has argued that Shakespeare may have written *Twelfth Night* in response to the so-called 'War of the Poets', a combination of fierce artistic competition and mutually beneficial advertising, which involved adult and child companies and their most prominent playwrights in the early 1600s:

> In the early years of the seventeenth century [. . .], the companies of child actors were at the height of their popularity, representing serious competition for their adult rivals. Many of the boys in these companies had

---

1   Bruce Smith (ed.), *Twelfth Night: Texts and Contexts* (Boston, Mass. and New York: Bedford and St. Martin's, 2001), p. 8.

started as choristers, and one source of their appeal was the quality of the music in their productions. In *Twelfth Night* Shakespeare may have been trying to beat them at their own game [since] all the songs are [unusually] taken by adults, in character.[2]

Ironically, a play devised to appeal to so many different social groups proved extremely unpopular when it was revived after the Restoration.[3] The diarist Samuel Pepys, who saw three productions on 11 September 1661, 6 January 1663 and 20 January 1669 was repeatedly and consistently unimpressed (see Introduction, p. 3). William Wycherley cleverly adapted the Olivia–Viola–Orsino triangle to suit the satirical register of his comedy *The Plain Dealer* (1674), but William Burnaby, the only early Augustan dramatist who attempted to rewrite the whole play, achieved disappointing results. His *Love Betray'd* was staged in February 1703 at Lincoln's Inn Fields and revived only once in 1705.[4]

Even more ironically, *Twelfth Night* was probably revived by Charles Macklin in 1741, along with *As You Like It* and *Merchant of Venice*, for no better reason than a sudden craze for 'breeches roles' (female roles which involved the use of a male disguise). Lois Potter points out that early nineteenth-century theatre-goers were still thrilled at the chance of seeing attractive actresses wearing trousers, as indicated by an 1820 review, which dwells at a shocking length on the leading actress's 'right feminine leg, delicate in foot, trim in ankle, and with a calf at once soft and well-cut, distinguished and unobtrusive'.[5] Fortunately, when critics stopped denigrating *Twelfth Night* for being an 'improbable fiction', leading actor-managers also started to see this play as more than a mere vehicle for the principal actor playing Malvolio or for beautiful actresses willing to cause a stir by showing off their legs!

'If music be the food of love': *Twelfth Night* on the Nineteenth-Century Stage

A genuine renewal of interest in the poetic and romantic aspects of *Twelfth Night* during the nineteenth century led to an unprecedented appreciation of its musical qualities. Musical adaptations proved particularly popular alongside memorable productions of Shakespeare's play, including those of Samuel Phelps in 1847 and 1858, Charles Kean in 1850 and Henry Irving in 1884. In 1820, Frederic Reynolds and Henry Bishop produced an operatic version of *Twelfth Night*, which included songs and musical versions of other Shakespearean poems, including several of his sonnets and the masque of Juno and Ceres from *The Tempest*. This version was staged and revived several times at Covent Garden. In 1893, Augustin Daly cut

---

2 Lois Potter, *Twelfth Night: Text and Performance* (Basingstoke: Macmillan, 1985), p. 34.
3 The Restoration marked the return of the Stuart monarchy after the Civil War, which started in 1642 and ended in 1649, when Charles I was beheaded, and the Interregnum (1642–60), when England was ruled by a republican government led by Lord Oliver Cromwell. All commercial theatres in London remained closed between 1642 and 1660.
4 For more details on Wycherley and Burnaby's adaptations of *Twelfth Night*, see Elizabeth Story Donno, *Twelfth Night: Or, What You Will*, The New Cambridge Shakespeare (Cambridge: Cambridge University Press, 1985), pp. 24–6.
5 Potter, *Twelfth Night: Text and Performance*, pp. 38–9.

Shakespeare's text fairly drastically in order to add new musical interpolations, including an opening sequence sung by fishermen and peasants. Daly's adaptation opened in New York and had a warm reception when it transferred to London in 1894. Those who saw it commended both the musical additions and the stunning beauty of the set, which could accommodate the violence of a storm and the peaceful tranquillity of a rose garden drenched in moonlight.

Clearly nineteenth-century audiences appreciated music and spectacle as much as Shakespeare's verse, but often at the expense of the comic sequences, which were substantially abridged. Laurie Osborne (see The Work in Performance, **pp. 120–1**) points out other patterns of revision, which show how changes in aesthetic taste went hand in hand with less obvious but ideologically significant adjustments to the text of *Twelfth Night*. The sequence of some scenes was rearranged in order to attune Shakespeare's characterisation to current moral and political ideals. If the transposition of Act 1 Scene 1 and Act 1 Scene 2 makes 'Viola seem more firmly in charge of her fate', the transposition of Act 2 Scene 1 and Act 2 Scene 2 'effectively underscores the sense that Sebastian appears as Viola's surrogate whenever the situation threatens to demand too much of her'.[6] If, in other words, the cult of Viola first introduced by Romantic critics like Hazlitt and Jameson (see Early Criticism, **pp. 51–3**) accorded her character greater prominence than in Shakespeare, nineteenth-century audiences expected Sebastian to compensate for the limitations intrinsically connected to Viola's femininity, now made clearly visible by the body of the actress underneath the breeches.

Some directors still rearrange the order to the opening scenes in the first and second acts of *Twelfth Night*. However, the nineteenth century had another, and far more influential, legacy on twentieth-century productions. Henry Irving's interpretation of Malvolio was coldly received by audiences on both sides of the Atlantic. However, when Irving's production opened at the Lyceum Theatre in London in 1884, Edward Aveling noticed how radically the 'tragic nuances' in Irving's interpretation of Malvolio's role departed from earlier, broadly humorous ones and welcomed the change: '[Irving's] conception may be new to us of today', Aveling remarked, '[but] I believe it would be old to Shakspeare' (see The Work in Performance, **p. 122**). Malvolio's 'real pain' and 'the sense of the grievous wrong done to him' were to re-emerge in the second half of the twentieth century as one of the defining approaches to this character. Tragic Malvolios, in turn, led to increasingly dark and disturbing interpretations of the play as a whole, which Benedict Nightingale described as 'prison-house productions',[7] thus stressing the extent to which Malvolio's experience in the 'dark room' in Act 4, Scene 2 affected their overall register.

'For the rain, it raineth every day': *Twelfth Night* on the Twentieth- and Twenty-first-Century Stage

The transition from the late nineteenth to the early twentieth century was marked by experimental productions of *Twelfth Night* that dispensed with spectacle and

---

6   Osborne, *The Trick of Singularity*, pp. 48, 49. For a full bibliographical reference, see p. 120.
7   Benedict Nightingale, 'Glandular Fever', *The New Statesman*, 22 June 1979, pp. 928–9.

elaborate setting in the name of authenticity. In 1901, Beerbohm Tree's production marked the apotheosis of the nineteenth-century practice of using lavish settings, by including a realistically terraced garden and real fountains. Around the same time, however, directors like William Poel and Harley Granville-Barker advocated a return to the early modern un-localised stage and to the staging conventions for which Shakespeare's plays had been written. Granville-Barker's comments on the detrimental effects that a mixed cast has on the reception of key moments in the play are extremely significant and worth analysing in detail, because they reveal a recurrent bias in the theatrical and critical reception of the play:

> The most important aspect of the play must be viewed, to view it rightly, with Elizabethan eyes. Viola was played, and was meant to be played, by a boy. See what this involves. To that original audience the strain of make-believe in the matter ended just where for us it must begin, at Viola's entrance as a page. Shakespeare's audience saw Cesario without effort as Orsino sees him; more importantly they saw him as Olivia sees him. . . . One feels at once how this affects the sympathy and balance of the love scenes of the play. One sees how dramatically right is the delicate still grace of the dialogue between Orsino and Cesario, and how possible it makes the more outspoken passion of the scenes with Olivia. Give to Olivia, as we must do now, all the value of her sex, and to the supposed Cesario none of the value of his, we are naturally quite unmoved by the business. Olivia looks a fool.[8]

By arguing that 'the strain of make-believe' would end for an early modern audience 'at Viola's entrance as a page', Granville-Barker implies that Viola's femininity was all but invisible when this character was played by a boy actor. This assumption, in turn, leads Granville-Barker to describe the homosocial relations between Orsino and Cesario as dignified and gracious and the 'more outspoken passion' of the exchanges between Olivia and Cesario as more credible. Interestingly, while Granville-Barker assumes that Viola's femininity was all but invisible when this character was played by a boy actor, he also assumes that Olivia's femininity, when her character was also played by a boy actor, was not, and that Shakespeare's audience would read the flirtatious exchange between Viola–Cesario and Olivia in Act 1, Scene 5 as normatively heterosexual. Conversely, when Granville-Barker laments the fact that from the Restoration (1660) onwards female characters were played by female actors, he assumes that it is Cesario's masculinity that has now become all but invisible. Curiously, if Cesario's masculinity becomes all but invisible when Viola is played by a female actor, thus making the exchanges between Orsino and Cesario normatively heterosexual, the homoerotic potential of the exchange between Olivia and Cesario makes Olivia a fool. While the *male* homoerotic potential of the exchanges between Orsino and Cesario on the early modern stage is believed to have been gracious and dignified, the *female* homoerotic potential between Olivia and Cesario on the modern

8   Harley Granville-Barker, *Prefaces to Shakespeare*, vol VI, ed. by B. T. Batsford (1974), 28–9.

stage is unaccountably dismissed as a silly affair. Maybe that is what Samuel Pepys found 'silly' about *Twelfth Night* when he saw it staged in the 1660s (see Introduction, **p. 3**), soon after the introduction of female actors to the English stage. And maybe Granville-Barker's bias in favour of *male* homosocial and homoerotic relations anticipated a similar bias, which was to re-emerge in Greenblatt's approach to *Twelfth Night* in the 1980s (see Modern Criticism, **pp. 82–90**).

Granville-Barker's 1912 production of *Twelfth Night* at the Savoy Theatre in London was one of the few notable productions in the first two decades of the twentieth century. In the 1930s and the 1940s, directors started to darken *Twelfth Night*, thus echoing some of the most memorable post-war critical readings of the play. Alec Guinness, for example, who played Sir Andrew in Tyrone Guthrie's production of 1937, revived the play in 1948–9, in a production dominated by a desperately sad and melancholic Feste. The vast majority of productions of the second half of the twentieth century were remarkably dark in register. Some productions chose to represent Malvolio as a tragic character, while others focused on the shattering effects of sexual desire.

A long line of tragic Malvolios started with Laurence Olivier in John Gielgud's Royal Shakespeare Company production of 1955. Despite exploiting the comic potential of this role, Olivier's Malvolio was also profoundly moving. As a contemporary reviewer pointed out, Olivier's Malvolio 'hardly seems a natural butt. It is not laughter but pathos that Sir Laurence is primarily concerned to produce – the pathos of a plain unlikeable man misplaced in a land of misrule and cruelly abused'.[9] John Russell Brown similarly reports that Olivier delivered Malvolio's last line as 'the natural, pained assertion of a "man who refuses to see himself as others see him"'.[10] Anthony Sher was possibly the most controversial Malvolio in the second half of the last century. Sher starred in Bill Alexander's 1987 Royal Shakespeare Company production (see The Work in Performance, **p. 124**), which was set in a Greek village. Penny Gay's extract draws attention to how the shift 'from an imaginary Illyria to a realistic Aegean community' signalled desire's transformation into sadism. Orsino looked more 'like a bad stepfather to the lost Viola/Cesario than a potential lover' and Sir Toby and Maria, who watched as Feste tortured Malvolio in the 'dark room', were 'sexually excited' by Feste's cruelty. Sher played Malvolio like somebody who is pushed over the edge and never recovers. As Robert Hewison reports, 'unlike most Malvolios, once maddened, he stays mad'.[11] Maria's scheme turns Sher's Malvolio into a raving lunatic. During the 'dark room' scene in Act 4, Scene 2, Sher was tied to a stake like a bear. Many reviewers found this stratagem too blunt and accused Sher's approach to be 'about as subtle as a run-away truck'.[12] Stanley Wells found Sher's interpretation unconvincing, arguing that 'if Malvolio has a tragedy, it is that he is irremediably sane'.[13] Simon Russell Beale offered another memorable interpretation of Malvolio in Sam Mendes' 2002 production at the Donmar Warehouse in London, which then transferred to Broadway in the autumn of the same year.

9 *The Times*, 22 April 1955, p. 16
10 John Russell Brown, *Twelfth Night* (New York: Applause Books, 2001), p. 159.
11 Robert Hewison, 'The Problems of Paternity', in *The Sunday Times Review*, 12 July 1987, p. 49.
12 Michael Ratcliffe, 'Thirteenth Night', in *The Observer*, 12 July 1987, p. 19.
13 Stanley Wells, 'Acting Out Illyria', in *Times Literary Supplement*, 17 July 1987.

According to Michael Dobson, Beale's Malvolio 'managed to combine prissiness, profound earnestness and an underlying sense of insecurity'. Although this Malvolio was clearly guilty of 'anxious self-regard' and 'preening solitary personal vanity' (see The Work in Performance, **p. 129**), setting Act 2, Scene 5 in his bedroom revealed the full scale of the violation that Maria and her associates perpetrate at his expenses. As Dobson notes, '[i]n 2002, this scene of transgressive voyeurism [had] suddenly become reminiscent of the agonies of reality TV' (see The Work in Performance, **p. 129**). Albeit radically different in their approach, Beale continued to convey the same sense of suffering and horror that late twentieth-century directors, actors and audiences had come to associate with Malvolio's ordeal.

Several late-twentieth-century productions also emphasised the dark quality of the main character's erotic fantasies and those desires, which the comic resolution leaves unfulfilled. Hilary Spurling praised Clifford Williams' 1966 production for dispensing with poetry and pathos, thus dispelling the 'misleading reputation [which] *Twelfth Night* had acquired down the ages . . . as an elegant and amiable piece of nonsense'. According to Spurling, '*Twelfth Night* was written for a magnificent and savage age', and its disquieting appeal was conveyed particularly well by Alan Howard, as he delivered Orsino's opening speech. 'The delivery', Spurling reports, 'shows a Renaissance delight in luxury and artifice'. Spurling also spotted 'more than a hint, in [Orsino's] eyes and sensuous lips, of Renaissance barbarity'.[14] Lighter productions have often found ways of defusing Orsino's threats against Olivia and Cesario in Act 5. John Russell Brown, for example, mentions how 'in a broadly comic production at the outdoor Delacorte Theatre in Central Park, New York [in 1989], Mary Elizabeth Mastrantonio as Viola, "her tears of longing still gleaming in her wide eyes, leap[t] on [Orsino's] back to celebrate the long-delayed reciprocation of her affections"'.[15] Possibly one of the most sexually charged productions of *Twelfth Night* was directed by Peter Gill in Stratford in 1974. As Michael Billington noted, Gill staged the play as an exploration of rampant bisexuality: 'Orsino hugs Cesario to his breast with rapturous abandon; Antonio is plainly Sebastian's long-time boyfriend; and Viola all but tears her hair in anguish at Olivia's unfulfilled passion for her'.[16] Another reviewer welcomed the fact that there was no room in Gill's production for 'romantic twaddle' or 'coy aside[s]'.[17] The clearly Ovidian slant (see Contextual Overview, **pp. 12–13**) in Gill's representation of desire in *Twelfth Night* was signalled by a large image of Narcissus staring at his own reflection, which dominated the setting. Desire in Gill's production was not only explicitly sexual but also obsessive and self-reflective. Irving Wardle wrote,

> Malvolio, in his own way, is the greatest narcissist of the lot (and the only one who finally resists cure). All are intoxicated with their own reflections, and the function of Viola and Sebastian is to put them

14 Hilary Spurling, 'Another Playwright Misunderstood', in *The Spectator*, 24 June 1966, pp. 789–90.
15 John Russell Brown, *Twelfth Night* (New York: Applause Books, 2001), p. 145.
16 Michael Billington, a review in *The Manchester Guardian*, 23 August 1974, p. 12.
17 Michael Conway, *The Financial Times*, 6 February 1975, p. 3.

through an Ovidian obstacle course from which they learn to turn away from the mirror and form real attachments.[18]

The ending attempted neither to resolve psychological inconsistencies nor to accommodate all desires. Michael Conway noted that 'at the play's end . . . [t]he lovers swirl and exit, perhaps still wrongly paired, it matters not; but they leave Antonio stranded in front of the painted Narcissus, a baffled figure, while Feste spits out his final song'.[19] Later productions have taken this disillusioned approach to the final scene further. What, for example, Michael Dobson liked best about the Globe 2002 production of *Twelfth Night* was '[Mark] Rylance's wonderful rendition of Olivia's sheer mortification at the public exposure of her misguided pursuit of Cesario' (see The Work in Performance, **p. 128**).

Not all twentieth-century productions of *Twelfth Night* emphasised its darker undertones. In fact, some cornerstone productions stressed the romantic qualities of the play. Among these, and much acclaimed, was Peter Hall's Royal Shakespeare Company production of 1958. Geraldine McEwan proved particularly popular, and her interpretation of Olivia as a 'rather silly, giggly [and] flirtatious'[20] young girl contributed to lighten the play's mixed register of comic and sombre voices. John Barton's melancholic but lyrical version of 1969–70 was inspired by Hall's production in making problematic aspects in the comedy seem less disquieting. Simon Gray, for example, pointed out that

> [Barton's] Feste is not Shakespeare's. The fool of the text . . . *enjoys* tormenting Malvolio. Mr Barton's Feste agrees in a tone of self-redeeming compassion to bring "the light, and paper, and ink" for Malvolio's letter, and so helps us to forget that Shakespeare's fool subsequently and callously fails to deliver the letter itself. Barton has humanely filled in Shakespeare's brutal blanks.[21]

Even Judy Dench's Viola, who is remembered by most for her tender attachment to Orsino, seemed to want to exorcise Dr Johnson's critical assessment of Viola as 'an excellent schemer' (see Critical History, **p. 40**), and she is visibly embarrassed by the consequences of her passionate addresses to Olivia in Act 1, Scene 5. Barton's production is also remembered for its evocative and yet minimalist set – a long, receding frame lit from the outside – and for its moving and suggestive use of music.

Also different from the 'prison-house' productions discussed above were two later Royal Shakespeare Company productions, which moved most of the action outdoors. Terry Hands's 1979 production marked the progression from the emotional paralysis caused by Orsino's and Olivia's initial self-absorption to the refreshing turmoil ushered in by Viola's arrival in Illyria by suggesting a seasonal shift from winter to spring. Elizabeth Story Donno, for example, relates that 'As

18 Irving Wardle, 'Turning Away from the Mirror', in *The Times*, 23 August 1974, p. 9.
19 Michael Conway, *The Financial Times*, 6 February 1975, p. 3.
20 Stanley Wells, *Royal Shakespeare: Four Major Productions at Stratford-upon-Avon* (Manchester: Manchester University Press, 1976), p. 44.
21 Simon Gray, 'Morally Superior', *New Statesman*, 29 August 1969, pp. 285–6.

the play advanced, Geoffrey Hutchings's austere Feste decorated the scene with narcissi'.[22] Hands's reliance on the setting to convey changes in mood and characterisation left some reviewers unimpressed. J. C. Trewin found the seasonal motif particularly intrusive: 'at first', he explains, 'it was obviously a hard Illyrian winter [. . .] When spring at length appeared, for some of us that early shiver stayed'.[23] Even more controversial was John Caird's decision to set the action around a vast tree placed right at the centre of the stage. According to Roger Warren, Robin Don's 'lumbering old-fashioned set [. . .] overwhelmed the play, obscured much of the action and distracted from the director's aim of exploring the emotional complexity of the characters'.[24] Even critics who found Don's design less objectionable pointed out that it had regrettable implications. Donno, among others, noted that 'the action lost its household setting and therefore something of what might be called its interior significance' and that 'the structures of pastoral idyll prevailed over those of domestic comedy'.[25]

Generally speaking, the popularity of *Twelfth Night* on stage has been steadily increasing throughout the second half of the twentieth century, and the British productions mentioned above are just a few of the better-known and most influential ones. *Twelfth Night* has also proved popular with recent directors of Shakespeare in North America. Most recently, two Shenandoah Shakespeare's productions of *Twelfth Night* offered interesting insights into the play by experimenting with original theatrical practices and conditions of performance. While in the 1995 production 'the revelers [in Act 2, Scene 3] chose their dancing partners from the audience', in the 2000–1 production, 'the actor playing Maria (David McCallum) doubled as Sebastian, thus creating a gendered ambivalence in both brother and sister'.[26] Also worth mentioning are recent productions by North American women directors. Melia Bensussen's *Twelfth Night*, for example, which was staged at the Oregon Shakespeare Festival in 1995, 'invited bemused contemplation of gender roles', by attracting the audience's attention to similarities in the twins' mannerisms and body language, as they delivered their soliloquies in Act 2, Scene 2 and Act 4, Scene 3.[27]

Twelfth Night, like most of Shakespeare's plays, has also been translated into foreign languages and performed worldwide, especially since the late twentieth century. While a comprehensive survey of foreign productions of *Twelfth Night* is beyond the scope of this study guide, a few versions are worth mentioning because they have clearly marked significant moments in the cultural history of the local communities who produced them and because they force us to reconsider the viability and desirability of more familiar and established

---

22 Elizabeth Story Donno (ed.), *Twelfth Night* (Cambridge: Cambridge University Press, 1985), p. 36.
23 J. C. Trewin, 'Shakespeare in Britain', *Shakespeare Quarterly* 31 (1980), p. 155.
24 Roger Warren, 'Shakespeare in England, 1983', *Shakespeare Quarterly* 34 (1983), p. 451.
25 Donno, *Twelfth Night*, p. 38.
26 John R. Ford, *Twelfth Night: A Guide to the Play*, Greenwood Guides to Shakespeare (Westport, Conn., and London: Greenwood Press, 2006), p. 157.
27 Felicia Hardison Londre, 'Performance Review', *Theatre Journal* 47 (1995), p. 414. For further details on this production, see also Nancy Taylor's chapter on *Twelfth Night* in her book *Women Direct Shakespeare in America: Productions From the 1990s* (Madison, NJ: Fairleigh Dickinson University Press, 2005).

ways of staging this play. *Twelfth Night* was, for example, one of the fourteen plays staged at the first China Shakespeare Festival in 1986, a landmark event that signalled a break with older political and cultural models. Tellingly, this production of *Twelfth Night*, which was adapted into Shaoxing opera,[28] also 'drew on Western drama, opera, and folksongs and on other Chinese opera-types'. What seems particularly interesting is that 'adaptor Zhou Shuihe and director Hu Weimin [. . .] added [. . .] two versified monologues that expressed [Viola's and Orsino's] mutual admiration'[29] when they first meet in Act 1, Scene 4, because they, like earlier readers of the play (see Early Criticism, **pp. 50–1**) and recent directors (see The Work in Performance, **pp. 111, 112–13**), must have felt that Orsino's marriage proposal to Viola/Cesario in Act 5 is too sudden and 'improbable'.

Other foreign productions of *Twelfth Night* in the late 1990s and the beginning of the new millennium invited their audiences to reflect on the legacy of the past at times of intense cultural and political change. Graham Keith Gregor, for example, has pointed out that, although *Hamlet* and *A Midsummer Night's Dream* are more often performed in Spain than the rest of Shakespeare's canon, 'no fewer than three productions of [*Twelfth Night*]' were staged in Madrid in 1996. One of them in particular, directed by Adrián Daumas, seems to have gone further than any of the British productions mentioned above to darken the play's mood and register. Even Sir Toby, as Gregor relates, 'came across as a nasty, vicious oaf, whose slicked-back hair and black braces seemed to invite comparisions with the falangist bully-boys of Spain's fascist past'.[30] Also suspended between a problematic past and the uncertainties of the future is another production of *Twelfth Night*, directed by Robert Sturua at the Ivan Vazov National Theatre in Sofia in 2001–2. The cultural climate in Bulgaria, in Boika Sokolova's words, 'has undergone a sea change since the early 1990s: the iconoclasm and enthusiasms of the first post-communist years has given way to a more sober picture of impasse, disappointment and lack of acknowledgement'. To some extent Sturua's production reflected the wish to register positive change by linking *Twelfth Night* to the celebrations of the new millennium. However, still according to Sokolova, Sturua's decision to intersect 'the events at Orsino's and Olivia's courts [with] added biblical scenes, outlining the progress of Christ from birth to crucifixion'[31] ultimately failed to make either the Shakespearean or the biblical material convey any convincing sense of genuine regeneration. Interestingly, the darkness of Shakespeare's comic vision in *Twelfth Night*, despite memorable exceptions, seems to have haunted late twentieth- and early twenty-first-century directors across different cultures, languages and geographical locations.

---

28 One style, or school, of traditional Chinese opera.
29 Zha Peide and Tian Jia, 'Shakespeare in Traditional Chinese Operas', *Shakespeare Quarterly* 39 (1988), p. 210.
30 Graham Keith Gregor, 'Spanish "Shakespeare-Manía": *Twelfth Night* in Madrid, 1996–97', *Shakespeare Quarterly* 49 (1998), p. 429.
31 Boika Sokolova, 'Relocating and Dislocating Shakespeare in Robert Sturua's *Twelfth Night* and Alexander Morfov's *The Tempest*', in Sonia Massai (ed.), *World-Wide Shakespeares: Local Appropriations in Film and Performance* (London: Routledge, 2005), p. 59.

'But that's all one, our play is done:' *Twelfth Night* on Film and Television

The play is obviously far from 'done'. Recent productions of *Twelfth Night* have offered memorable, (re)visionary interpretations of its characters, like Mark Rylance's Olivia or Simon Russell Beale's Malvolio. However, *Twelfth Night* has also risen to the challenge of pleasing new and younger audiences who more and more often encounter Shakespeare not in the theatre but through imaginative adaptations for the television or the big screen. By far the most popular and most widely distributed film inspired by *Twelfth Night* was a cinematic version directed by Trevor Nunn in 1996.[32] Nunn's main departures from the play include Feste's transformation into Shakespeare's dramatic persona. Ben Kingsley's Feste over-looks Viola running away from Orsino's guards as she is washed ashore in Act 1, Scene 2 and gives Cesario the necklace that Viola had dropped on the beach towards the end of Act 5, Scene 1, thus confirming that he was able to see through Cesario's disguise all along. As he sings his last song, Feste watches all the char-acters who cannot benefit from the 'happy wreck' of Act 5 leave Olivia's house. As he reaches the final line, he stares straight into the camera and sings 'And *I'll* strive to please you every day' thus reinforcing this notion that Feste is the char-acter who most closely represents Shakespeare's own outlook on the fictive world of the play. Another major departure from the play was Nunn's addition of a controversial opening sequence. Carol Chillington Rutter reads this sequence as a 'farewell [to] difference' and to 'differentiating claims to what men and women "owe" in love' (see The Work in Performance, **p. 132**). Other critics and reviewers have also argued that the idealised setting (Orsino's castle is perched on a dra-matic stretch of the Cornish coastline and Olivia lives in a stunning National Heritage country house), period (late nineteenth century) and customs (Olivia is distinctly Pre-Raphaelite when she casts off her mourning black and wears a turquoise dress which sets off her curly dark red hair) create a nostalgic tension towards a past which restores a unitary and normative sense of personal, sexual and national identity.[33] Sexuality does not seem to be the only aspect of Nunn's film to be firmly anchored to traditional notions of personal identity. Laurie Osborne, for example, has noticed that by expanding Act 2 Scene 4 and by inter-spersing Orsino and Cesario's exchange with other scenes. Nunn, therefore, makes Orsino's impromptu proposal in the final scene psychologically more credible.[34]

If Nunn's Illyria is Victorian, rural and idyllic, Tim Supple's television version broadcast by Channel 4 in Britain in 2003 and based on his 1998 stage production

32 Other versions include Charles Kent's ten-minute long silent film (1910); Friedland's 1955 film *Dvenadtsataia noch* (Russian) and Dieter Dorn's 1980 film *Was ihr wollt* (German); John Dexter's first television version in English (1968); the 1980 BBC Series version and Paul Kafno's 1988 television version based on Kenneth Branagh's Renaissance Theatre Company production.

33 See, for example, Marla F. Magro and Mark Douglas, 'Reflections on Sex, Shakespeare and Nostalgia in Trevor Nunn's *Twelfth Night*', in D. Cartmell, I. Q. Hunter and I. Whelehan (eds), *Retrovisions: Reinventing the Past in Film and Fiction* (London: Pluto Press, 2001), pp. 41–58.

34 Laurie Osborne, 'Cutting Up Characters: The Erotic Politics of Trevor Nunn's *Twelfth Night*', in Courtney Lehmann and Lisa S. Starks (eds), *Spectacular Shakespeare: Critical Theory and Popular Cinema* (Madison, NJ: Fairleigh Dickinson University Press, 2002), pp. 89–109.

at the Young Vic, is contemporary, urban and extremely violent. Although Antonio gives Sebastian his purse and an A-to-Z map of London on his arrival at Orsino's court, Supple's Illyria resembles a southern Mediterranean or South American sprawling city run by powerful warlords. Like Nunn's film, Supple's adaptation has an opening sequence that provides additional information about the twins' background besides what Shakespeare's audiences find out in Act 1, Scene 2 and Act 2, Scene 1. The film starts somewhere on the Indian subcontinent. Viola (Parminder Nagra) and Sebastian (Ronny Jhutti) are surprised in their own home at night by a group of armed men wearing military uniforms. They shoot their father dead and drag away their mother, a family member who is curiously never mentioned in Shakespeare's play. Viola and Sebastian jump through a window into an incongruously starry sky and flee the country in a small boat crammed with other refugees. Trauma in Supple's film precedes the shipwreck. Interestingly, the storm, a long sequence in Nunn's film, is reduced to a bright flash that fills the screen for a few seconds. The violence of the elements and ill fortune have been replaced by the evil perpetrated against the twins and their family by a brutal military regime.

Supple's Illyria is not altogether different from the violent homeland from which the twins are forced to flee. A palpable sense of impending danger infects Supple's Illyria like the plague. Orsino (Chiwetel Ejiofor) is surrounded by bodyguards wearing dark glasses and dark pin-striped suits. Olivia's garden is separated from a dangerous and shabby-looking back street by iron gates constantly monitored by CCTV cameras. Illyria is a world where Cesario does need Orsino's protection and Sebastian is genuinely relieved by Olivia's intercession, when she puts an end to the dangerous brawl initiated by Sir Toby (David Troughton) in Act 4, Scene 1. Sebastian is also clearly struck both by Olivia's beauty and by her ability to put an end to the senseless violence. In this sense, she truly 'purge[s] the air of pestilence'. Sir Toby, Maria and Feste's revenge against Malvolio is similarly fierce. The box-tree is replaced by a security camera, through which Malvolio's enemies watch the contents of the fake letter take hold of Malvolio's imagination. The dark room is Olivia's cellar, and Malvolio, taunted by Feste, thrashes about smashing bottles and trampling on broken glass. The chance of getting seriously hurt is never completely dispelled by the 'happy ending': Orsino's homicidal threats against Olivia and Cesario in the final scene represent a realistic, altogether too familiar alternative, to the final reconciliation between the two main couples, who kiss and embrace each other under the same improbable starry sky which framed the brutal attack against Viola and Sebastian's family in the opening sequence.

The first filmed version of *Twelfth Night* in the twenty-first century echoes in many ways the dark productions in the second half of the last century. Sir Toby's callousness and his penchant for 'cakes and ale' barely hide a deep-rooted sense of his own mortality, as suggested by the fact that he breaks down in Olivia's chapel when he catches a glimpse of scattered photographs of her dead father and brother. Olivia herself (Claire Price) bursts out crying when she finds old photographs in the cellar just minutes before the end of the film. Like most late twentieth-century productions, Supple's version is also sexually charged. However, Supple's exploration of homoerotic desire is not consistently developed in his treatment of Cesario's intimate exchanges with Olivia and his growing friendship with Orsino. While, for example, Supple allows Olivia's infatuation with a very feminine Cesario to manifest itself quite explicitly, he uses special effects to distance Orsino from his increasingly sexual attraction towards Cesario, as shown by Supple's reworking of Act 2, Scene 4. In this sequence, Ejiofor's Orsino literally makes division of himself and remains seated when Nagra admits 'I am all the daughters of my father's house, / And all the brothers too' (see Key Passages, **p. 164**), while his double stands up and gets tantalizingly close to undoing Nagra's shirt. Overall, sexuality is less prominent than the themes of exile, loss and displacement, which make Supple's multi-ethnic adaptation particularly poignant and attuned to current preoccupations with the escalation of local and global conflicts and the problematic balance between personal security and intrusive surveillance, self-preservation and retaliation, hope and mourning.

Twelfth Night and the Place of the Early Modern Stage

From **Laura Levine, *Men in Women's Clothing: Anti-Theatricality and Effeminization, 1579–1642*** (Cambridge: Cambridge University Press, 1994), pp. 12, 19, 43, 71–2

Laura Levine's extract offers helpful insights into how the convention of casting boy actors to play female roles on the early modern stage was perceived by theatre audiences, by anti-theatrical pamphleteers like Philip Stubbes (see Contemporary Documents, **pp. 25–6**) and by Shakespeare himself, judging from how he tackles the issues of cross-dressing and effeminisation in some of his plays. Although Levine only focuses on Shakespeare's *Troilus and Cressida* and *Antony and Cleopatra*, her comments can be usefully applied to *Twelfth Night*. According to Levine, cross-dressing in the theatre became the focus of cultural anxieties about human nature and its assumed malleability and tendency to degenerate to the level of the monstrous. Viola's remark in Act 2, Scene 1 – 'Disguise, I see thou art a wickedness' (see Key Passages, **p. 155**) – can be read as a symptom of Shakespeare's own divided response to the anti-theatrical prejudice, which, still according to Levine, projected such anxieties onto the androgynous body of the boy actor. In some ways, Shakespeare seems to have endorsed the anti-theatrical assumption that masculinity was particularly endangered by men's failure to act in a manly fashion. Shakespeare may, therefore, have decided to expose Cesario's mock masculinity and Sir Andrew's effeminacy by contrasting their unwillingness to fight with Sebastian's readiness to use violence to defend himself. However, Shakespeare is unlikely to have condemned theatricality per se, first and foremost because he devoted his professional life to the stage. Besides, as Levine observes, in some of his later plays, like *Troilus and Cressida* and *Antony and Cleopatra*, 'theatricality [is] simply the constitutive condition of existence itself'. Also noteworthy is Levine's theory that theatricality was directly associated with Queen Elizabeth's explicit use of ritual, pageantry and portraiture as part of her sustained attempt to present an image of ideal monarchy to her people. As Levine explains, later characters like Cleopatra can be read as a nostalgic tribute to the Queen's sustained effort to stage her public persona before her people, a practice which was abandoned by her crowd-shy successor, James I. Cesario's failure to transform himself back into Viola may similarly betray Shakespeare's veiled tribute to a queen who had described herself as having 'the body of a weak and feeble woman, but . . . the heart and stomach of a king'.[1]

[T]he model of the self implicitly held by anti-theatricalists is profoundly contradictory, for, according to its logic, the self is both inherently monstrous and inherently nothing at all. To manage this contradiction, the men who held this model of the self seemed to project it outward. And from this point of view, the actor became the ideal repository for such a projection: the male actor, dressed in women's clothing, seemed to lack an inherent gender, and this seemed to make him monstrous. In this way, the fantasy of effeminization which came to dominate anti-theatrical tracts became a repository for a profound contradiction in the way a certain segment of the English Renaissance saw the self.
[. . .]
If we found that anti-theatricalists regularly fixed their attention on things which were both monstrous and lacked intrinsic natures, we would seem to be justified in saying that they had found a repository for their own conflicts about the self. This is, indeed, exactly what they do. Significantly, anti-theatrical tracts from *School of Abuse*[2] onward grow increasingly obsessed with the idea of the effeminized man – the thing that has no inherent nature because it has no inherent gender and is monstrous precisely because of this fact. Phillip Stubbes' *Anatomie of Abuses* calls men who wear women's clothes "monsters, of both kindes, half women, half men".[3] He defines the monstrous itself in terms of that which has no essential nature – because it has no essential gender. At least in this tract we can see the antithesis between the two opposites "monstrous" and "no inherent nature" collapse in the idea of the androgyne. For writers of these tracts, the hermaphroditic actor, the boy with the properties of both sexes, becomes the embodiment of all that is frightening about the self.
[. . .]
In an even deeper way [than *Troilus and Cressida*], *Antony and Cleopatra* seems implicated in this kind of anti-theatricality [. . .]. *Antony and Cleopatra* presents as history, as actual, what was, in effect, the central cautionary tale at the heart of the period's anti-theatrical literature itself, the story of the warrior who loses his masculinity because he fails to perform it, to "act" like a man. [. . .]

---

1   For a complete version of this speech, which Queen Elizabeth delivered at Tilbury on the eve of the defeat of the Spanish Armada in 1588, see *Elizabeth I: Collected Works*, ed. Leah Marcus, Janel Mueller and Mary Beth Rose (Chicago, Ill. and London: University of Chicago Press, 2000).
2   *The Schoole of Abuse, conteining a pleasant invective against Poets, Pipers, Plaiers, Jesters, and such like Catterpillers of a Commonwelth* is a popular anti-theatrical tract written by Stephen Gosson and first published in London in 1579.
3   See Contemporary Documents, pp. 25–6.

The play's "defense" of theatre, then, is made not on any moral ground, lies not in any capacity to salvage theatre from the critiques both the play and the period supply, but on what are virtually ontological grounds: if things fail to exist apart from their own theatricalizations, then what is enacted is simply more "real" than what is not, theatricality [being] simply the constitutive condition of existence itself. [. . .]

But in light of this it is striking that it *is* the woman, Cleopatra, not Antony [. . .] who gets to stage herself: her "triumph" in staging her death is not just the capacity to "represent" her self in an abstract sense as if that self already existed, but the capacity to create that self, to constitute it. In performing her death, she creates a self.

Does the play then celebrate the very female theatricality that the tracts abhor, celebrate it in the full recognition of its effeminizing, even fatal power to dissolve those men it is aimed at? [. . .]

Perhaps Shakespeare is not so much celebrating the power of female theatricality as he is mouring its loss: for the cost of Cleopatra's last performance is, indeed, her life. And at what more timely moment would Shakespeare mourn such a loss than at one in which his own world has passed from the hands of a woman monarch, whose theatricality swept its populace into itself in a rhetoric of love, to the hands of a male king who, though he [. . .] spoke the rhetoric of universal peace, took his theatricality indoors to the world of court masques where it would not be achieved "in the public eye"?

From **Paul Yachnin, 'Revels of Fortune: Shakespeare, Middleton and the Puritans'**, *English Literary History* 70 (2003), pp. 776–7

Paul Yachnin investigates the culture of playgoing in London in order to overcome author-centred approaches that ignore the theatrical and social context within which a play like *Twelfth Night* was first written and performed. As Yachnin explains in another article called 'The Populuxe Theatre',[1] Elizabethan players operated in 'an area of trade that centered on the selling of popular, relatively inexpensive versions of deluxe goods'.[2] According to Yachnin, public playhouses gave their paying audiences the chance 'to play with the pleasures of the elite – with their language, clothing, music, masquing, even with their virtual bodies'.[3] Yachnin, therefore, argues that playgoing could hardly have functioned 'as a form of collective protest against aristocratic licence'.[4] This approach naturally affects Yachnin's views on Shakespeare's representation of the aristocracy in *Twelfth Night*. If Orsino's dismissive attitude towards the musicians in Act 1, Scene 1 seems to encourage a critical view of the court, the ambiguous social status of the twins and their elevation through marriage encourage

---

1 Paul Yachnin, 'The Populuxe Theatre', in Anthony B. Dawson and Paul Yachnin, *The Culture of Playgoing in Shakespeare's England: A Collaborative Debate* (Cambridge: Cambridge University Press, 2001), pp. 38–65.
2 Yachnin, 'The Populuxe Theatre', p. 40.
3 Yachnin, 'The Populuxe Theatre', p. 41.
4 Yachnin, 'The Populuxe Theatre', p. 53.

the audience to fantasise about social advancement, thus 'underscor[ing] the
charisma of the nobility'.

The structure of desire in the play around the high center of court culture (the
play even begins with a snippet of courtly music), and the resolution of the action
according to the principle of rank and gender difference, might seem an answer to
recent arguments for Shakespeare's antipopulist bias and obsession with royalty.[5]
This view certainly lines up with much in the play, like the sea captain's comment,
"What great ones do, the less will prattle of" (1.2.29)—and *he* is one of the
prattling (that is, infantilized) "less." While *Twelfth Night* provides a more or less
rapt reproduction of court culture (its music, poetry, clothing, jewels, fencing,
and over-wrought emotional and sexual register), it does so for a mixed, paying
audience at the Globe, in preference to either the courtiers at Whitehall or the law
students at the Middle Temple.

The populuxe orientation of *Twelfth Night* gives rise to a critical element
within Shakespeare's retailing of courtliness. This is hinted at in the opening scene
by the duke's casual disregard for the paid, highly skilled work of the court
musicians, who must (on command) play, stop playing, repeat the phrase, stop
playing again—all because Orsino likes their music so much that he wants to be
made sick of it (and thereby lose his appetite for love):

> If music be the food of love, play on,
> Give me excess of it; that surfeiting,
> The appetite may sicken, and so die.
> That strain again, it had a dying fall;
> O, it came o'er my ear like the sweet sound
> That breathes upon a bank of violets,
> Stealing and giving odor. Enough, no more,
> 'Tis not so sweet as it was before.
>
> (see Key Passages, **p. 141**)

The subtle comedy of the scene remains only a playing possibility (easily realized
by an indication of exasperation from the musicians and/or the courtiers).[6] The
actors can, of course, choose to play it straight, but it nevertheless connects with a
broader critical element in the play, one defined by Viola's reflections on how
hard it is to earn a livelihood by courtly fooling. Not only does Feste have to
endure the meanness of spoilsports like Malvolio ("I marvel your ladyship takes
delight in such a barren rascal" [1.5.79–80]), but his apparent spontaneity
in fact requires planning and toil ("This is a practice / As full of labor as a wise
man's art" [see Key Passages, **p. 176**]). Courtly music and fooling—and play-
acting, as Viola discovers for herself—are forms of work carried out by people who

---

5   [Yachnin's note.] See Gary Taylor, 'Forms of Opposition: Shakespeare and Middleton', in *English
     Literary History*, 24 (1994), 283–314.
6   [Yachnin's note.] For a charming version of this playing possibility, see *Twelfth Night*, dir Trevor
     Nunn, Fine Line Features, 1996.

need to earn a living. That courtly glamour depends on the trade in elite forms of art and entertainment does not so much darken the impression of aristocratic luster, as suggests something about both Shakespeare's company's situation as hard-working producers of populuxe drama (and drama at court) as well as the broad public angle of their courtly artifice.

Twelfth Night also plays games with the rank of the twins. Are Viola and Sebastian of the nobility, and hence suitable partners for the Duke and Countess, or do they embody fantasies of social advancement, so that the gentlewoman Viola emerges as interchangeable with the gentleman Malvolio (except that he fails to rise and is punished, while she succeeds in penetrating the closed ranks of the nobility)? The play has it both ways: most of the time the twins seem no higher than of gentle rank, but Orsino assures Olivia that Sebastian is a good match for her: "right noble is his blood" (see Key Passages, **p. 183**). Such indeterminacy cuts two ways, since it opens up a question about the authenticity of the demarcations that prevent members of one rank from marrying members of another, and since, by inviting everyone in the audience to fantasize about eroticized social advancement, it underscores the charisma of the nobility.

From **Jason Scott-Warren, 'When Theaters Were Bear-Gardens: Or, What's at Stake in the Comedy of Humors'**, *Shakespeare Quarterly* 54 (2003), pp. 65–6, 74–7

> While Yachnin claims that Shakespeare's paying audience would have relished the courtly elements in *Twelfth Night*, Jason Scott-Warren highlights an interesting connection between the gulling of Malvolio in *Twelfth Night* and bearbaiting. According to Scott-Warren, 'the point of framing humans, as of baiting animals, was to reveal their inner natures' and 'the arena [or the stage] became a kind of psychological anatomy theatre'. By arguing that Shakespeare's audience would have responded to *Twelfth Night* as a 'comedy of humours', Scott-Warren provides a useful counterpoint to Yachnin's reading of *Twelfth Night* as an example of 'populuxe' drama.

Twelfth Night contains several references to animal-baiting.[1] Sir Andrew Aguecheek, introduced by Sir Toby Belch as a man who "speaks three or four languages word for word without book," turns out not to know what "*pourquoi*" means and wishes that he "had bestow'd that time in the tongues that I have in fencing, dancing, and bear-baiting" (1.3.24–5, 90–1). Fabian nurses a grudge against Olivia's steward Malvolio because "he brought me out o'favor with my lady about a bear-baiting here" (see Key Passages, **p. 166**). More poetically, Olivia, having employed "a shameful cunning" to reveal her love for Cesario (3.1.115), asks Orsino's servant how he interprets the deceit:

---

1   [Scott-Warren's note.] The following paragraphs draw heavily on Dickey's article ['Shakespeare's Mastiff Comedy', *Shakespeare Quarterly* 42 (1991), pp. 255–75] and its precursor, Ralph Berry's '*Twelfth Night*: The Experience of the Audience', in *Shakespeare Survey* 34 (1981), pp.111–19.

What might you think?
Have you not set mine honor at the stake,
And baited it with all th' unmuzzled thoughts
That tyrannous heart can think?

(II. 116–19)

Here the language of bear-baiting expands into a larger field of references to hunting, as we catch an echo of Orsino's Actaeon-like metamorphosis at the first sight of Olivia:[2] "That instant was I turn'd into a hart, / And my desires, like fell and cruel hounds, / E'er since pursue me" (see Key Passages, **p. 142**).

But this is a play that does more than just mention bears and hounds in passing; in the gulling of Malvolio, it has been argued, *Twelfth Night* actually stages a bear-baiting. When Fabian complains about the steward's spoilsport tactics, Sir Toby vows revenge: "To anger him we'll have the bear again, and we will fool him black and blue, shall we not, Sir Andrew?" (see Key Passages, **p. 167**). Thereafter, with the support of Sir Toby, Fabian, and Sir Andrew, Malvolio is taunted by Maria, whose feigned letter encourages him to indulge fantasies above his station, and by Feste in the guise of Sir Topas the curate, who attempts (unsuccessfully) to push the incarcerated Malvolio over the edge into madness. Finally, Malvolio promises his revenge and exposes the bear-garden dramaturgy of the plot against him in the line that is his parting shot: "I'll be reveng'd on the whole pack of you" (see Key Passages, **p. 184**). And, as if one blood sport weren't enough for a play, Sir Toby lays on a different kind of match as a sideshow when he sets up a duel between Sir Andrew and Viola/Cesario. Neither wants to duel, and each is informed that the other is implacable and highly dangerous. Before the encounter, Fabian tells Sir Toby how Sir Andrew "pants and looks pale, as if a bear were at his heels" (3.4.285–6); and after Sebastian has stepped into his sister's shoes, Sir Andrew and Sir Toby end up with "bloody coxcomb[s]" (5.1.174), the phrase evoking the cockpit where birds, spurred like knights, fought to the death.

[. . .]

[. . . T]he pleasure of animal-baiting did not arise merely from the challenge it posed to cultural demarcations of the human and the bestial. Rather, it followed from the way that the bearpits and cockpits enabled animals to become objects of knowledge, exposing their inner natures to outward view.[3] For this reason, the anthropomorphism implicit in baiting did not necessarily lead to sympathy; rather, where comic detachment was lacking, a quasi-scientific objectivity could come to dominate. The arena became a kind of psychological anatomy theater, revealing the courage, nobility, and artistry, the "peculiar or

---

2   See also Contextual Overview, **pp. 12–13** and Modern Criticism, **pp. 60–1**.
3   [Scott-Warren's note.] That the language of inwardness long predates the advent of romanticism is demonstrated by Katharine Eisaman Maus in *Inwardness and Theater in the English Renaissance* (Chicago[, Ill.]: Chicago University Press, 1995) and by John Martin in "Inventing Sincerity, Refashioning Prudence: The Discovery of the Individual in Early Modern Europe", *American Historical Review* 102 (1997), 1309–42. Both Maus and Martin relate developments in the inner/outer dichotomy to confessionalization. For another stimulating discussion of early modern interiority, see John Lee, *Shakespeare's* Hamlet *and the Controversies of the Self* (Oxford: Clarendon Press, 2000)

proper" character of the animals that were exposed to the public gaze. This is also the key to baiting's kinship with the public theater of Shakespeare and Jonson.

At the end of the sixteenth century, dramatists discovered a new mode: the comedy of humors. The Galenic medical theory of the four humors, bodily substances that in their various combinations determined personality, remained extremely influential.[4] Conscripted for the purposes of creating theatrical characters, Galenism issued in the "humorist," the individual marked out by a single trait or habit of speech [. . .].

Commercialism is indeed central to a proper understanding of this craze. The humors were not just a principle for the creation of character; they were also a way of marketing dramatic entertainment. That much is clear from the metatheatricality of humors-plots, which frequently use internal dramatists to create—and internal onlookers to frame—the action, thereby consciously selling the mirth to the audience. The celebrated box-tree scene of *Twelfth Night* (2.5) is paradigmatic in this respect. Malvolio is the victim of a plot requiring the involvement of an internal plotter—effectively a surrogate playwright—in the shape of Maria. There is also an onstage audience, made up of Sir Toby, Sir Andrew, and Fabian, framing the action that will frame Malvolio. And that audience repeatedly expresses its pleasure in Maria's wares, saying such things beforehand as "If I lose a scruple of this sport, let me be boil'd to death with melancholy" (see Key Passages, **p. 166**) and afterward as "I will not give my part of this sport for a pension of thousands to be paid from the Sophy" (see Key Passages, **p. 172**). [. . .]

The point of framing humans, as of baiting animals, was to reveal their inner natures. So, in *Twelfth Night*, Maria's playlet is designed rapidly to disclose what Maria herself has already divined from her previous acquaintance with Malvolio:

> he is . . . an affection'd ass, that cons state without book, and utters it by great swarths [i.e., swathes]; the best persuaded of himself, so cramm'd (as he thinks) with excellencies, that it is his grounds of faith that all that look on him love him; and on that vice in him will my revenge find notable cause to work.
>
> (2.3.142–47)

The gulling of Malvolio turns him inside out, exposing his vice of self-love to the eyes of the world both within and without the play. And, as we watch Maria's intensely theatrical and improbably perfect plot unfold, it is hard not to believe that the theater was made for such exposés. Humors comedy offers a voyeuristic promise of disclosure. Surface pretension will be stripped away, and the audience will obtain privileged glimpses into private selves.

---

4 [Scott-Warren's note.] The most recent studies of humoral theory in early modern literature are Michael C. Schoenfeldt, *Bodies and Selves in Early Modern England: Physiology and Inwardness in Spenser, Shakespeare, Herbert and Milton* (Cambridge: Cambridge [University Press], 1999) and Gail Kern Paster, *The Body Embarrassed: Drama and the Disciplines of Shame in Early Modern England* (Ithaca, NY: Cornell [University Press], 1993).

Twelfth Night and Nineteenth-Century Performance Editions

From **Laurie E. Osborne, *The Trick of Singularity: 'Twelfth Night' and the Performance Editions*** (1996), (Iowa City, Iowa: University of Iowa Press, 1996), pp. 47–9, 56–7

The following extract focuses on the interesting changes, revisions and adjustments which nineteenth-century editors introduced in performance editions based on contemporary stage productions. As Laurie E. Osborne explains, 'these performance editions are not authoritative in any sense that the textual bibliographer would accept', because they deliberately change the Folio text of 1623 (see Further Reading, **p. 190**) to register contemporary stage practices. However, these editions enjoy a special kind of authority as they 'display the multiplicity of the play's material existence in a historical continuum'. Osborne, in other words, regards *Twelfth Night* 'as a series of texts rather than a single text'.[1] Interestingly, some of the changes first introduced in the nineteenth century survived in major twentieth-century productions, thus reinforcing Osborne's view that *Twelfth Night* is not simply a play as it was printed in 1623 but a long tradition of critical and theatrical responses, which new generations of critics, readers, and directors challenge and appropriate from their own standpoint.

The second type of alteration[2] affecting the performance editions, the pervasive rearrangements of the Folio *Twelfth Night*'s scenic order, significantly reworks the comedy's structure. Nine performance editions between 1808 and 1900, including individual as well as collective editions, open *Twelfth Night* with Viola's entrance (1.2) and thus substantially change the play's initial emphasis. In terms of performance, this shift makes sense. The development of the proscenium stage and scenery meant that it was more theatrically convenient to get the seashore scene out of the way and consolidate the interior scenes in Orsino's and Olivia's houses. These scenic features in the nineteenth-century theatre materially change the texts and alter their sense. When Viola appears first, the initial emphasis of a production is on loss and mourning, not the melancholy of love. The sea captain's view of Olivia, mourning and bereft, is our first impression of her, not the Duke's invocation of what she will be like when she loves. Moreover, if the Duke follows her onstage, Viola seems more firmly in charge of her fate. Instead of entering a situation that already exists theatrically, she introduces Orsino and Olivia and chooses between them.

[. . .]

Of course, performance critics often discuss the rearrangement of the first few scenes, but nineteenth-century performance editions enact other major redesigns

---

1   Osborne, *The Trick of Singularity*, p. 21.
2   The first type of alteration is what Osborne refers to as 'sweeping cuts', *The Trick of Singularity*, p. 47.

in scenic structure, perhaps less obvious because of the well-known inversion of the opening. All but one of the nine editions which change the opening also move the scene introducing Sebastian and Antonio (2.1). As it stands in the Folio, Sebastian's first appearance in the play intervenes between Olivia's discovery of her passion, which drives her to send Malvolio after Cesario with the ring in act 1, scene 5, and Malvolio's "return" of the ring to Cesario in act 2, scene 2. According to the most frequent changes in nineteenth-century performances, the sequence runs 1.5, 2.2, 2.1: Olivia's interview with Viola and request that Malvolio "return" the ring, then Viola's receipt of the ring and acknowledgment of Olivia's love, and only after that Sebastian's first appearance in the comedy.

This second change in sequence also creates a new set of theatrical possibilities. In the Folio, no sooner does Olivia express her desire for the unattainable Cesario than Viola's eminently suitable twin appears. The Folio text seems to provide a substitute here, much as Orsino's desire for the unattainable Olivia in the Folio text's opening is followed immediately by the arrival of another eligible young woman, also in mourning for *her* brother. In the order suggested by the performance editions, Sebastian's appearance, following Viola's assertion that the situation is a knot she cannot untie, seems a response to Viola's dilemma rather than Olivia's desire.[3] This sequence effectively underscores the sense that Sebastian appears as Viola's surrogate whenever the situation threatens to demand too much of her—when Olivia falls in love with her, when Sir Andrew and Sir Toby try to pursue the duel, and when Antonio, the Duke, and Olivia are all claiming her loyalty at the end of the comedy. The emphasis in act 2 moves from a pattern of desire and displacement in the Folio to one of demand and duplication in the performance editions.

Malvolio's Metamorphosis: From Comic Butt to Tragic Gull

From **Edward Aveling, *Our Corner*,** July 1884, in G. Salgado, *Eyewitnesses of Shakespeare: First Hand Accounts of Performances, 1590–1890* (London: Sussex University Press, 1975), pp. 214–15

Edward Aveling wrote an enthusiastic review of Henry Irving's interpretation of Malvolio as a tragic character, which marked the beginning of a long theatrical tradition, memorably appropriated, among others, by Anthony Sher in 1987 (see The Work in Performance, **pp. 124–6**) and Simon Russell Beale in 2002 (see The Work in Performance, **pp. 128–30**).

Until Tuesday night I did not know the character of Malvolio. So new was the conception, so startling, so thoroughly carried out, and withal so true, that I

---

3   [Osborne's note.] John Weaver argues that the Folio defuses Viola's anxiety before we witness it, in 'The Other Twin: Sebastian's Relationship to Viola and the Theme of *Twelfth Night*', in *Essays in Honor of Esmond Linworth Marilla* (Baton Rouge [, La.]: Louisiana State University, 1970), pp. 89–100.

confess to being staggered. Unfortunately, the majority of the audience without a doubt, either did not understand at what Irving was aiming, or, if they understood, did not agree with his reading. My own impression is that they did not in the least degree comprehend what he meant to convey. And this, from no fault of his, but from the novelty of idea, and from the natural denseness of English audiences.

[. . .]

The gradual growth of the great idea in his mind that Olivia loved him was shown as I believe none other could show it, and with that growth came as gradually the first indication of the new line he meant to take. He intended us to pity Malvolio, to weep for if not with him. From the moment when we see how completely he, the sport of others, is self-deceived, a feeling of incipient sympathy takes hold on us. At the end of the scene his exit was not with a pompous swaggering strut, Malvolio passed out with his face buried in his hands, strangely moved, overwhelmed with his good fortune. Then we began to see what real pain this foolish jest of Maria was, like most foolish jests, about to cause. But how much and how real the pain, was not conceived until Malvolio was seen in prison. The scene is so arranged, with a wall, that of his cell, built down the centre line of the stage, that we see both his tormentors and the man himself. On the right hand are Maria and the plaguing clown. On the other lies Malvolio. He is in darkness. The mental and physical horror of darkness and the longing yearning for deliverance from a prison cell were never so realised, I think, before. And with all this agony (it is literally agony) there is the sense of the grievous wrong done to him, and the utter hopelessness of redress. My readers may be inclined to smile at me, but I declare in all seriousness the effect of this scene from the comedy of 'Twelfth Night' on me was that of the intensest tragedy.

The critics, as a rule, do not appear to grasp what Irving intended them to grasp any better than did the first night audience. When it dawns slowly on them, controversy will set in as to whether this reading of Malvolio is true, or whether the old, broadly humorous one, that only moves men to inextinguishable mirth, is right. For my part, I have decided, or rather Irving has decided for me. His conception may be new to us of to-day. I believe it would be old to Shakspere.

Authentic Shakespeare? *Twelfth Night* at the Middle Temple (1897)

From **Marion F. O'Connor, 'The Theatre of the Empire'**, in J. E. Howard and M. F. O'Connor, *Shakespeare Reproduced: The Text in History and Ideology* (New York and London: Routledge, 1987), pp. 70–1

Marion F. O'Connor has studied William Poel's production of *Twelfth Night* at the Middle Temple in 1897 in the context of turn-of-the-century attempts to conjure the spirit of a very specific Elizabethan past, which could justify and celebrate England's role as an imperialist super-power. O'Connor focuses on Poel's use of the Fortune's fit-up in the Great Hall at the Middle Temple, 'a

Victorian image of Shakespeare's theatre . . . superimposed on the Elizabethan architecture', as an emblematic example of how 'the authority of Shakespeare is appropriated to serve particular political ends'.[1] This extract should be read alongside Michael Dobson's review of another revival of *Twelfth Night* at the Middle Temple in 2002 (see The Work in Performance, **pp. 126–8**), because both extracts show how even productions which attempt to be 'authentic', far from recovering the original performance (which is lost for ever), inevitably end up adjusting early modern staging conventions to suit current aesthetic and ideological agendas.

[. . .] The earlier event[2] was the first of three performances of Shakespeare's *Twelfth Night* which William Poel's Elizabethan Stage Society gave in the hall of the Middle Temple on 10, 11 and 12 February 1897. The Elizabethan Stage Society was a play-producing society, a club that sponsored productions of non-commercial drama. This particular play-producing society had been founded to serve an end which programmes for its earliest productions variously defined as 'the principle that Shakespeare should be accorded the build of stage for which he designed his plays' and 'the principle that Shakespeare's plays should be accorded the conditions of playing for which they were designed'. Staging *Twelfth Night* in Middle Temple Hall, the Elizabethan Stage Society had such a build of stage and such conditions of playing immediately at hand, built into the very fabric of their venue. [. . .]

The programme for the 1897 Elizabethan Stage Society performances of *Twelfth Night* in Middle Temple Hall reprinted the diary passage twice over, in manuscript facsimile and in printed transcript. In effect an invocation of the Ghost of Candlemas Past, the programme invited the audience to pretend that time had been reversed and to savour some imaginary aura of place. Having thus conjured up the *genius loci*,[3] the production paid no regard to the physical place itself. Setting aside the principle(s) for which he had founded the Elizabethan Stage Society and ignoring the incomparably appropriate set which was the architecture of Middle Temple Hall, Poel brought into that hall the flagrantly fake Elizabethan stage which he regularly erected on the stages of proscenium theatres for Elizabethan Stage Society productions. This fake Elizabethan stage was known as the 'Fortune fit-up' – the substantive designating the kind of collapsible and adaptable stage used by small Victorian touring companies playing one-night stands in the covered markets, parish halls, etc., of provincial towns and villages too small to have regular theatre buildings. [. . .] The conjunction of this tawdry specimen of low-budget late Victorian stagecraft with the mid-Tudor carpentry and joinery of Middle Temple Hall must have been startling. Visual aesthetics aside, a Victorian image of Shakespeare's theatre was

---

1   O'Connor, 'The Theatre of the Empire', p. 3.
2   The later event to which Marion O'Connor relates the three performances of Poel's *Twelfth Night* at the Middle Temple is the Duchess of Devonshire's fancy-dress ball, which took place in the summer of 1897 as part of the celebrations for Queen Victoria's Diamond Jubilee.
3   A synonym for what O'Connor calls 'some imaginary aura of place'.

superimposed on the Elizabethan architecture which had accommodated Shakespeare's company playing Shakespeare's text; an ersatz Elizabethan structure was erected in a genuine Elizabethan space; and history was at once remade and revisited.

'Prison-House' Productions: *Twelfth Night* in the 1980s

From **Michael Billington (ed.),** *Directors' Shakespeare: Approaches to 'Twelfth Night'* (London: Nick Hern, 1990), p. 75

The following extract stems from a two-day long discussion, which was arranged, moderated and then turned into a book by theatre critic Michael Billington. The four participants to this event, including Bill Alexander, had directed Royal Shakespeare Company productions of *Twelfth Night* between the late 1960s and the late 1980s. In this extract, Alexander explains how his research into the social status of the steward within the hierarchical organisation of an Elizabethan household had helped him realise that Malvolio's suffering is heightened by the fact that his aspirations were not entirely unrealistic or misplaced.

When I did my production, I spent some time doing research into the structure of an Elizabethan household and finding out exactly what the steward was in that context. I was interested to discover that he was a far more important figure than I had thought, far more than just a glorified butler. He was a very highly trained, highly educated person, responsible for all aspects of the house, gardens, and land. He was often a very erudite person, a very well-educated person, and probably an expert huntsman and expert archer. He had to have a very good economic sense in that he ran and organised the books. You could well imagine how he was key figure in a large Elizabethan household.

It's the importance of his role that gives the character its interest and ambivalence in dramatic literature, I think. When Malvolio says to himself, musingly, 'The lady of the Strachey married the yeoman of the wardrobe,' he may be quoting a slightly ridiculous topical example, but unless you take the aspiration of Malvolio as a realisable one then I think you undermine the comedy of the play and make it purely fantastical and farcical. The fact that it is an outrageous thought to Sir Toby that Malvolio should aspire to marry Olivia is neither here nor there — that tells you something about Sir Toby, not about the reality of what Malvolio wants for himself.

If you don't accept that it is a possible social movement, as it indeed *was* in the Elizabethan period, which was a time of great social mobility, then you simply have to come to the conclusion that the man is completely mad, in which case the *driving* of him mad or nearly mad loses its complexity, the play becomes thinner and more obvious.

From **Penny Gay, As She Likes It: Shakespeare's Unruly Women**
(London and New York: Routledge, 1994), pp. 44–7

Penny Gay provides further insights into Bill Alexander's 1987 Royal Shakespeare Company production of *Twelfth Night*. Alexander's production seems
worth focusing on because it touched upon controversial issues that prompted
fairly extreme responses and still affect recent approaches to the play (see
Modern Criticism, **pp. 67–80**). If, as Gay points out, the realistic quality of
Alexander's production reflects 'the conservative and selfish society of the
1980s', his interest 'in the alienation of his characters [rather] than their sexuality' seems to match Tim Supple's focus on the experience of dislocation and
exile (see The Work in Performance, **pp. 111–13**).

Much the same tone pervaded Bill Alexander's 1987 production: the only major
change was in the design, which moved from 1983's darkly romantic *capriccio* by
Robin Don to the central square of a realistic Aegean village, the design of Kit
Surrey. Alexander justified this by claiming that

> *Twelfth Night* is a very realistic play in the timbre of its dialogue, in the
> aspects of human behaviour that it's exploring, in the whole feel of it . . .
> you have to account for behaviour [. . .].[1]

Donald Sumpter's Orsino was a balding, bad-tempered, middle-aged village
tyrant – more like a bad stepfather to the lost Viola/Cesario than a potential
lover. There was no sexual chemistry between him and Viola, and correspond-
ingly little eroticism in their scenes together, despite his near-nakedness (ascribed
to insomnia) in II.4. 'It always amazes me,' said Michael Coveney, 'when contemporary productions miss out, as does this one, on the obvious sexual interplay
of the cross-gender comedy'. Alexander, one might infer, found the alienation of
his characters more engaging than their sexuality – the 'madness' of his formula
privileged over the 'love'. Like Orsino, the melancholy imperious Olivia (Deborah
Findlay) seemed not very interested in the boy-ambassador. In fact desire only had
a place among the hangers-on of these rather glum gentry: Sir Toby (Roger Allam)
was a youngish, good-looking, mellifluous drunk, who was clearly having an
affair with Maria. [. . .] Billington noted that Sir Toby and Maria were 'sexually
excited by the cruelty and the torture of Malvolio'. Bill Alexander explained:
'The comedy becomes a meaningless game if it's just a jolly come-uppance for
Malvolio: it's not, it's viciously cruel, what they do, and part of the cruelty is an
excitement at seeing people suffer'.[2] Thus even desire, in this dark production,
was corrupted into sadism.

1   [Gay's note.] Bill Alexander in Michael Billington, *Directors' Shakespeare: Approaches to 'Twelfth
     Night'* (London: Nick Hern Books, 1990), p. xvii.
2   [Gay's note.] Also in Billington, p. 91.

Or into a self-regarding priapism[3] – Malvolio (Antony Sher) was also well under middle-age: a young upstart in the community, costumed, rather oddly, as a Greek Orthodox priest. His display to Olivia was absolutely manic – he flashed not only a yellow codpiece, but long yellow pockets in his gown; his black Greek hat became a phallic yellow clown's cone: his capers, high kicks, and furious energy were typical of the extraordinary physicality audiences have come to expect from Sher in any role. [. . .] What emerges from these 'dark' productions of *Twelfth Night* in the 1980s is a sense of the repression of desire, both in the *dramatis personae* and in the audience. Love is difficult (if it exists at all), sex is egoistic greed, laughter is cruel, and any beauty is fraught with melancholy or danger. By displacing the play from an imaginary Illyria to a realistic Aegean community, Bill Alexander offered a metaphor for the conservative and selfish society of the 1980s; but he was also, paradoxically, thereby putting up a barrier against the play's ability to titillate and disturb.

Twelfth Night Comes of Age, 1602–2002 (Rylance and Mendes)

From **Michael Dobson, 'Shakespeare Performances in England, 2002'**, *Shakespeare Survey* 56 (2003), pp. 258–62

> Michael Dobson's comments about the casting in Mark Rylance's 2002 Middle Temple production of *Twelfth Night* reinforce Marion O'Connor's conclusions about William Poel's experimental production at the Middle Temple in 1897 (see The Work in Performance, **pp. 122–4**), by stressing how even this production, far from recovering the original performance of 1602, allowed current concerns to override what theatre scholars know about the material conditions of production on the early modern stage. Dobson's review of Mendes' 2002 productions is particularly useful for its focus on interesting departures from the Folio text (see Further Reading, **p. 189**) and the theatrical tradition, including Mendes' decision to set Act 2, Scene 5 in Malvolio's bedroom rather than Olivia's garden.

Given the return to the play's first recorded venue and all the authenticity-hungry Elizabethan trimmings, one might have expected the production itself to try harder to conform as far as possible to what we know of the theatrical conventions of 1602, but Rylance's programme note admitted that his company would be using 'some original playing practices and some modern', and this was certainly the case. It seems very unlikely, for one thing, that theatrical performances in the

---

3   From Priapus, Greek and Roman god of fertility and procreation; his statues, which were marked by a prominent and erect penis, were placed in vineyard and gardens to protect them from depredators (*Oxford English Dictionary*, 2).

halls of the Inns[1] weren't a good deal more end-on than the almost traverse arrangement adopted on this occasion, with much smaller stages: but what was most striking about this production was the composition of its company. This was all-male, and as such quite unlike the sort of company one would normally expect to see performing *Twelfth Night* in 2002; however, it was also quite unlike the sort of all-male company that one would have expected to see performing *Twelfth Night* in 1602, since as well as being racially mixed (apparently sexual discrimination can be permitted in the name of historical authenticity, but not racial), it cast a younger actor for only one of the play's three female roles, Viola (and not that much younger, either; a Cambridge undergraduate, Eddie Redmayne). As Maria, Paul Chahidi was more like a nineteenth-century pantomime Dame than either an Elizabethan or a modern Maria, and as Olivia Mark Rylance was – well, was Mark Rylance, further developing the special, anachronistic, and in its own way rather charming species of drag act which he tried out as Cleopatra at the Globe in 1997. [. . .] With an ensemble who were for the most part inconspicuously competent, in a solid, slightly amateur-dramatic manner, the *mise-en-scène*[2] for this show carried an unusual amount of weight: the melancholy music, the dark wood panelling of the hall itself, the large solid table that dominated the scenes at Olivia's house, and above all the costumes. Oliver Cotton's Malvolio was a senior, tall, heavy figure in long black robes – but for his steward's chain, just like a picture of Lord Burleigh[3] – who in 1.3 brought Olivia a large pile of what might have been state papers to look over and sign as she sat solemnly at the head of the table; all his inferiors in the household were also in black, in conformity with their mistress's grief, and there was a strong sense that this was the normal state of affairs in Illyria, here a rather grave country throughout rather than a fantastical realm in which one particular countess was temporarily wearing a black veil as an affectation. His face made-up almost pure white, and wearing a large farthingale[4] under which he took artificially tiny and rapid steps so as to arrive on the stage like a waxwork travelling on invisible wheels, Rylance as Olivia looked something like a well-built Tudor geisha girl and something like the portrait of Elizabeth I visible at the far end of the hall, but he was more dignified than either, and more pained, reproving Malvolio's uncharity towards Feste with a sort of sad absent generosity (as if Feste's joke about not mourning that her brother was in Heaven hadn't amused Olivia in the present but had just succeeded in awakening some poignant memory of past laughter now gone forever). The whole play became principally the story of how this orderly, dutiful world was comprehensively disrupted by the incursion of Viola and Sebastian, neither of whom gave very vibrant or engaging performances, but who achieved their considerable impact by wearing the same comparatively light-hearted-looking clothes, based on that famous Hilliard miniature of the youth in the hat with the cape on one shoulder.[5]

---

1   See Footnote 1 on **p. 1**.
2   The realisation of the play within the physical space of the stage.
3   Sir William Cecil, Lord Burleigh, (1520/1–1598), chief advisor of Queen Elizabeth I.
4   A framework of hoops, usually of whalebone, worked into some kind of cloth, formerly used for extending the skirts of women's dresses (*Oxford English Dictionary*).
5   Nicholas Hilliard (1547–1619) was a goldsmith and famous miniaturist who was often hired by Queen Elizabeth I and James I. Most of his miniatures are held at the Victoria & Albert Museum in London.

Even Redmayne's Viola did little to upstage this outfit (quietly and sorrowfully effeminate throughout), and so one was left with a rather sinister sense of two eerily identical and only partly inhabited white silk outfits invading the decorous hall and deluding poor Olivia into betraying herself. In the final scene the histrionics of Terence Maynard's Othello-like[6] Orsino, the reunion of the parted siblings and the return of Malvolio very much took second place to Rylance's wonderful rendition of Olivia's sheer mortification at the public exposure of her misguided pursuit of Cesario and its sequels: undoubtedly the best and most painfully funny single moment of the production came when an insensitively jubilant Sebastian, his tactless delight at the situation clearly not shared by his new wife, blurted out 'So comes it, lady, you have been mistook' (5.1.257), to be answered only by a half-wincing little shake of the head, eyes cast down, and a little waving-away gesture of one hand. [. . .]

At the other end of the year, Sam Mendes's Donmar Warehouse production of the same play had by contrast an almost absurdly strong company throughout, and was emphatically a director's ensemble piece rather than a showcase for a single star. The design, executed by Anthony Ward, revolved around a conceit apparently borrowed from the proxy wooing scenes[7] in Michael Boyd's *Henry VI* sequence for the RSC the previous year: apart from candles and small lamps suspended from ropes above the actors' heads, the Donmar's tiny acting area was usually dominated by a single large gilded empty picture-frame, behind which absent members of the cast being imagined or described could pose, motionless, sometimes for whole scenes at a time. To cite only a few instances, the performance opened with Mark Strong's appealingly Byronic[8] Orsino, seated on a single chair directly in front of this frame, contemplating what appeared to be a three-dimensional portrait of the veiled Olivia; implausibly fierce incarnations of Viola and Aguecheek respectively appeared while Sir Toby was exaggerating the valour of each to the other in 3.4, and Sebastian appeared like a mirror-image of his twin when Antonio rebuked Cesario for denying his acquaintance after the ensuing duel (3.4.351–62); and, in the sole instance of a character being made visible in this way despite being largely forgotten by those onstage, Malvolio could be seen beyond the frame throughout most of his imprisonment. This may sound tricksy and intrusive, but it worked remarkably well, both to underline the extent to which this play's characters are trapped in their own and one another's fantasies, and simply to articulate its structure, since with this convention in place many scenes turned out, conveniently, to begin as the character last brooded over stepped forward out of the frame and into action.

[. . .]

Simon Russell Beale, meanwhile, was simply the best and most closely observed Malvolio I have ever seen, at once the funniest and the most heartbreaking: [. . .] He managed to combine prissiness, profound earnestness and an underlying sense

---

6   Orsino, who threatens to kills Cesario to spite Olivia in the final scene, is here compared to Shakespeare's Othello, who, blinded by jealousy, kills his innocent wife Desdemona.

7   Dobson is here referring to Suffolk's proxy wooing of Princess Margaret on the King's behalf in *1 Henry VI* (Act 5, Scene 5).

8   In the style of George Gordon Noel, sixth Baron Byron, better known as Lord Byron (1788–1824), Romantic poet, whose self-conscious melancholy was widely imitated by his admirers both during his lifetime and after his death.

of insecurity, to a whole range of effects, all of them beautifully highlighted by a visibly cherished Hercule Poirot[9] moustache and an Edward VII[10] beard which struggled in vain to confer an air of distinction on his dumpy chin. He had a specially unctuous, slow-spoken, would-be suave tone of voice in which to show off his judiciousness to a bored Olivia in 1.5, which was abruptly replaced on receipt of the command 'Call in my gentlewoman' (see Key Passages, **p. 147**) by the manner he reserved for his inferiors. The first word of his 'Gentlewoman, my lady calls' (see Key Passages, **p. 147**) became a deafeningly imperious, harsh, petulant, contemptuous squawk; on the comma he looked affectedly at his watch, tut-tutting until Maria arrived, and then 'my lady calls' was performed for Olivia's benefit as a condescending and undeserved reproof. The sources not only of Maria's exasperation with the steward but of her sense that he was 'a time-pleaser, an affectioned ass' (2.3.142) were entirely clear from this single tiny encounter: this Malvolio, it transpired when he came downstairs in tightly tied dressing gown and pyjamas to rebuke the revellers in 2.3, even had enough anxious self-regard to sleep in a hairnet, his sense of his own identity apparently depending, in isolation from anyone he could regard as a social equal, on a preening solitary personal vanity. The full ghastly intimate horror of Maria's ensuing vengeance was enhanced by a bold and highly effective change of location for the letter scene, 2.5: instead of lurking behind a potted shrub in an imagined garden, Sir Toby, Sir Andrew and Fabian were covertly ushered by Maria into what was clearly Malvolio's private room in the servants' quarters (a narrow single bed was placed stage left beside the single chair), where 'the box-tree' had dwindled into a screen ornamented with a horticultural design (stage right). As the three trespassing conspirators looked on from behind the screen (and as the veiled Olivia once more appeared as image in the gilded frame, stage centre), Malvolio returned to his room for a short interlude from his duties, the whole audience transfixed with a kind of delighted horror at this artfully intensified violation of his privacy. In 2002, this scene of transgressive voyeurism has suddenly become reminiscent of the agonies of reality TV, and Russell Beale rose to the occasion with a magnificent fussy naturalism: he carefully removed his jacket and meticulously hung it over the back of the chair to avoid creases, and then sniffed each armpit of his shirt to check their freshness before lying on his back on the little bed to console himself with his pathetic daydream of being Count Malvolio. He had a small black book to read – perhaps a Bible – but it turned out that this prop was of less use to him as a source of wisdom than as a repository for the flimsy evidence with which he shored up his sustaining erotic fantasy of upward mobility: on 'There is example for't: the Lady of the Strachey married the yeoman of the wardrobe' (see Key Passages, **p. 168**) he at once furtively and triumphantly produced a treasured press cutting from between its pages and held it up towards the audience, nodding wide-eyed as if demanding our reassuring assent. As he read the forged letter, he came to occupy exactly the position before Olivia's framed image earlier adopted by Orsino, and at the climax of his joyous

---

9 Famous fictional detective in novels by Agatha Christie.
10 Eldest son of Queen Victoria (1841–1910) and King of England between 1901 and 1910; he sported a full beard immortalised in portraits by W. and D. Downey (1868) and George Frederic Watts (c. 1874), now held at the National Portrait Gallery.

faith in its contents – 'every reason excites to this, that my lady loves me' (see Key Passages, p. 171) – she lingeringly removed her veil before his rapt gaze, just as she had earlier removed it in person for Cesario. After his departure, Sir Toby's already half-appalled 'Why, thou hast put him in such a dream that when the image of it leaves him, he must run mad' (2.5.186–8) seemed only a literal state-ment of the case. Malvolio's subsequent cross-gartering was the funnier for being invisible beneath his sober suit (save for its effect on his gait), indicated on the relevant lines by smiling, eminently misunderstandable gestures, and his confine-ment – seated on the same wooden chair from his little room, but in a straitjacket – seemed crueller than ever. In the final scene, his suddenly immobile face, as the deception was explained to him, seemed at once to age and, beard and moustache already ruined, to empty of all its characteristic expression: everything that had earlier supported Malvolio's precariously maintained sense of himself had been taken away, and the voice that spoke the line 'I'll be revenged on the whole pack of you' as he stalked hastily off in shame and defiance, though it retained some-thing of the harshness earlier directed at Maria, was quite unlike that of the early acts' oily upper servant. The underlying pain and aggression were no longer fil-tered through deference and self-consciousness, and they sounded altogether more frightening.

A Cinematic Appropriation of *Twelfth Night* (dir. Nunn, 1996)

From **Carol Chillington Rutter, 'Looking at Shakespeare's Women on Film'**, in R. Jackson (ed.), *The Cambridge Companion to Shakespeare on Film* (Cambridge: Cambridge University Press, 2000), pp. 248–50

> Reviewers and critics who write about Trevor Nunn's 1996 film often focus on the long opening sequence, which shows Viola and Sebastian working as profes-sional entertainers onboard a luxury cruiser just before it sinks, probably because their routine seems to comment directly on the instability of the signs through which we are encouraged to identify the twins as either male or female. Carol Chillington Rutter believes that this sequence 'literalises the common terms of gender differentiation but also suggests gender erasure'. However, other critics have interpreted Nunn's additions to the opening scene as an attempt to exorcise the threat of gender instability.[1]

No film proposes the question about how we read the gendered body so wonder-fully – and disconcertingly – as Trevor Nunn's *Twelfth Night* (1995) with its teasing opening sequence. The camera pans across a scene below deck on a sailing

---

1   See, for example, Maria F. Magro and Mark Douglas, 'Reflections on Sex, Shakespeare and Nostalgia in Trevor Nunn's *Twelfth Night*', in Deborah Cartmell, I. Q. Hunter, and Imelda Whelehan (eds), *Retrovisions: Reinventing the Past in Film and Fiction* (London: Pluto Press, 2001), pp. 41–58.

ship where the passengers, outlandish in late-Victorian fancy dress, are ignoring a rising gale. The camera settles on identical twins, at the piano to do their 'turn', stunningly got-up in harem costume, veils covering their lower faces, a concealment that only emphasises their seductive eyes. From the shadows, Antonio, in mariner's uniform, gazes hungrily. We read them as women. Until mid-way through the soprano chorus of 'O mistress mine' they 'sing both high and low', and 'low' booms out in a bass voice! Which of them is the man? Which of them does Antonio desire? Eyes narrowing, the piano-playing twin moves to unmask the impersonator, pulling aside the first twin's veil to expose what's underneath. A moustache! Frowning, that former 'she' (now written 'he') reciprocates, pulls aside the second twin's veil, and discloses – another moustache.

These 'monster' androgynes – women's kohled eyes over men's hirsute lips – appeal helplessly to their audience who roar delight at each disclosure. Again, the first twin reaches out. S/he tugs the corner of the opposite moustache – and pulls it off! So *that's* the sister! But there's still another moustache. And just as the bare-faced twin grimly reaches for it – the comic rhythm of the sequence working to make us project the next step, imagine *it* ripping off, leaving us where we started – the ship runs aground.

There's chaos: rigging falls, the piano slides across the deck, the twins stagger below, Sebastian pulling off his wig – but not his moustache – as they throw belongings into the trunk that is going to wash ashore with Viola: clothes, a sepia photograph, a wooden box of theatrical make-up. That close-up on the possessions that make the twins what they are (skirts vs. shirts, a child of each sex flanking the father in the photograph) literalises the common terms of gender differentiation but also suggests gender erasure, for the box of greasepaint significantly remembers what the masquerade so disconcertingly taught us: gender is what we 'read', nothing more, perhaps, than a performance slapped on with the Leichner no. 5.[2] If so, farewell difference; farewell differentiating claims to what men and women 'owe' in love.

---

2   Leichner produce grease paint for actors; Leichner No. 5 is ivory-coloured.

3

Key Passages

Introduction

Samuel Pepys wrote in his famous diary that *Twelfth Night* is a silly play and that its title is misleadingly unrelated to its subject matter (see Introduction, **p. 3**). Roughly 200 years later, William Archer was similarly critical about the structure of the play: 'the elements of beauty and of humour', he claims, 'are kept very much apart in *Twelfth Night*'. The play, Archer continues, 'contains two actions in one frame – a romantic intrigue borrowed from Italy, and a pair of practical jokes [. . .] invented by Shakespeare'. According to Archer, 'these two actions can be said really to touch at only one point, and then as it were, unwillingly; for it is where Viola's blade crosses Sir Andrew's. . . . The play has just as much unity as two spheres in contact' (see Early Criticism, **p. 56**). These comments usefully challenge us to establish whether the different strands in the plot of *Twelfth Night* do in fact relate to each other in meaningful ways.

The quick succession of short scenes at the beginning of Act 1 shows quite effectively how different characters and situations can be mutually reinforcing in highlighting a common source of psychological and dramatic interest. Excess is the dominant trait defining all the major characters introduced in the play's opening sequence, namely Orsino, Duke of Illyria,[1] Olivia, a countess, and Sir Toby, her uncle. If Orsino's unrequited love for Olivia is boundless and 'Receiveth as the sea' (see Key Passages, **p. 141**), Sir Toby refuses to be confined 'within the modest limits of order' when it comes to 'quaffing and drinking' (see Key Passages, **p. 143**). Olivia is similarly trapped in a behavioural pattern that threatens to destroy her: the excessive quality of the 'debt of love' (see Key Passages, **p. 142**) that she plans to pay to her dead brother involves mourning in secluded isolation for a period of seven years. Illyria seems paralysed by the compulsive, excessive behaviour of its inhabitants. When Viola is washed ashore and assumes that her brother Sebastian has died during the shipwreck, her opening lines ring ominously appropriate: 'And what should I do in Illyria? / My brother he is in Elysium' (1.2.3).[2] By placing the words 'Illyria' and 'Elysium' at the end of each line,

---

1   Orsino's title is 'Duke' in stage directions and speech prefixes, but he is often referred to as 'Count' in the dialogue.
2   The state and place (Elysian Fields) of perfect happiness achieved by the blessed after death in Greek mythology.

Shakespeare draws our attention to their phonetic similarity. Their assonance, in turn, suggests that Viola may well have arrived in Elysium, in a world frozen by a deadly paralysis of the will. However, Viola's arrival introduces an unexpected and welcome development. Her decision to adopt a male disguise and a new identity as Cesario turns her into an irresistible androgynous creature, who diverts Orsino from his obsession for Olivia (Act 1, Scene 4) and Olivia from her plan to mourn her brother's death for seven years (Act 1, Scene 5).

Act 2 opens with a short scene, which introduces two new characters, Sebastian, Viola's brother, and Antonio, who rescued him from the 'breach of the sea' (see Key Passages, p. 153) and has lovingly provided for him since. While Sebastian's announcement that he is 'bound to the Count Orsino's court' (see Key Passages, p. 153) provides an interesting clue as to how the Orsino–Viola–Olivia love triangle will be resolved in Act 5, Scene 1, Antonio's feelings for Sebastian reinforce the impression that sexual desire is predominantly homoerotic at this stage in the play. Although Viola effectively disproves Orsino's misogynist views in Act 2, Scene 4, thus paving the way for Orsino's marriage proposal in Act 5, transgressive desires prevail in Act 2, both in Orsino's and Olivia's emotional worlds and among the members of Olivia's unruly household. Even the steward Malvolio is tricked into revealing his ambition to marry Olivia and become 'Count Malvolio', when Maria, Olivia's lady-in-waiting, forges a love letter, which he reads as a genuine, if cryptic, declaration of Olivia's secret feelings for him.

When even Malvolio gives in to his secret fantasies and desires, madness breaks loose and takes hold of every aspect of Illyrian life. Even words become unstable: Malvolio's attempt to decipher the forged letter and to 'crush' the meaningless sequence of letters 'M.O.A.I' into an abbreviation of his own name is closely linked to Feste's allusion to the slippery quality of language in Act 3, Scene 1. Gender, class and meaning itself are shown to be nothing but the provisional effect of transgressive and idiosyncratic desires. In Act 3, comments such as Olivia's 'this is very midsummer madness' (3.4.54) and Fabian's 'More matter for a May morning' (3.4.140) show how appropriately the title *Twelfth Night* links the play to traditional holiday periods, when festive inversions and carnivalesque disorder prevail over the norms that regulate ordinary life (see Critical History, pp. 43–5). Although the overall register has been festive this far into the play, violence lurks just below the surface and breaks out when Sir Toby tricks Sir Andrew and Viola into fighting each other (Act 3, Scene 4). Sir Toby, who becomes increasingly sinister, is also responsible for taking the gulling of Malvolio a bit too far. Malvolio's ordeal, when he is locked up in a dark room in Act 4, Scene 2 and is challenged by Feste disguised as Sir Topas the curate to prove that he is not mad, has dark, potentially tragic, undertones.

Sebastian's arrival in Illyria in Act 3, Scene 3 does not restore order. On the contrary, it predictably generates further opportunities for farcical confusion due to the fact that Viola/Cesario and Sebastian look identical. In Act 3, Scene 4 Antonio joins the sword fight between Sir Andrew and Viola, having mistakenly assumed the latter to be Sebastian. When Orsino's guards arrest Antonio for attacking Orsino's ships and stealing their cargo, Antonio is understandably shocked by Viola's failure to come to his rescue. In Act 4, it is Sebastian's turn to be taken for Viola, first by Feste, then by Sir Toby and Sir Andrew, and finally by Olivia (Act 4, Scene 1), who is overjoyed to find Viola finally willing to return her feelings for her. Sebastian is naturally overwhelmed and wonders whether he or the Illyrians have suddenly gone mad. Sebastian's comic ordeal in Act 4, Scene 1 is subtly linked to Malvolio's tragic ordeal in Act 4, Scene 2: both scenes interestingly show that sanity is not an absolute state of mind but that it merely depends on other people's willingness to endorse our own perceptions, our own certainties regarding what time of day it is, whether it is day or night, or whether what we see is real or not. Sebastian does wonder whether Olivia is mad, but the mere fact that everybody around her supports and indulges her delusion, makes her 'sane' to Sebastian's eyes. However, Sebastian's conclusion that Olivia is not mad does not justify the fact that he agrees to marry her straight after their first meeting (Act 4, Scene 3).

In the final scene, Viola is once again mistaken for Sebastian, first by Antonio, then by Olivia, who calls her husband, and, finally, by Sir Andrew and Sir Toby, who get a good bashing, when Sebastian proves a more valiant adversary than Viola. Confusion reaches a climatic moment, and violence threatens to erupt again, as Orsino swears to kill Viola to spite the cruel Olivia. This is a revelatory moment: Orsino's couplet – 'I'll sacrifice the lamb that I do love / To spite a raven's heart within a dove' (see Key Passages, p. 181) – shows the strength of Orsino's feelings *before* Viola's 'true' identity is revealed a few lines later. The tension between Orsino's heterosexual fantasies about Olivia and his homoerotic attachment towards Viola/Cesario is far from resolved at this stage in the final scene. Similarly, instead of bringing about a speedy resolution, Sebastian's entrance in Act 5, Scene 1 ushers in an exceptionally long, emotional recognition scene between Viola and Sebastian, which deflects our attention from the conventional comic resolution. Besides, whether or not directors and critics choose to regard Olivia's feelings for Sebastian, or Orsino's feelings for Viola/Cesario, as genuine or at least dramatically credible, the 'happy' ending is substantially qualified by the fact that several characters are disappointed: Antonio, Malvolio and Sir Andrew have no share in the 'happy wreck'; Sir Toby, who has secretly married Maria, does not rejoin the celebrations; and Feste sings a song, which, like many other songs in this play, reminds us that although we may bask in the illusion of a happy Illyrian dream, the dream is drawing to an end.

Unlike several other Shakespearean plays, *Twelfth Night* was not printed individually before being included in the First Folio edition of Shakespeare's dramatic works in 1623. The text in the following extracts is based on the text of *Twelfth Night* as it appears in the First Folio. Spelling and punctuation have been modernised, speech prefixes normalised and stage directions expanded to clarify entrances, exits, stage action and mode of delivery (when a speech is delivered as an aside or when there is a change of addressee within the same speech). Square brackets signal editorial intervention while accents indicate that the suffix -ed is stressed because of the requirement of metre. Line numbers are keyed to Stanley Wells and Gary Taylor, with John Jowett and William Montgomery (eds), *The Complete Works* (Oxford: Oxford University Press, 1986).

List of Key Passages

Editions Cited

The following editions are cited in the Key Passages below.

Bevington   David Bevington (ed.), *The Complete Works of Shakespeare*, 4th edn (New York: Longman, 1997).

Donno   Elizabeth Story Donno (ed.), *Twelfth Night*, The New Cambridge Shakespeare (Cambridge: Cambridge University Press, 1985).

Lothian and Craik   J. M. Lothian and T. W. Craik (eds), *Twelfth Night*, The Arden Shakespeare, 2nd series (London: Methuen, 1975).

Mahood   M. M. Mahood (ed.), *Twelfth Night*, The New Penguin Shakespeare (London: Penguin, 1968).

Warren and Wells   Roger Warren and Stanley Wells (eds), *Twelfth Night*, The Oxford Shakespeare (Oxford: Oxford University Press, 1994).

Key Passages

Dramatis Personae

The Folio text of 1623 (see Further Reading, **p. 189**) did not include a list of dramatis personae. The first list appeared in Nicholas Rowe's 1709 edition of Shakespeare's *Works*. The following list includes only the characters who appear in the Key Passages below. The remaining characters are: the sea captain (and sailors from the wrecked ship) who tells Viola about Illyria and its inhabitants in Act 1, Scene 2; the priest who marries Olivia and Sebastian after they exit at the end of Act 4, Scene 3 and then testifies that he has joined them in matrimony in Act 5, Scene 1; and a handful of generically named officers, servants and attendants in Olivia and Orsino's households.

ORSINO,[1] Duke[2] of Illyria
CURIO and VALENTINE, his attendants
FIRST OFFICER

OLIVIA, a Countess
SIR TOBY Belch, her uncle
MALVOLIO,[3] her steward
FESTE, her jester
MARIA, her waiting-woman
FABIAN, her attendant
SIR ANDREW Aguecheek, her suitor

---

1 Although Leslie Hotson's theory according to which *Twelfth Night* was first performed at Court on 6 January 1601, as a tribute to the Queen and her guest Don Virginio Orsino, Duke of Bracciano, has been confuted, Shakespeare is nevertheless believed to have been inspired by the young Italian aristocrat and to have named Orsino after him, when he wrote *Twelfth Night* later in the year.
2 See Footnote 1, **p. 135.**
3 See Footnote 10, **p. 100.**

VIOLA, Sebastian's twin sister, disguised as CESARIO
SEBASTIAN, Viola's twin brother
ANTONIO, a sea captain

Musicians and attendants.

Act 1, Scene 1, lines 1–41: Orsino in love

'If music be the food of love, play on': a most poetical opening for the most
poetical of Shakespeare's romantic comedies. *Twelfth Night* greets its spectators
and readers with music and flowing blank verse. Yet, excessive passions break
the elegant surface of this opening scene. Orsino describes his love for Olivia
as a violent appetite and demands more music in order to feed it, or rather, to
glut it, so that, 'by surfeiting', it may die. Orsino's account of his distracting
passion for Olivia is openly at odds with Act 2, Scene 4, where he blames
women for falling prey to violent and inconstant sexual appetites (see Key
Passages, pp. 163–4).

Shakespeare's use of the hunting metaphor in the second half of this short
opening scene emphasises the brutal, destructive quality of sexual passion.
Although Curio encourages Orsino to go hunting and the latter fantasises
about a time when Cupid will strike Olivia with his 'golden shaft', an allusion to
the popular Ovidian myth of Actaeon and Diana (see Contextual Overview,
pp. 12–13 and Modern Criticism, pp. 60–1) effectively turns Orsino, and not
Olivia, into the hunted hart. Sexual passion, it seems, does not only manifest
itself as a violent appetite, but it also turns the lover into a prey of his own
desires. Interestingly, Olivia's plan to mourn her brother for seven years par-
takes of the narcissistic quality of Orsino's feelings for her. Sigmund Freud, the
founder of psychoanalysis, believed that narcissism is the basis both of mourning
and of our romantic investment in a 'love object' (the beloved).[1] According to
Freud, we love and miss others less for being who they are than for how we see
ourselves reflected in them. The eyes of the beloved, in other words, function
like the reflecting surface of Narcissus's pool (see Modern Criticism, pp. 61–3).
Freud's work on narcissism and mourning highlights interesting similarities in
Orsino's and Olivia's characters. Orsino is self-absorbed, isolated, metaphoric-
ally transformed into the hunted hart by the violence of his own desires. Similarly, Olivia has cut herself off from the world and is consumed by the violence
of her grief.

Orsino and Olivia's self-consuming narcissism tinges this opening scene
with a decadent melancholy. However, some scholars have interpreted Orsino's
character in socio-historical, rather than in psychological, terms. Paul Yachnin,

1   See, for example, his essays 'On Narcissism: An Introduction' (1914) and 'Mourning and
Melancholia' (1917), in *The Standard Edition of the Complete Psychological Works of Sigmund
Freud*, Vol. XIV (Harmondsworth: Penguin, 1984), pp. 73–102, 243–58.

for example, has argued that 'the duke's casual disregard for the paid, highly skilled work of the court musicians, who must (on command) play, stop playing, repeat the phrase, stop playing again' (see The Work in Performance, **p. 116**) may represent a subtle critique of aristocratic self-indulgence and a sardonic comment on the actors' role as professional entertainers at court. Although theatrical companies increasingly depended on the revenue generated by the paying audiences, they still relied on royal patronage both for profit and protection.

For all its poetical qualities, the opening scene in Twelfth Night has dark, disquieting undertones. Reflecting on the fact that nineteenth-century directors often inverted the order of Act 1, Scene 1 and Act 1, Scene 2 as they appear in the Folio, Laurie Osborne suggests that 'the development of the proscenium stage and scenery meant that it was more theatrically convenient to get the seashore scene out of the way and consolidate the interior scenes in Orsino's and Olivia's houses' (see The Work in Performance, **p. 120**). However, stage and film directors who interpret Twelfth Night as a romantic comedy also invert the order of Act 1, Scene 1 and Act 1, Scene 2 in order to downplay Orsino's melancholy and to foreground Viola's arrival, which is going to bring new life into Orsino and Olivia's decadent households (see, for example, The Work in Performance, **pp. 130–1**).

Enter ORSINO, *Duke of Illyria*, CURIO, *and other lords.*

ORSINO   If music be the food of love, play on;
    Give me excess of it, that, surfeiting,[2]
    The appetite may sicken and so die.[3]
    That strain[4] again, it had a dying fall;[5] [*Music starts*]
    O, it came o'er my ear, like the sweet sound   5
    That breathes upon a bank of violets,
    Stealing and giving odour. Enough! No more. [*Music stops.*]
    'Tis not so sweet now as it was before.
    O spirit of love, how quick and fresh art thou
    That, notwithstanding thy capacity,[6]   10
    Receiveth as the sea: nought enters there,
    Of what validity[7] and pitch[8] so e're,
    But falls into abatement[9] and low price,
    Even in a minute. So full of shapes is fancy,
    That it alone is high fantastical.   15

2 Feeding to excess.
3 The death of appetite is also the death of sexual desire, as suggested by the Elizabethan erotic sense of the verb 'to die', meaning 'to experience a sexual orgasm'.
4 Melody, tune, piece of music.
5 A lowering of the note, or cadence.
6 Ability to receive or contain.
7 Value.
8 Height.
9 Lowering of value.

CURIO   Will you go hunt, my lord?

ORSINO   What, Curio?

CURIO   The hart.

ORSINO   Why so I do, the noblest that I have.[10]
O, when mine eyes did see Olivia first,
Methought she purged the air of pestilence.[11]   20
That instant was I turned into a hart
And my desires, like fell and cruel hounds,
E'er since pursue me.

Enter VALENTINE.

How now, what news from her?

VALENTINE   So please my lord, I might not be admitted,
But from her handmaid do return this answer: 25
The element[12] itself, till seven years' heat,[13]
Shall not behold her face at ample view,
But, like a cloistress,[14] she will veilèd walk
And water once a day her chamber round
With eye-offending brine – all this to season[15]   30
A brother's dead love, which she would keep fresh
And lasting in her sad remembrance.

ORSINO   O, she that hath a heart of that fine frame
To pay this debt of love but to a brother,
How will she love when the rich golden shaft[16]   35
Hath killed the flock of all affections else
That live in her; when liver, brain, and heart,
These sovereign thrones,[17] are all supplied, and filled
Her sweet perfections,[18] with one self king![19]
Away before me to sweet beds of flowers: 40
Love-thoughts lie rich when canopied with bowers.

                                                   Exeunt.

---

10 Pun on 'hart' and Orsino's 'heart'.
11 Plague.
12 Sky.
13 Seven summers.
14 Female tenant of a cloister, a nun.
15 Preserve in brine (tears).
16 Cupid's golden arrow, which caused his victims to love; Cupid also had a leaden arrow, which
    quenched love.
17 Shakespeare's contemporaries understood the passions in *physiological* rather than *psychological*
    terms. The liver, the brain and the heart were believed to be seats of love (and valour), judgement
    and the emotions and to be far nobler organs than the palate, which was conventionally associated
    with sexual and gastronomic appetites (see also Key Passages, **p. 163**). For more details on early
    modern models of human physiology, see Bruce R. Smith, *Twelfth Night: Texts and Contexts*
    (Boston, Mass. and New York: Bedford and St. Martin's, 2001), pp. 187–94.
18 'Her sweet perfections filled' (punctuation and note from Bevington).
19 Romantic love, as opposed to sisterly love; or the object of Olivia's passion, as imagined by Orsino,
    that is Orsino himself.

Act 1, Scene 3, lines 1–11: Quaffing and drinking 1

Sir Toby's penchant for 'quaffing and drinking' introduces another type of excessive behaviour, which, unlike Orsino's and Olivia's immoderate passions, has often been interpreted as intimately connected to life, growth and *joie de vivre*. C. L. Barber and Michael Bristol (see Modern Criticism, **pp. 64–7 and pp. 70–3**), for example, associate Sir Toby and his refusal to be confined 'within the modest limits of order' with the traditional role of the 'Lord of Misrule', who was appointed to preside over seasonal holidays and was then uncrowned when ordinary life resumed. Barber and Bristol disagree exactly as to whether normality did indeed resume at the end of the holiday period (or whether normality is restored at the end of the play). Recent critics have qualified both Barber's conservative views on festivity and Bristol's utopian views on the Carnival. Karin Coddon, for example, regards Malvolio and Feste as equally, if not more disruptive and transgressive, than Sir Toby (see Modern Criticism, **pp. 73–5**). Keir Elam, on the other hand, points out that Sir Toby is indeed a 'Belch', a 'humoral symptom', and that his invocations against death, Olivia's mourning and recurrent references to the plague establish him as a life-affirming character. Besides, Elam associates Sir Toby not only with the declining tradition of popular carnivals and festivals but also, and more crucially, with 'the life of the comedy, of the playhouse, of the actor and his performance (see Modern Criticism, **pp. 76–80**).

Enter SIR TOBY *and* MARIA.

SIR TOBY   What a plague[1] means my niece to take the death of her
    brother thus? I am sure care's an enemy to life.

MARIA   By my troth, Sir Toby, you must come in earlier a-nights.[2] Your
    cousin, my lady, takes great exceptions to your ill hours.[3]

SIR TOBY   Why, let her except before excepted.[4]   5

MARIA Ay, but you must confine yourself within the modest limits of
    order.[5]

SIR TOBY   Confine? I'll confine myself no finer[6] than I am. These
    clothes are good enough to drink in, and so be these boots too;
    and they be not, let them hang themselves in their own straps.   10

MARIA   That quaffing[7] and drinking will undo you.

---

1   What on earth.
2   At night.
3   Late nights.
4   Pun on *exceptis excipiendis*, a legal phrase meaning 'due exceptions having been made'.
5   Decent behaviour.
6   '(1) "I will accept no further constraints", (2) "I refuse to dress more finely". Sir Toby plays upon
    chimes of sound and sense between "confines" and "finer"' (note from Donno).
7   Copious, immoderate drinking.

Act 1, Scene 4, lines 1–41: Viola in love

In Act 1, Scene 2 the boy actor playing Viola announces her plan to adopt a male disguise and to offer her services to Orsino. At the beginning of Act 1, Scene 4, the boy actor playing Viola enters 'in man's attire', disguised as Cesario. While recent critics, including Laura Levine (see The Work in Performance, pp. 113–15), help us establish how Shakespeare's audience responded to the convention of cross-dressing on the commercial stage, this scene shows how other characters respond to Viola–Cesario.

Orsino, for example, never openly suspects that Cesario may be a woman in disguise. However, his sexually charged use of the words 'lip', 'pipe' and 'the maiden's organ', which signal simultaneously the mouth, the throat and the voice of a woman *and* the vagina, the neck of the womb and womb itself, suggests that he is attracted by the fluid combination of Cesario's male and female attributes. Rather than revealing 'an apparent [male] homoeroticism in all sexuality', as Greenblatt argues (see Modern Criticism, **p. 90**), the complex mixture of masculine *and* feminine traits would seem to make Cesario's appeal *panerotic* rather than *homoerotic*.[1] What charms Orsino in this scene and Olivia in the next is the fact that Cesario, the source of all desires, is simultaneously male *and* female, or 'what you will'.

Enter VALENTINE *and* VIOLA [as CESARIO] *in man's attire*.

VALENTINE   If the Duke continue these favours towards you, Cesario, you are like to be much advanced: he hath known you but three days, and already you are no stranger.

VIOLA   You either fear his humour[2] or my negligence, that you call in question the continuance of his love. Is he inconstant, sir, in his   5
favours?

VALENTINE   No, believe me.

Enter Duke [ORSINO], CURIO, *and Attendants*.

VIOLA   I thank you. Here comes the Count.

ORSINO   Who saw Cesario, ho?

VIOLA   On your attendance, my lord, here.   10

ORSINO   [to CURIO and Attendants] Stand you a while aloof.[3] [*to* VIOLA] Cesario,
Thou know'st no less but all: I have unclasped
To thee the book even of my secret soul.

---

1   For a full discussion of Viola/Cesario's panerotic appeal, see Bruce Smith (ed.), *Twelfth Night: Texts and Contexts* (Boston, Mass. and New York: Bedford and St. Martin's, 2001), pp. 201–36.
2   Disposition.
3   At a distance.

Therefore, good youth, address thy gait[4] unto her,
Be not denied access, stand at her doors,   15
And tell them there thy fixèd foot shall grow
Till thou have audience.

VIOLA   Sure, my noble lord,
If she be so abandoned to her sorrow
As it is spoke, she never will admit me.

ORSINO   Be clamorous and leap all civil bounds[5]   20
Rather than make unprofited return.[6]

VIOLA   Say I do speak with her, my lord, what then?

ORSINO   O, then unfold the passion of my love,
Surprise[7] her with discourse of my dear faith.
It shall become thee well to act my woes: 25
She will attend it better[8] in thy youth
Than in a nuncio's[9] of more grave aspect[10].

VIOLA   I think not so, my lord.

ORSINO   Dear lad, believe it,
For they shall yet belie thy happy years
That say thou art a man. Diana[11]'s lip   30
Is not more smooth and rubious;[12] thy small pipe[13]
Is as the maiden's organ, shrill and sound;[14]
And all is semblative a woman's part.[15]
I know thy constellation[16] is right apt
For this affair. [To attendants] Some four or five attend him;   35
All, if you will, for I myself am best
When least in company. [to VIOLA] Prosper well in this
And thou shalt live as freely[17] as thy lord,
To call his fortunes thine.

VIOLA   I'll do my best
To woo your lady – [aside] yet, a barful[18] strife: 40
Whoe'er I woo, myself would be his wife.

                                                    Exeunt.

---

4 Go.
5 Limits imposed by good manners.
6 Come back without results.
7 Take her by surprise and/or force (military image).
8 Pay more attention.
9 Messenger's (the genitive case is redundant but not infrequent in Shakespearean usage).
10 Literally 'of more serious, reverend appearance', but also 'older', given Orsino's reference to
    Cesario's youth in the previous line.
11 Roman goddess of hunting and protectress of married chastity and childbirth, also known among
    the Greeks as Artemis.
12 Red.
13 Voice.
14 Clear and unbroken.
15 'All about Cesario is feminine'; also, meta-theatrical allusion to the fact that a boy actor is playing
    Viola's 'part' (or role).
16 Disposition determined by astrological influence.
17 Lavishly, free of care.
18 Full of bars, or hindrances.

Act 1, Scene 5, lines 134–274: Olivia in love

'I will not be compelled to listen to your sonnets', says the independently minded Mistress Carol to her would-be suitor Fairfield in James Shirley's comedy Hyde Park (1632). Mistress Carol's views on sonnets signal the decline of Petrarchan conventions (See Contextual Overview, **pp. 13–14**), which was well underway by the time Shakespeare wrote Twelfth Night. Mistress Carol would agree with Olivia and dismiss Orsino's protestations of love as conventional and, therefore, fake. The following exchange is a masterly display of rhetorical invention: Viola, who is wooing Olivia on Orsino's behalf, progresses from using the conventional language of courtship drawn from Petrarch to forging a new, intimate language of love, which infects Olivia's soul as quickly as Viola's androgynous looks infect her eyes and heart.

Viola almost spoils her chances with Olivia by insisting on delivering her 'well penned' message from Orsino. The conventional opening of Orsino's message – 'Most radiant, exquisite, and unmatchable beauty' (161) – prompts Olivia to insinuate that Viola is a mere comedian, namely, somebody who has learned lines written by somebody else and does not mean what she says. Viola parries Olivia's provocation remarkably well: her reply, 'I am not that I play' (not a mere servant? not a boy?), clearly arouses Olivia's interest, who identifies herself as the lady of the house (173–4). Viola loses Olivia's good will again, as she insists on resuming her conventional 'speech of praise'. When Maria threatens to escort Viola out, the latter raises the stakes and appeals to Olivia's modesty to be granted the chance to speak to her alone. Viola's intimation that she shares Olivia's investment in 'maidenhead'– 'what I am and what I would are as secret as maidenhead' (197–8) – secures Olivia's undivided attention. As Maria leaves, Olivia becomes defensive again and defiantly asks the young messenger to deliver Orsino's text. Olivia's use of the words 'text' and 'chapter' at lines 203–5 suggests that she views Orsino's feelings as bookish and conventional. Olivia's views are retrospectively validated by Orsino's use of the same metaphor in Act 2, Scene 4, when he says to Viola: 'I have unclasped / To thee the book even of my secret soul' (12–13). Once again, Viola rises to the challenge by asking Olivia to unveil. Olivia realises that Viola is 'now out of [her] text'. Viola is indeed improvising a fresh, more personal, approach, rather than simply following Orsino's orders. Olivia tries to hide her uneasiness by implying that Viola is not genuinely praising her beauty but using the hackneyed Petrarchan convention of the blazon (see Contextual Overview, **pp. 13–14** and Contemporary Documents, **pp. 33–5**). She accordingly compares her face to a painting so perfect as to seem artificial ('Is't not well done?') and her beauty to an asset so rare and precious as to deserve a mention in her will ('It shall be inventoried and every particle and utensil labelled to my will'). By exposing the sinister logic of Orsino's and Viola's language of praise, which turns the beloved into a commodity, Olivia challenges Viola to stay 'out of [her] text'. Viola's next speech at lines 234–42 is one of the most frequently quoted extracts from Twelfth Night and from Shakespeare's canon as a whole. Although it is as carefully constructed as a Petrarchan sonnet, Viola's 'willow cabin' speech forges a new language of love. Through a skilful use of assonance (see Modern Criticism, **pp. 57–9**), Shakespeare managed to make Viola's speech sound like a 'genuine' outburst of raw emotions.

Viola's appeal to 'maidenhead' and her teasing remark that 'he' is not what 'he' plays suggest that Olivia responds narcissistically to Viola's feminine qualities. However, Lorna Hutson has pointed out that Olivia is attracted by Viola's rhetorical skills, rather than her androgynous looks and that a transgression of class boundaries rather than sexual normativity represents the most radical aspect of this exchange (see Modern Criticism, **pp. 96–99**). Undoubtedly, approaches that focus on sexuality *and* class seem to do more justice to the complexity of Olivia's character, who, according to Sir Toby, may be refusing Orsino's advances because she is determined not to 'match above her degree' (1.3.105–6). Extracts in the Contemporary Documents section (see **pp. 19–25**) highlight the socially transgressive quality of Olivia's wish to marry Viola/ Cesario. Those extracts also show how the potentially tragic outcome of such matches is defused, if not altogether neutralised, by Orsino's isolated and sudden reference to the fact that the twins' blood is 'right noble' in Act 5, Scene 1.

Enter MALVOLIO.[1]

MALVOLIO Madam, yon[2] young fellow swears he will speak with you.

[. . .]

OLIVIA What kind o' man is he? 145

MALVOLIO Why, of mankind.

OLIVIA What manner of man?

MALVOLIO Of very ill[3] manner: he'll speak with you, will you or no.

OLIVIA Of what personage[4] and years is he?

MALVOLIO Not yet old enough for a man, nor young enough for a 150 boy: as a squash[5] is before 'tis a peascod,[6] or a codling[7] when 'tis almost an apple; 'tis with him in standing water[8] between boy and man. He is very well-favoured[9] and he speaks very shrewishly.[10] One would think his mother's milk were scarce out of him.

OLIVIA Let him approach. Call in my gentlewoman. 155

MALVOLIO Gentlewoman, my lady calls.

Exit [MALVOLIO].

1 Olivia and some of her attendants are already on stage.
2 That.
3 Rude.
4 Appearance.
5 The unripe pod of a pea.
6 Pea-pod.
7 A variety of apple, but also figuratively applied to a raw youth.
8 At the turn of the tide, between two ages, boyhood and adulthood.
9 Handsome.
10 Like a shrew, that is sharply and in a high-pitched voice.

Enter MARIA.

OLIVIA   Give me my veil; come, throw it o'er my face.
We'll once more hear Orsino's embassy.

Enter VIOLA[11] [*as* CESARIO].

VIOLA   The honourable lady of the house, which is she?
OLIVIA   Speak to me, I shall answer for her. Your will?   160
VIOLA   Most radiant, exquisite, and unmatchable beauty – I pray you
tell me if this be the lady of the house, for I never saw her. I would
be loath to cast away my speech, for besides that it is excellently
well penned, I have taken great pains to con it.[12] Good beauties, let
me sustain no scorn; I am very comptible,[13] even to the least sinister 165
usage.
OLIVIA   Whence came you, sir?
VIOLA   I can say little more than I have studied, and that question's out
of my part. Good gentle one, give me modest assurance if you be the
lady of the house, that I[14] may proceed in my speech.   170
OLIVIA   Are you a comedian?[15]
VIOLA   No, my profound heart; and yet, by the very fangs of malice, I
swear I am not that I play. Are you the lady of the house?
OLIVIA   If I do not usurp myself, I am.
VIOLA   Most certain, if you are she, you do usurp yourself, for what 175
is yours to bestow is not yours to reserve. But this is from my
commission.[16] I will on with my speech in your praise and then
show you the heart of my message.
OLIVIA   Come to what is important in't; I forgive[17] you the praise.
VIOLA   Alas, I took great pains to study it, and 'tis poetical.   180
OLIVIA   It is the more like to be feigned. I pray you keep it in. I heard
you were saucy[18] at my gates, and allowed your approach rather to
wonder at you than to hear you. If you be not mad, be gone; if you
have reason, be brief. 'Tis not that time of moon with me to make
one in so skipping a dialogue.[19]   185
MARIA   Will you hoist sail, sir? Here lies your way.

---

11 *Violenta* in the First Folio (see Further Reading, **p. 189**).
12 To commit it to memory.
13 Sensitive.
14 All modern editions insert 'I' here, although 'I' only appears as a catchword in the First Folio
    (see Further Reading, **p. 189**), that is, as a single word at the bottom right-hand corner of the page,
    and not in the text of the dialogue.
15 Meant as an insult, but ironically apt since Cesario is not only a boy actor playing Viola in disguise,
    but he is also playing the part of the wooer by proxy on Orsino's behalf.
16 Order, instruction.
17 Excuse.
18 Rude, ill-mannered.
19 Olivia explains that she is not under the influence of the moon (lunatic, mad) and that she is,
    therefore, unwilling to engage in a silly conversation with Viola.

VIOLA   No, good swabber, I am to hull²⁰ here a little longer. Some
mollification²¹ for your giant,²² sweet lady. Tell me your mind, I am
a messenger.

OLIVIA   Sure you have some hideous matter to deliver, when the   190
courtesy of it is so fearful. Speak your office.

VIOLA   It alone concerns your ear. I bring no overture²³ of war, no
taxation of homage.²⁴ I hold the olive²⁵ in my hand. My words are
as full of peace as matter.

OLIVIA   Yet you began rudely. What are you? What would you?   195

VIOLA   The rudeness that hath appeared in me have I learned from
my entertainment. What I am and what I would are as secret as
maidenhead: to your ears, divinity;²⁶ to any other's, profanation.²⁷

OLIVIA   Give us the place alone, we will hear this divinity.

[*Exit* MARIA]

Now, sir, what is your text?   200

VIOLA   Most sweet lady –

OLIVIA   A comfortable doctrine,²⁸ and much may be said of it. Where
lies your text?

VIOLA   In Orsino's bosom.

OLIVIA   In his bosom? In what chapter of his bosom?   205

VIOLA   To answer by the method, in the first of his heart.

OLIVIA   O, I have read it: it is heresy. Have you no more to say?

VIOLA   Good madam, let me see your face.

OLIVIA   Have you any commission²⁹ from your lord to negotiate with
my face? You are now out of your text.³⁰ But we will draw the   210
curtain and show you the picture. [OLIVIA *unveils*] Look you, sir,
such a one I was this present. Is't not well done?

VIOLA   Excellently done, if God did all.³¹

OLIVIA   'Tis in grain,³² sir, 'twill endure wind and weather.

VIOLA   'Tis beauty truly blent, whose red and white   215

---

20 Viola responds to Maria's order to 'hoist sail', that is, to leave, by wittily calling her a 'swabber'
(petty officer who cleans the decks on a ship) and by stressing that she is 'to hull' (to keep the sails
furled, and, therefore, to stay) a little longer.

21 Viola is asking Olivia to pacify Maria.

22 Ironic reference to Maria's size. Another allusion to Maria's size occurs at 3.2.63, where Sir Toby
refers to Maria as 'the youngest wren of mine' (or 'nine', a common emendation in modern editions).

23 Declaration.

24 Levy or tax due to a lord, possibly implying that Orsino's rank is higher than Olivia's.

25 Symbol of peace and reconciliation. See Genesis 8:11, where Noah realises that the rain will stop
and the waters will recede when a dove flies towards him carrying an olive branch, the symbol of
God's reconciliation with mankind.

26 Theology, the noblest of sciences in medieval times.

27 Blasphemy.

28 Olivia mocks Viola's use of theological vocabulary at line 198 by referring to the conventional
opening 'Most sweet lady—' as a 'comfortable doctrine', that is comforting, but also familiar and
predictable.

29 See Footnote 16.

30 Olivia accuses Viola of departing from Orsino's instructions.

31 Cheeky allusion to the fact that Olivia may be wearing make-up.

32 Fast-dyed.

Nature's own sweet and cunning hand laid on.[33]
Lady, you are the cruell'st she alive,
If you will lead these graces to the grave
And leave the world no copy.[34]

OLIVIA   O, sir, I will not be so hard-hearted. I will give out divers 220
schedules[35] of my beauty. It shall be inventoried and every particle
and utensil labelled to my will as: *item*,[36] two lips, indifferent red;
item, two grey eyes, with lids to them; *item*, one neck, one chin, and
so forth. Were you sent hither to praise me?

VIOLA   I see you what you are, you are too proud.   225
But if you were the devil, you are fair.
My lord and master loves you. O, such love
Could be but recompensed,[37] though you were crowned
The nonpareil[38] of beauty!

OLIVIA   How does he love me?

VIOLA   With adorations, fertile[39] tears,   230
With groans that thunder love, with sighs of fire – [40]

OLIVIA   Your lord does know my mind, I cannot love him.
Yet I suppose him virtuous, know him noble,
Of great estate, of fresh and stainless[41] youth;
In voices well divulged,[42] free,[43] learned and valiant,   235
And in dimension and the shape of nature[44]
A gracious person. But yet I cannot love him.
He might have took[45] his answer long ago.

VIOLA   If I did love you in my master's flame,
With such a suffering, such a deadly[46] life,   240
In your denial I would find no sense,
I would not understand it.

OLIVIA   Why, what would you?

VIOLA   Make me a willow[47] cabin at your gate

---

33 By referring to Nature as a painter, Viola is alluding to Olivia's description of her own face as a
picture at line 211.
34 Copy of the picture, Olivia's face, but also a child. In the following reply, Olivia responds only to
the literal sense of Viola's plea.
35 Inventories.
36 Latin term meaning 'likewise', 'also', or 'moreover', and used as a heading for individual entries in
a formal list or different sections or parts in a legal document, such as a will.
37 Requited.
38 Paragon.
39 Abundant.
40 A full stop follows 'fire' in the First Folio (see Further Reading, **p. 189**) and in most modern
editions. The dash suggests that Olivia interrupts Viola, as she resumes what sounds like
conventional Petrarchan language (see Contextual Overview, **pp. 13–14**).
41 Unblemished.
42 People speak well of Orsino.
43 Generous.
44 In appearance.
45 Taken.
46 Death-like.
47 Symbol of unrequited love. There are other well-known examples in Shakespeare: Ophelia, spurned
by Hamlet, drowns when she falls off a willow that grows over a brook (*Hamlet* 4.7.138), while
Desdemona sings a 'song of willow' shortly before Othello murders her (*Othello* 4.3.27).

And call upon my soul within the house;
Write loyal cantons[48] of contemnèd[49] love   245
And sing them loud even in the dead of night;
Halloo[50] your name to the reverberate[51] hills
And make the babbling gossip of the air[52]
Cry out 'Olivia!' O, you should not rest
Between the elements of air and earth,   250
But you should pity me!
OLIVIA   You might do much.
    What is your parentage?
VIOLA   Above my fortunes,[53] yet my state[54] is well.
    I am a gentleman.
OLIVIA   Get you to your lord.
    I cannot love him. Let him send no more,   255
    Unless, perchance, you come to me again
    To tell me how he takes it. Fare you well.
    I thank you for your pains. [OLIVIA *gives* VIOLA *money*] Spend
        this for me.
VIOLA   I am no fee'd post,[55] lady. Keep your purse.
    My master, not myself, lacks recompense.   260
    Love make his heart of flint that you shall love,
    And let your fervour, like my master's, be
    Placed in contempt. Farewell, fair cruelty.
                                                            Exit [VIOLA]
OLIVIA   'What is your parentage?'
    'Above my fortunes, yet my state is well.   265
    I am a gentleman'. I'll be sworn thou art.
    Thy tongue, thy face, thy limbs, actions and spirit
    Do give thee five-fold blazon.[56] Not too fast! Soft, soft!
    Unless the master were the man.[57] How now?
    Even so quickly may one catch the plague?[58]   270
    Methinks I feel this youth's perfections
    With an invisible and subtle stealth

48 Songs.
49 Rejected.
50 Shout.
51 Resounding, echoing.
52 Echo, the nymph who was transformed into a mere echoing sound by the strength of
    her unrequited love for Narcissus (see Contextual Overview, **p. 12** and Modern Criticism,
    pp. 61–3).
53 Better than my present employment as a servant suggests.
54 Status, rank.
55 Hired go-between, who expects to be paid.
56 Device as on a shield; see also Contextual Overview (**pp. 13–14**) and Contemporary Documents
    (**pp. 33–5**).
57 Unless Orsino were Viola.
58 Fall in love. Shakespeare's contemporaries believed that falling in love caused actual changes in the
    body, like a disease or an infection.

To creep in at mine eyes.[59] Well, let it be.
What ho, Malvolio!

Act 2, Scene 1, lines 1–36: Antonio in love

This scene introduces two more characters: Sebastian, Viola's twin brother, who
is until now presumed dead by Viola *and* by those readers and theatre-goers who
are unfamiliar with the play, and Antonio, the sea captain who rescues him from
the shipwreck. The timing of this short scene, which is positioned just after Act 1,
Scene 5, where Olivia first realises that she is in love with Viola/Cesario, suggests
that the following exchange can be read as an anticipation of how Sebastian's
climactic reunion with Viola at the end of Act 5 will resolve the Orsino–Olivia–
Viola love triangle. However, Act 2, Scene 1 can also be read as another opening
sequence, which replicates Act 1, Scene 1 in many interesting ways. Like Olivia,
Sebastian is mourning the death of a sibling and is unable to return another
character's feelings for him. This time the spurned friend (or lover?) is the sea
captain Antonio. In Act 1, Scene 1, the intensity of Olivia's mourning for her
brother was matched by the intensity of Orsino's passion for her; in Act 2, Scene
1, the intensity of Sebastian's mourning for his sister is matched by the intensity
of Antonio's passion for him. If Orsino's passion for Olivia turns him into a
metaphorical prey of his own desires, Antonio is prepared to sacrifice his own life
by following Sebastian to Orsino's court, from where he is banned due to his
involvement in trade wars that have inflicted personal and financial loss upon
Orsino's family. It is, therefore, worth wondering whether Act 2, Scene 1 adds
fresh complications, rather than a glimpse of a possible resolution, to the tangled
knot of passions and desires introduced in Act 1.

Enter ANTONIO *and* SEBASTIAN.

ANTONIO   Will you stay no longer, nor will you not that I go with you?
SEBASTIAN   By your patience, no. My stars shine darkly over me. The
    malignancy[1] of my fate might perhaps distemper[2] yours, therefore I
    shall crave of you your leave that I may bear my evils alone. It were
    a bad recompense for your love to lay any of them[3] on you.   5
ANTONIO   Let me yet know of you whither you are bound.[4]

---

59 Shakespeare's contemporaries believed that the brain delivered the image of the beloved from the
    eyes to the heart, and that the impression made by that image would alter the balance of humours
    in the body and cause the beloved to experience sexual desire. For further details, see Bruce Smith
    (ed.), *Twelfth Night: Texts and Contexts* (Boston, Mass. and New York: Bedford and St. Martin's,
    2001), pp. 187–94.

1 Evil influence.
2 Affect negatively.
3 Referring to 'my evils'.
4 Where you are going.

SEBASTIAN   No, sooth,[5] sir. My determinate[6] voyage is mere extrava-
gancy.[7] But I perceive in you so excellent a touch of modesty that
you will not extort from me what I am willing to keep in; therefore
it charges me in manners the rather to express my self. You must   10
know of me then, Antonio, my name is Sebastian, which I called
Roderigo.[8] My father was that Sebastian of Messaline[9] whom I
know you have heard of. He left behind him myself and a sister,
both born in an hour.[10] If the heavens had been pleased, would we
had so ended.[11] But you, sir, altered that, for some hour before you   15
took me from the breach[12] of the sea was my sister drowned.

ANTONIO   Alas the day!

SEBASTIAN   A lady, sir, though it was said she much resembled me,
was yet of many accounted beautiful. But though I could not with
such estimable wonder overfar believe that,[13] yet thus far I will   20
boldly publish[14] her: she bore a mind that envy could not but call
fair. She is drowned already, sir, with salt water, though I seem to
drown her remembrance again with more.[15]

ANTONIO   Pardon me, sir, your bad entertainment.[16]

SEBASTIAN   O good Antonio, forgive me your trouble.   25

ANTONIO   If you will not murder me for my love, let me be your servant.

SEBASTIAN   If you will not undo what you have done, that is, kill him
whom you have recovered, desire it not. Fare ye well at once. My
bosom is full of kindness[17] and I am yet so near the manners of
my mother[18] that upon the least occasion more mine eyes will tell   30
tales of me[19]. I am bound to the Count Orsino's court. Farewell.

Exit

ANTONIO   The gentleness[20] of all the gods go with thee!
I have many enemies in Orsino's Court,
Else[21] would I very shortly see thee there.

---

5 In truth.
6 Intended.
7 Aimless wandering.
8 Although I called myself Roderigo until now.
9 Possibly Messina or Marseilles, but also fictitious location, which may have a literary origin in
   Plautus's *Manaechmi*, a comedy which Shakespeare had used as his main source in *The Comedy
   of Errors*, as established by G. Salingar in an article published in *Shakespeare Quarterly* 9 (1958),
   pp. 117–39.
10 Therefore, twins.
11 Died together.
12 Surf.
13 A difficult sentence, which can be freely paraphrased as follows: 'Though I never thought that I
    deserved such admiration'.
14 'Make public', therefore 'talk openly' about Viola.
15 More salt water, that is, his tears.
16 If Antonio had known about Sebastian's recent loss, he would have been more considerate; or
    Antonio's entertainment has not been adequate to Sebastian's wealthy (aristocratic?) background.
17 Tenderness.
18 Feminine propensity to tears.
19 My tears will reveal my young age (and naivety).
20 Favour.
21 Otherwise.

But come what may, I do adore thee so   35
That danger shall seem sport, and I will go.

Exit

Act 2, Scene 2, lines 17–41: Knots, tangles and love triangles

The following soliloquy is preceded by a brief exchange where Malvolio, the 'churlish messenger' of line 23, returns what he believes to be Orsino's ring to Viola. Having left no ring with Olivia, Viola correctly works out that Olivia is sending, rather than returning, the ring, and that the ring is a love token. Viola's soliloquy can be read as a moral set-piece. Unlike the disguised heroines in Shakespeare's sources, who openly admit that disguise grants them exceptional autonomy and mobility (see Contemporary Documents, **pp. 26–30**), Viola describes disguise as a devilish 'wickedness' and pities the poor lady Olivia, who is fallen in love with her 'outside', that is, with her assumed identity as Orsino's page, Cesario. This soliloquy, therefore, echoes contemporary anti-theatrical pamphleteers, such as Philip Stubbes (see Contemporary Documents, **pp. 25–6**), who condemned cross-dressing and the practice of casting boy actors to play the role of female characters in early modern commercial theatres. However, the postponement of Cesario's transformation into Viola beyond the end of the play may signal Shakespeare's divided attitude towards disguise and impersonation, which are fundamental practices at the very heart of theatricality itself (see The Work in Performance, **pp. 113–15**). Also complex is the significance of this soliloquy within the dramatic structure of the play as a whole. On the one hand, Viola's appeal to Time, straight after Sebastian's first appearance in the previous scene, can be read as another anticipation of the happy ending in Act 5. On the other hand, as with Act 2, Scene 1, we can choose *not* to read this soliloquy as an anticipation of an assumedly normative ending, which dispels confusing dreams and quenches transgressive passions, since time does indeed run out before Viola is given a chance to switch her male disguise for her 'maiden weeds'.

VIOLA   I left no ring with her. What means this lady?
Fortune forbid my outside[1] have not charmed her!
She made good view of me, indeed so much
That methought her eyes had lost her tongue,[2]   20
For she did speak in starts,[3] distractedly.
She loves me sure! The cunning of her passion
Invites me in this churlish messenger.[4]

---

1   Male appearance.
2   What she saw left her speechless.
3   More commonly in the phrase 'by fits and starts'.
4   Malvolio.

None of my lord's ring?[5] Why, he sent her none.
I am the man! If it be so, as 'tis,   25
Poor lady, she were better love a dream.
Disguise, I see thou art a wickedness,
Wherein the pregnant[6] enemy does much.
How easy is it for the proper false[7]
In women's waxen hearts to set their forms?[8]   30
Alas, our frailty is the cause, not we,
For such as we are made of, such we be.[9]
How will this fadge?[10] My master loves her dearly,
And I, poor monster, fond as much on him,
And she, mistaken, seems to dote on me.   35
What will become of this? As I am man,
My state[11] is desperate[12] for my master's love;
As I am woman, now alas the day,
What thriftless[13] sighs shall poor Olivia breathe?
O Time, thou must untangle this, not I;   40
It is too hard a knot for me t'untie.

                                                                      [*Exit*]

Act 2, Scene 3, lines 1–108: Quaffing and drinking II

Like Act 1, Scene 3, Act 2, Scene 3 begins by inverting the 'normal order of day and night typical of Carnival and other forms of misrule' (see Modern Criticism, p. 71). Sir Toby exploits ambiguity in language – 'early' can mean both 'betimes', that is 'in good time' and 'in the early hours of the morning' – to prove that to stay up late is to go to bed early, thus sanctioning the inversion of night and day, of sleep and wake. Sir Andrew and Sir Toby also reject the early modern notion that health and happiness rested on the balance of the four humours in the body (microcosm), which in turn corresponded to the harmonious blend of the four elements which constituted all created matter

5   Viola is imagining, rather than quoting, Olivia's pretended rejection of Orsino's ring, since she exits
    before Olivia instructs Malvolio to return the ring at the end of Act 1, Scene 5.
6   A crafty enemy, capable of many tricks, i.e., the Devil.
7   Handsome but deceitful men.
8   To stamp their images on women's soft and, therefore, impressionable, hearts.
9   Although I follow most modern editors in emending the First Folio's 'Alas, O frailtie is the cause,
    not wee, / For such as we are made, if such we bee:', it is worth stressing that the original line has
    occasionally been regarded not only as grammatically viable but also as crucially different from the
    misogynistic reading implied by the emendation (see Osborne, 'The Texts of *Twelfth Night*', in
    Further Reading, p. 190). See also the indisputably chauvinist, 'Frailty, thy name is woman', in
    Hamlet 1.2.146.
10 Turn out.
11 Situation.
12 Hopeless.
13 Unprofitable.

(macrocosm). Health and happiness, according to the carnivalesque logic invoked by Sir Toby, rest instead on 'eating and drinking' and the satisfaction of bodily appetites.

Feste's arrival introduces other key elements of festivity – laughter, songs and revelry – thus making Act 2, Scene 3 a vivid dramatisation of the spirit which would have prevailed during seasonal holidays (see Introduction, **pp. 2–3** and Critical History, **pp. 44–5**). According to Michael Bristol, Malvolio's attempt to restrain Sir Toby and his associates can therefore be read as a clash between the forces of Carnival and the principle of Lent (see Modern Criticism, **pp. 70–3**). Sir Toby's objection – 'Dost thou think, because thou art virtuous, there shall be no more cakes and ale?' – stresses the opposition between excess and restraint, pleasure and duty, holiday and work, order and disorder. However, Bristol downplays the significance of Maria's reference to Malvolio as 'a kind of Puritan' (2.3.135). Puritans endorsed religious ideals, which were distinctly more extreme and radical than those introduced by the Protestant Reformation, the religious and political movement that marked a split with Catholicism and Rome during the reign of King Henry VIII in the early 1530s (see Contextual Overview, **p. 9**). Puritan religious zeal went hand in hand with moral, economic and social values, such as probity, industry and self-improvement, which became increasingly associated with upwardly mobile social groups, who interpreted economic and social success as a sign of God's approval of their orderly lifestyle. As Bruce Smith has pointed out, 'Maria identifies the Puritan in Malvolio as a matter of social ambition and exaggerated self-worth'.[1] The clash between Sir Toby and Malvolio can, therefore, be read not only as the cyclical alternation of Carnival and Lent but also as the historical tension generated by the decline of the landed aristocracy and the rise of increasingly powerful political, professional and religious groups, associated with aggressive reformist and proto-capitalist values. Malvolio, in other words, embodies radical forces of change in Shakespeare's England, which would eventually lead to the overthrow of the monarchy and its aristocratic supporters at the outbreak of the English Civil War in 1642. If Malvolio suffers a humiliating defeat in the second half of the play, 'laughter at Malvolio', as Bruce Smith points out, 'was *nervous* laughter'.[2] Similarly, Feste's second song, which reminds the revellers that 'present mirth hath present laughter' (42), and that 'youth's a stuff will not endure' (46), stresses not only the inevitability of personal decline towards old age and death, but also the steady decline of the traditional celebration of seasonal periods of holiday, excess and carnivalesque inversions.

---

1   Smith, *Twelfth Night: Texts and Contexts*, p. 320.
2   Smith, *Twelfth Night: Texts and Contexts*, p. 321.

Enter SIR TOBY *and* SIR ANDREW.

SIR TOBY   Approach, Sir Andrew. Not to be abed[3] after midnight is to
be up betimes;[4] and, *diluculo surgere,*[5] thou know'st.

SIR ANDREW   Nay, by my troth, I know not. But I know to be up late
is to be up late.

SIR TOBY   A false conclusion. I hate it as an unfilled can. To be up   5
after midnight and to go to bed then is early, so that to go to bed
after midnight is to go to bed betimes. Does not our lives consist of
the four elements?[6]

SIR ANDREW   Faith, so they say, but I think it rather consists of eating
and drinking.   10

SIR TOBY   Thou'rt a scholar! Let us therefore eat and drink. Marian,
I say, a stoup[7] of wine!

Enter Clown [FESTE].

SIR ANDREW   Here comes the fool, i'faith.

FESTE   How now, my hearts? Did you never see the picture of 'we
three'[8]?   15

SIR TOBY   Welcome, ass. Now let's have a catch.[9]

SIR ANDREW   By my troth, the fool has an excellent breast.[10] I had
rather than forty shillings I had such a leg[11] and so sweet a breath
to sing, as the fool has. In sooth,[12] thou wast in very gracious fooling
last night, when thou spokest of Pigrogromitus, of the Vapians pass-   20
ing the equinoctial of Queubus.[13] 'Twas very good, i'faith. I sent
thee sixpence for thy leman;[14] hadst it?

FESTE   I did impeticos thy gratillity:[15] for Malvolio's nose is no

---

3 In bed.
4 In good time, therefore, early.
5 From the Latin proverb, '*Diluculo surgere saluberrimun est*', 'to get up early is most healthy'.
6 Earth, air, fire and water, corresponding to the four humours or fluids – melancholy (or black
bile), blood, choler (or yellow bile) and phlegm – which, according to Galen (see Contextual
Overview, **pp. 10–11**) circulated within the human body. Shortly after William Shakespeare
wrote *Twelfth Night*, William Harvey's study on the circulation of the blood – *Exercitatio ana-
tomica ... de circulatione sanguinis* (1628) – would challenge and gradually replace Galenic
physiology.
7 A drinking vessel of varying dimensions.
8 Since Sir Andrew has greeted Feste as 'fool' in the previous line, Feste retorts by pointing out that
Sir Toby and Sir Andrew are also fools, as in a popular picture where two fools hold up a mirror,
which captures the reflection of the viewer, thus turning the latter into the third fool.
9 Short song, for three or four voices, who sing the same lines in turns; also 'a round'.
10 Lungs, voice.
11 Ability to dance or curtsey.
12 Truth.
13 These names are clearly made up.
14 Sweetheart.
15 Possibly, 'I did pocket thy gratuity'. Feste, unlike Elbow in *Measure for Measure* or Dogberry in
Much Ado About Nothing, uses nonsensical malapropisms on purpose, possibly to mock Sir
Andrew.

whipstock,[16] my lady has a white hand, and the Myrmidons[17] are
no bottle-ale houses.   25
SIR ANDREW   Excellent! Why, this is the best fooling, when all is done.
Now a song!
SIR TOBY   Come on, there is sixpence for you. Let's have a song.
SIR ANDREW   There's a testril[18] of me too. If one knight give a – [19]
FESTE   Would you have a love song, or a song of good life?[20]   30
SIR TOBY   A love song, a love song.
SIR ANDREW   Ay, ay. I care not for good life.[21]
FESTE   (*sings*)
    O mistress mine, where are you roaming?
    O stay and hear, your true love's coming,
    That can sing both high and low.   35
    Trip no further, pretty sweeting.[22]
    Journeys end in lovers meeting,
    Every wise man's son doth know.
SIR ANDREW   Excellent good, i'faith.
SIR TOBY   Good, good.   40
FESTE   [*sings*]
    What is love? 'Tis not hereafter,[23]
    Present mirth hath present laughter.
    What's to come is still unsure.
    In delay there lies no plenty,
    Then come kiss me, sweet and twenty;[24]   45
    Youth's a stuff will not endure.
SIR ANDREW   A mellifluous voice, as I am true knight.
SIR TOBY   A contagious[25] breath.
SIR ANDREW   Very sweet and contagious, i'faith.
SIR TOBY   To hear by the nose, it is dulcet in contagion.[26] But shall we   50
make the welkin[27] dance indeed? Shall we rouse the night-owl in a

---

16 Handle of a whip.
17 Achilles' personal army of loyal soldiers; see Homer's *Iliad* II.684, and Shakespeare's *Troilus and Cressida*, 5.5.33.
18 A sixpenny coin.
19 Accidental omission in the First Folio (see Further Reading, **p. 189**); alternatively, Sir Andrew loses the train of his thoughts, or is brutally interrupted.
20 A drinking song, and not a moral, virtuous one, as Sir Andrew's remark at line 32 implies. Once again, Sir Andrew sounds naïve and foolish.
21 See Footnote 20.
22 Darling.
23 In the future.
24 Twenty is used here as an intensive; therefore, 'most sweetly'.
25 Literally, that can be caught like a disease; therefore Sir Toby is punning on 'catch' (see Footnote 9), and 'catchy'.
26 Sir Toby develops the simile introduced at line 48 between a contagious disease and a tune by pointing out that since Feste's song was sweet, hearing his song by the nose (most diseases, including the plague, were believed to be air-borne) will cause them to become sweetly ('dulcet') infected.
27 Sky.

catch[28] that will draw three souls out of one weaver?[29] Shall we
do that?

SIR ANDREW   An[30] you love me, let's do't. I am dog[31] at a catch.

FESTE   By'r Lady, sir, and some dogs will catch well.   55

SIR ANDREW   Most certain. Let our catch be, 'Thou knave'.

FESTE   'Hold thy peace, thou knave', knight? I shall be constrained
in't, to call thee knave, knight.

SIR ANDREW   'Tis not the first time I have constrained one to call me
knave. Begin, fool. It begins, 'Hold thy peace'.   60

FESTE   I shall never begin if I hold my peace.

SIR ANDREW   Good, i'faith. Come, begin. (*Catch sung*)

Enter MARIA.

MARIA   What a caterwauling[32] do you keep here? If my lady have not
called up her steward Malvolio and bid him turn you out of doors,
never trust me.   65

SIR TOBY   My lady's a Cathayan,[33] we are politicians,[34] Malvolio's a
Peg-o'-Ramsey,[35] and [*sings*] 'Three merry men be we'. Am not I
consanguineous?[36] Am I not of her blood? Tilly-vally,[37] lady! [*sings*]
'There dwelt a man in Babylon, lady, lady'.

FESTE   Beshrew me,[38] the knight's in admirable fooling.   70

SIR ANDREW   Ay, he does well enough if he be disposed, and so do I
too. He does it with a better grace, but I do it more natural.[39]

SIR TOBY   [*sings*] 'O' the twelfth day of December'[40] –

MARIA   For the love o'God, peace!

Enter MALVOLIO.

MALVOLIO   My masters, are you mad? Or what are you? Have you   75
no wit, manners, nor honesty, but to gabble[41] like tinkers[42] at this
time of night? Do ye make an alehouse of my lady's house, that

---

28 See footnote 9, p. 157.
29 Many weavers in Shakespeare's times were 'Calvinist refugees from the Low Countries' (see
     Mahood, p. 152), who had a reputation for being devout and serious-minded and were, therefore,
     not easily moved by catchy drinking songs.
30 If.
31 Good at.
32 The noise made by mating cats.
33 'Chinese', but also 'Catharan', that is 'Puritan', and therefore: 'My lady is an extreme, rigid moral-
     ist, whereas we are flexible politicians' (Warren and Wells, p. 127).
34 Here meant in a derogatory sense as 'crafty plotters'.
35 Title of a popular song.
36 Related by blood.
37 An exclamation of impatience, therefore 'Nonsense'.
38 A humorous, playful curse.
39 'More easily', but also 'more like a natural', that is, 'more like a fool'.
40 A possible allusion to the title, if Sir Toby is alluding to the carol, 'The Twelve Days of Christmas'
     (see, Warren and Wells, p. 128).
41 Chatter, prattle.
42 Itinerant craftsmen; more generally, vagrants associated with disorderly behaviour and drunkenness.

ye squeak out your coziers'[43] catches without any mitigation or remorse of voice? Is there no respect of place, persons, nor time in you?   80

SIR TOBY   We did keep time, sir, in our catches. Sneck up![44]

MALVOLIO   Sir Toby, I must be round[45] with you. My lady bade me tell you that, though she harbours[46] you as her kinsman, she's nothing allied to[47] your disorders. If you can separate yourself and your misdemeanours, you are welcome to the house; if not, an it   85 would please you to take leave of her, she is very willing to bid you farewell.

SIR TOBY   [to MARIA, singing] 'Farewell, dear heart, since I must needs be gone'.[48]

MARIA   Nay, good Sir Toby.   90

FESTE   [sings] 'His eyes do show his days are almost done'.

MALVOLIO   Is't even so?

SIR TOBY   [sings] 'But I will never die'.

FESTE   [sings] 'Sir Toby, there you lie'.

MALVOLIO   This is much credit to you.   95

SIR TOBY   [sings] 'Shall I bid him go?'

FESTE   [sings] 'What an if you do?'

SIR TOBY   [sings] 'Shall I bid him go, and spare not?'

FESTE   [sings] 'O no, no, no, no, you dare not.'

SIR TOBY   [to FESTE] Out o'tune,[49] sir, ye lie! [to MALVOLIO] 100 Art any more than a steward? Dost thou think, because thou art virtuous, there shall be no more cakes and ale?

FESTE   Yes, by Saint Anne, and ginger shall be hot i'th'mouth too.

SIR TOBY   Thou'rt i'th'right. – Go, sir, rub your chain with crumbs.[50] A stoup[51] of wine, Maria!   105

MALVOLIO   Mistress Mary, if you prized my lady's favour at anything more than contempt, you would not give means for this uncivil rule.[52] She shall know of it, by this hand.

Exit

---

43 Cobblers were renowned for singing at work.
44 Go hang!
45 Open, direct.
46 Provides lodgings.
47 She does not approve of.
48 The lines Sir Toby and Feste sing at lines 88–99 are freely adapted from a popular song (Mahood, p. 154).
49 Often emended to read 'Out o' time', in response to Malvolio's accusation that the revellers have 'no respect of place, persons, nor time'.
50 'Clean your chain', that is, continue to act as a subservient employee.
51 See Footnote 7.
52 Barbarous behaviour (or self-rule).

Act 2, Scene 4, lines 13–40 and 72–122: Viola's sister in love

Act 2, Scene 4 reveals ironic inconsistencies between Orsino's professed feelings for Olivia and his misogynistic attitude towards women in general, which can be interpreted both as psychological limitations in Orsino's character and, more interestingly, as clashing cultural mindsets. Orsino, for example, first explains that true lovers are fickle and changeable in everything but their devotion to 'the constant image' of their beloved (16–19), but then warns Viola that men's desires are in fact 'giddy and unfirm' (32). Feste's comments about Orsino's changeable and fickle mind – 'the tailor make thy doublet of changeable taffeta' (72–3) – highlight this unflattering trait in Orsino's character. Orsino then claims that women are physiologically unable to experience love and that they are merely prone to 'appetite[s] [. . .] That suffer surfeit, cloyment and revolt' (95–7). Orsino's misogynist remark is clearly at odds with his description of his own feelings for Olivia in the opening scene as a boundless 'appetite' that 'Receiveth as the sea' (see Key Passages, **p. 141**). Orsino's simultaneous idealisation and degradation of women is symptomatic of patriarchal cultures that privilege homosocial over heterosexual relations. Both *Twelfth Night* and Shakespeare's main literary sources (see Contemporary Documents, **pp. 26–30**) would seem to encourage a captivating fantasy by showing how heterosexual bonds stem seamlessly from the homoerotic relationships between male characters and heroines donning a male disguise. However, far from endorsing such a fantasy, this scene exposes Orsino's contradictory attitudes towards women and grants Viola a golden opportunity to disprove his misogynist remarks. Commentators and critics from Anna Jameson (see Early Criticism, **pp. 52–3**) to Juliet Dusinberre have remarked on Viola's moral stature in this scene. Dusinberre has attributed Shakespeare's sympathetic representation of his female characters, in general, and of Viola, in particular, to changing views on marriage and the role of women in sixteenth- and seventeeth-century England (see Modern Criticism, **pp. 81–2**). More recently, Catherine Belsey has argued that the semiotic complexity of Viola/Cesario as a sign (the boy actor, playing Viola, disguised as Cesario) and the even more complex association between Viola and Cesario's father's pining daughter who 'never told her love' (108) are also important strategies whereby Shakespeare disrupts 'the system of differences on which sexual stereotyping depends' (see Modern Criticism, **p. 92**).

Enter Duke [ORSINO], VIOLA, CURIO, *and* [*musicians*].

[. . .]

ORSINO   [*to* CURIO] Seek him¹ out, and [*to musicians*] play the tune
                the while.²   [*Exit* CURIO]
                                                        (*Music plays*)
        [*to* VIOLA] Come hither, boy. If ever thou shalt love,
        In the sweet pangs of it remember me,   15
        For such as I am, all true lovers are,
        Unstaid³ and skittish⁴ in all motions⁵ else,
        Save in the constant image of the creature
        That is beloved. How dost thou like this tune?
VIOLA   It gives a very echo to the seat   20
        Where Love is throned.⁶
ORSINO   Thou dost speak masterly.
        My life upon't, young though thou art, thine eye
        Hath stayed upon some favour⁷ that it loves.
        Hath it not, boy?
VIOLA   A little, by your favour.⁸
ORSINO   What kind of woman is't?
VIOLA   Of your complexion.⁹   25
ORSINO   She is not worth thee, then. What years, i'faith?
VIOLA   About your years, my lord.
ORSINO   Too old, by heaven! Let still the woman take
        An elder than herself, so wears she¹⁰ to him,
        So sways she level¹¹ in her husband's heart.   30
        For, boy, however we do praise ourselves,
        Our fancies are more giddy and unfirm,
        More longing, wavering, sooner lost and worn,¹²
        Than women's are.
VIOLA   I think it well, my lord.
ORSINO   Then let thy love be younger than thyself,   35
        Or thy affection cannot hold the bent.¹³
        For women are as roses, whose fair flower
        Being once displayed,¹⁴ doth fall that very hour.
VIOLA   And so they are. Alas, that they are so:
        To die even when they to perfection grow.   40

---

1 Feste.
2 In the meantime.
3 Unstable.
4 Fickle.
5 Emotions.
6 The heart.
7 Face.
8 By your leave; also 'like you in feature' (see Mahood, p. 156).
9 Literally, 'colouring' (see Warren and Wells, p. 135), or, 'temperament' (see Donno, p. 82).
10 She adjusts.
11 Swings in synchrony.
12 Worn out.
13 'Remain constant'; literally, 'remain stretched, like a bow, without breaking'.
14 'In bloom', but also, 'revealed', with a sexual innuendo at the devalued 'price' of an unmarried
    woman, once she has lost her virginity.

Enter CURIO *and* [FESTE]

[. . .]

Feste performs a melancholy love song. Orsino then dismisses him, giving him
money for his service. Feste's parting lines are addressed to Orsino.

FESTE   Now, the melancholy god[15] protect thee, and the tailor make thy
doublet of changeable taffeta,[16] for thy mind is a very opal.[17] I would
have men of such constancy[18] put to sea, that their business might be
everything and their intent everywhere, for that's it that always   75
makes a good voyage of nothing.[19] Farewell.

Exit

ORSINO   Let all the rest give place.   [*Exeunt* CURIO *and attendants.*]
[*to* VIOLA] Once more, Cesario,
Get thee to yond same sovereign cruelty.
Tell her my love, more noble than the world,
Prizes not quantity of dirty lands;[20]   80
The parts that fortune hath bestowed upon her,
Tell her, I hold as giddily[21] as fortune.
But 'tis that miracle and queen of gems
That nature pranks[22] her in attracts my soul.

VIOLA   But if she cannot love you, sir?   85

ORSINO   It cannot be so answered.

VIOLA   Sooth,[23] but you must.
Say that some lady, as perhaps there is,
Hath for your love as great a pang of heart
As you have for Olivia. You cannot love her;
You tell her so. Must she not then be answered?   90

ORSINO   There is no woman's sides
Can bide[24] the beating of so strong a passion
As love doth give my heart; no woman's heart
So big to hold so much. They lack retention.[25]
Alas, their love may be called appetite,   95
No motion of the liver, but the palate,

15 Saturn.
16 Glossy silk that changes colour according to the angle of view.
17 Gemstone, which, like taffeta, changes colour as the light changes, hence, 'changeable'.
18 Constant only in being inconstant.
19 Achieves nothing (proverbial).
20 The land Olivia has inherited.
21 Lightly.
22 Adorns.
23 In truth.
24 Bear.
25 Medical term indicating the body's ability to retain (and digest, at line 99).

That suffer surfeit, cloyment and revolt;[26]
But mine is all as hungry as the sea,
And can digest as much. Make no compare
Between that love a woman can bear me   100
And that I owe Olivia.
VIOLA   Ay, but I know –
ORSINO   What dost thou know?
VIOLA   Too well what love women to men may owe.
    In faith, they are as true of heart as we.
    My father had a daughter loved a man   105
    As it might be, perhaps, were I a woman,
    I should your lordship.
ORSINO   And what's her history?
VIOLA   A blank, my lord. She never told her love,
    But let concealment, like a worm i'th'bud,
    Feed on her damask[27] cheek. She pined in thought,   110
    And with a green and yellow[28] melancholy
    She sat like Patience on a monument,
    Smiling at grief. Was not this love indeed?
    We men may say more, swear more, but indeed
    Our shows are more than will; for still we prove   115
    Much in our vows, but little in our love.[29]
ORSINO   But died thy sister of her love, my boy?
VIOLA   I am all the daughters of my father's house,
    And all the brothers too; and yet I know not.
    Sir, shall I to this lady?
ORSINO   Ay, that's the theme.[30]   120
    To her in haste. Give her this jewel; say
    My love can give no place, bide no denay.[31]

Exeunt

---

26 The liver was regarded as the seat of noble passions, like love and valour, whereas the palate was
    associated with shallow gastronomic and sexual appetites, which are easily satisfied ('suffer surfeit'
    and 'cloyment') or cause repulsion ('revolt'). See also Modern Criticism, **p. 77** and Footnote 17
    on **p. 142**.
27 Red and white; see also Footnote 4, **p. 35**.
28 Pale and sallow, but also an allusion to a condition commonly known as 'green sickness' (or
    'erotomania'), which was believed to affect young women when their sexual desires were
    unrequited or repressed.
29 What we say or show is more than we can or will do to keep our words.
30 Topic of conversation; Orsino's initial, half-line response may suggest that both Orsino and Viola
    are overwhelmed by the turn their conversation has taken. In some productions, Orsino and Viola
    almost touch (as in Barton's Royal Shakespeare Company production (1969–70), see The Work in
    Performance, **p. 108**) or they almost kiss (as in Trevor Nunn's cinematic adaptation (1996), see The
    Work in Performance, **p. 111**). In other productions, Orsino and Viola get close to revealing
    their feelings for each other when Viola confesses to be 'all the daughters of my father's house,
    / And all the brothers too' (118–19). In Peter Gill's 1974 Royal Shakespeare Company production
    (see The Work in Performance, **p. 107**), Orsino turned Viola's face towards him; special effects in
    Tim Supple's 2003 television version allow Orsino to 'make division' of himself and to reach
    towards Viola while remaining seated and in control of his emotions (see The Work in Perform-
    ance, **pp. 111–13**).
31 Denial.

Act 2, Scene 5, lines 1–155: Malvolio in love

While Act 2, Scene 4 shows that Orsino's feelings for Olivia do not preclude the flow of homoerotic desire from master to 'male' servant and vice versa, Act 2, Scene 5 suggests that class is a formidable barrier that makes the counter-flow of desire from male servant to mistress the target of harsh mockery and denigration. Early critics tended to regard Malvolio's secret ambition to marry Olivia as an unnatural and abominable breach of decorum. Émile Montégut, for example, argued that although all characters in this play have dreams, only some come true, because 'Nature accepts only [those] which are in harmony with grace, with poesy, and with beauty [. . .] and thrusts aside as a revolt and a sin, every dream wherein ugliness intrudes' (see Early Criticism, **p. 55**). Montégut's logic implies that the class system reflects a natural and aesthetic order, which should not be changed or upset. Only in the second half of the twentieth century did Marxist critics like Elliot Krieger start to point out that it is not 'Nature', but the 'ruling-class ideology [that] operates within the play', which endorses Orsino's passion for Olivia as noble and dignified and dismisses Malvolio's ambition to marry Olivia as a ridiculous breach of decorum which deserves to be punished (see Modern Criticism, **p. 69**).

Several critics, including Jason Scott-Warren, have noticed that 'in the gulling of Malvolio, [. . .] *Twelfth Night* actually stages a bear-baiting' (see The Work in Performance, **p. 118**). Lines 1–10 establish a strong link between this popular entertainment, which involved setting dogs to attack a bear chained to a stake, and the comic but cruel trick which Maria devises to punish Malvolio. Act 2, Scene 5 can, indeed, be read as a prelude to Act 4, Scene 2, where Malvolio is locked up in a dark room and treated like a madman. Antony Sher, who performed Malvolio in Act 4, Scene 2 wearing a big chain around his neck, may have been inspired by the opening of Act 2, Scene 5. However, the gulling of Malvolio is also very funny and uncannily apt. As a 'kind of Puritan' (2.3.135) Malvolio would have opposed not only bear-baiting, as Fabian points out in this extract, or excessive drinking, as shown in Act 2, Scene 3, but also all forms of popular entertainment, including the theatre. Maria's stratagem is, therefore, ironically appropriate because it forces Malvolio to enact his private fantasies while he is being watched by Sir Toby, Sir Andrew and Fabian. As Scott-Warren has noted, the gulling of Malvolio functions like a 'comedy of humours', a popular dramatic form that flourished around the time when *Twelfth Night* was first performed and that aimed to expose and ridicule a specific humour, or character trait, like Malvolio's self-love and his yearning for power and self-advancement.

Malvolio is not the only character to be ridiculed and denigrated in Act 2, Scene 5. The letters which resemble his mistress's handwriting most closely – 'These be her very c's, her u's, and her t's, and thus makes she her great P's' (76–7) – spell out a bawdy reference to Olivia's genitals (cut) and to her urinary incontinence (great P's). According to Gail Paster, the joke's "lowness" effects a shift from one category of constructing women by class, which recognizes the social differences *between* women, to constructing women by gender, in which all such differences are subsumed in the body. [. . .] Olivia is reduced to the lowly status of generic female by that specifically shameful female signifier – the "cut" '.[1]

Although both Olivia and Malvolio are ridiculed, Act 2, Scene 5 is hardly a normative endorsement of the class system as a natural and desirable order. Both Malvolio's habit of practising courtly gestures 'to his own shadow' (14–5) and the advice Malvolio finds in the fake letter to *act* 'strange' (144) and 'surly' (128) with the servants, to *train* his tongue to speak about 'arguments of state' (114) and to *affect* eccentricity and originality of character suggest that class is not an innate quality but a set of actions which anybody can imitate. Several conduct books written during the early modern period, like Baldassare Castiglione's *The Book of the Courtier* (English translation, 1588) and Richard Brathwait, *The English Gentleman* (1630), encouraged their readers to assume that courtliness was the result of meticulous discipline, training and education. Although Malvolio gets his comeuppance for daring to try and rise above his station, thus reinforcing a traditional belief in a divinely ordained and stable cosmic and social universe, Shakespeare's contemporaries were becoming increasingly confident that education, knowledge and self-motivation could help anybody become anything they wanted. Shakespeare himself, the son of a glovemaker from Stratford, who had made a name for himself in the dubious and disreputable world of the London theatres, successfully applied for a coat of arms on his father's behalf in 1596.

Enter SIR TOBY, SIR ANDREW, *and* FABIAN.

SIR TOBY   Come thy ways,[2] Signor Fabian.

FABIAN   Nay, I'll come. If I lose a scruple[3] of this sport, let me be boiled to death with melancholy.[4]

SIR TOBY   Wouldst thou not be glad to have the niggardly[5] rascally sheep-biter[6] come by some notable shame?   5

FABIAN   I would exult, man. You know he brought me out o'favour with my lady about a bear-baiting[7] here.

---

1   Gail Kern Paster, *The Body Embarrassed: Drama and the Disciplines of Shame in Early Modern England* (Ithaca, NY and London: Cornell University Press, 1993), p. 33.
2   Come along.
3   If I miss even a small part.
4   'Die of melancholy'; Fabian's remark is a joke, since melancholy is a cold and dry humour.
5   Who behaves like a 'niggard', that is a miser.
6   A 'censorious, malicious fellow', often applied to Puritans; Maria describes Malvolio as 'a kind of Puritan' at 2.3.135.
7   Popular entertainment which involved setting dogs to attack a bear chained to a stake. See The Work in Performance, p. 106 and pp. 117–20.

SIR TOBY   To anger him we'll have the bear again, and we will fool him black and blue – shall we not, Sir Andrew?

SIR ANDREW   An[8] we do not, it is pity of our lives.[9]   10

Enter MARIA.

SIR TOBY   Here comes the little villain. – How now, my metal of India?[10]

MARIA   Get ye all three into the box-tree. Malvolio's coming down this walk. He has been yonder i'the sun practising behaviour[11] to his own shadow this half hour. Observe him, for the love of mockery,   15 for I know this letter will make a contemplative idiot of him. Close,[12] in the name of jesting! [*All hide while* MARIA *drops the letter*] Lie thou there, for here comes the trout that must be caught with tickling.[13]

Exit

Enter MALVOLIO.

MALVOLIO   'Tis but fortune; all is fortune. Maria once told me she did   20 affect me;[14] and I have heard herself come thus near, that, should she fancy, it should be one of my complexion.[15] Besides, she uses me with a more exalted respect than anyone else that follows her. What should I think on't?

SIR TOBY   Here's an overweening[16] rogue!   25

FABIAN   O, peace! Contemplation makes a rare turkey-cock[17] of him; how he jets[18] under his advanced plumes.

SIR ANDREW   'Slight,[19] I could so beat the rogue!

SIR TOBY   Peace, I say.

MALVOLIO   To be Count Malvolio!   30

SIR TOBY   Ah, rogue!

SIR ANDREW   Pistol him,[20] pistol him!

SIR TOBY   Peace, peace!

---

8 If.
9 We do not deserve to live.
10 Precious metal, since India was renowned for its mines.
11 Elegant deportment, posture, and gestures.
12 Hide.
13 Flattery.
14 Olivia liked me.
15 Literally, 'colouring' and 'appearance'; more generally, 'temperament'. See also footnote 9 on p. 162.
16 Conceited, arrogant.
17 Proud like a turkeycock, or, more commonly, like a peacock, as both birds display their tail-feathers; hence Fabian's next remark on Malvolio's 'advanced plumes'.
18 Struts.
19 By God's light.
20 Shoot him.

MALVOLIO   There is example for't: the Lady of the Strachy married
the yeoman of the wardrobe.[21]   35

SIR ANDREW   Fie on him, Jezebel![22]

FABIAN   O, peace! Now he's deeply in.[23] Look how imagination blows
him.[24]

MALVOLIO   Having been three months married to her, sitting in my
state –   40

SIR TOBY   O, for a stone-bow[25] to hit him in the eye!

MALVOLIO   Calling my officers about me, in my branched[26] velvet
gown,[27] having come from a day-bed, where I have left Olivia
sleeping –

SIR TOBY   Fire and brimstone!   45

FABIAN   O, peace, peace!

MALVOLIO   And then to have the humour of state,[28] and, after a
demure travel of regard,[29] telling them I know my place as I would
they should do theirs, to ask for my kinsman Toby.

SIR TOBY   Bolts and shackles!   50

FABIAN   O, peace, peace, peace! Now, now.

MALVOLIO   Seven of my people with an obedient start make out[30]
for him. I frown the while, and perchance wind up my watch, or
play with my[31] – some rich jewel. Toby approaches, curtsies there
to me –   55

SIR TOBY   Shall this fellow live?

FABIAN   Though our silence be drawn from us with cars,[32] yet peace.

MALVOLIO   I extend my hand to him thus, quenching my familiar[33]
smile with an austere regard of control[34] –

---

21 Topical allusion to a lady who married (or had an affair with) a yeoman, that is a servant in a noble
household, ranking between a squire and a page; or, possibly, David Yeomans, the wardrobe
master at the Blackfriars Theatre, who may have become involved with William Strachy's wife.
William Strachy was a shareholder in the same theatre company and died in 1621. For more
details, see C. J. Sisson, *New Readings in Shakespeare*, 2 vols (Cambridge: Cambridge University
Press, 1956), Vol. I, pp. 188–91.

22 In the Bible, the deceitful wife of Ahab, King of Israel (2 Kings 9:30–7).

23 Caught up in his own fantasies.

24 Inflates him with pride.

25 A cross-bow used for shooting stones.

26 Embroidered with gold or needlework, representing foliage and branch patterns.

27 Sumptuary laws regulated what type of clothes different social groups could wear. According to
Elizabeth's 1957 *A Proclamation Enforcing Statutes and Proclamations of Apparel*, no one 'under
the degree of a knight', except members of the Queen's own household, could wear 'velvet
in gowns, cloaks, coats, or other uppermost garments' (Smith, *Twelfth Night: Texts and Contexts*,
p. 252). Malvolio's reference to the 'branched velvet gown' he will wear when he is married to
Olivia is, therefore, in keeping with his fantasy of social advancement.

28 To adopt a dignified manner or attitude.

29 Looking solemnly at the company gathered around the room.

30 Go out.

31 Several editors have suggested that Malvolio is about to mention his steward's chain, but then
stops, as it occurs to him that, as Count Malvolio, he would no longer wear it.

32 By torture; 'cars', or 'carts', were used to pull the body of a prisoner in different directions to force
him/her to speak.

33 Friendly.

34 Authoritative look.

SIR TOBY   And does not Toby take[35] you a blow o'the lips then?   60

MALVOLIO   Saying, 'Cousin Toby, my fortunes having cast me on your niece, give me this prerogative of speech' –

SIR TOBY   What, what?

MALVOLIO   'You must amend your drunkenness.'

SIR TOBY   Out, scab!   65

FABIAN   Nay, patience, or we break the sinews of our plot.

MALVOLIO   'Besides, you waste the treasure of your time with a foolish knight' –

SIR ANDREW   That's me, I warrant you.

MALVOLIO   'One Sir Andrew'–   70

SIR ANDREW   I knew 'twas I, for many do call me fool.

MALVOLIO   [picks up the letter] What employment[36] have we here?

FABIAN   Now is the woodcock near the gin.[37]

SIR TOBY   O, peace! And the spirit of humours intimate reading aloud to him.[38]   75

MALVOLIO   By my life, this is my lady's hand. These be her very c's, her u's, and her t's;[39] and thus makes she her great P's.[40] It is in contempt of question[41] her hand.

SIR ANDREW   Her c's, her u's, and her t's? Why that?[42]

MALVOLIO   [reads] 'To the unknown beloved, this, and my good   80
wishes.' Her very phrases! By your leave, wax.[43] Soft! And the impressure[44] her Lucrece,[45] with which she uses to seal. 'Tis my Lady! To whom should this be? [opens the letter]

FABIAN   This wins him, liver[46] and all.

MALVOLIO   [reads]   'Jove knows I love,   85
                         But who?
                         Lips, do not move,
                         No man must know.'

'No man must know'. What follows? The numbers[47] altered. 'No man must know.' If this should be thee, Malvolio?   90

---

35 Give.
36 Business.
37 Aphetic for 'engine', meaning 'trap'.
38 May he read the letter aloud.
39 The three letters Malvolio reads aloud spell out the word 'cut', which was slang for female genitals.
40 Malvolio thinks he recognises Olivia's distinctive capital Ps, but his wording is also an obscene allusion to Olivia's urinary incontinence. Although Malvolio seems unaware of this double meaning, his remark harks back to Orsino's claim that 'women lack retention' (2.4.94). Malvalio's remark is also in keeping with Galenic physiology, according to which the body of a woman was more liquid and more prone to incontinence than the body of a man. For more details, see Paster, *The Body Embarrassed*, especially pp. 29–34.
41 Beyond doubt.
42 Sir Andrew, as usual, misses the joke.
43 Conventional phrase indicating that Malvolio is about to break the seal on the letter.
44 Impression made by the seal on the wax.
45 Renowned Roman matron who committed suicide after being violated by Sextus Tarquinius, son of the last King of Rome, Lucius Tarquinius. Many late medieval and early modern poets, including Chaucer, Shakespeare and Thomas Heywood, wrote versions of her story.
46 Seat of love and valour; see also footnote 17, **p. 142** and footnote 26, **p. 164**.
47 Metre.

SIR TOBY   Marry, hang thee, brock![48]

MALVOLIO   'I may command where I adore;
                                  But Silence, like a Lucrece knife,
                                  With bloodless stroke my heart doth gore.[49]
                                  M.O.A.I. doth sway[50] my life.'   95

FABIAN   A fustian[51] riddle!

SIR TOBY   Excellent wench, say I.

MALVOLIO   'M.O.A.I. doth sway my life'. Nay, but first, let me see, let
me see, let me see.

FABIAN   What dish o' poison has she dressed him!   100

SIR TOBY   And with what wing the staniel[52] checks at it!

MALVOLIO   'I may command where I adore.' Why, she may command me: I serve her, she is my lady. Why, this is evident to any
formal capacity.[53] There is no obstruction in this.[54] And the end –
what should that alphabetical position[55] portend? If I could make   105
that resemble something in me! Softly! 'M.O.A.I.' –

SIR TOBY   O ay,[56] make up that! He is now at a cold scent.[57]

FABIAN   Sowter[58] will cry upon't for all this, though it be as rank as a
fox.[59]

MALVOLIO   'M' – Malvolio! 'M'! Why, that begins my name.   110

FABIAN   Did not I say he would work it out? The cur is excellent at
faults.[60]

MALVOLIO   'M' – but then there is no consonancy[61] in the sequel.
That[62] suffers under probation:[63] 'A' should follow, but 'O' does.

FABIAN   And 'O' shall end,[64] I hope.   115

SIR TOBY   Ay, or I'll cudgel him,[65] and make him cry 'O!'

---

48 Badger (derogatory).
49 See Footnote 45.
50 Control.
51 Literally 'rough cloth'; hence, 'ridiculously lofty, inflated, but meaningless', especially in relation to
    language or speech.
52 The reading preserved in the First Folio (Further Reading, p. 189) – 'stallion' – is now com-
    monly emended to read 'staniel', that is 'kestrel', in keeping with 'wing'. However, 'stallion',
    Elizabethan slang for 'prostitute', may not be a typographical mistake in the First Folio, since
    Malvolio is associated with lewd women elsewhere (Peg-o'-Ramsey at 2.3.67 and Jezebel at
    2.5.36).
53 Normal intelligence.
54 No doubt or problem in the interpretation of this line.
55 Sequence.
56 Echoing Malvolio.
57 Malvolio is compared to a hunting dog that loses the scent of its quarry; for other hunting
    metaphors, see Key Passages, p.142. (See also Contextual Overview, pp. 13–14 and Contemporary
    Documents, pp. 30–3).
58 An uncommon dog's name.
59 'Even though the trail has been crossed by a fox', whose strong smell obliterates the scent of the
    quarry (see Warren and Wells, p. 148).
60 Finding the scent again, after it was lost.
61 Logical order.
62 Referring to 'sequel'.
63 Does not bear scrutiny.
64 'O' may stand for the hangman's noose, as suggested by Samuel Johnson in his edition of 1765, or
    'misery' (see Donno, p. 92); in either case, Fabian hopes that Malvolio shall meet a miserable end.
65 Beat him with a club.

MALVOLIO   And then 'I' comes behind.

FABIAN   Ay, an you had any eye behind you, you might see more detraction at your heels than fortunes before you.

MALVOLIO   'M.O.A.I.' This simulation[66] is not as the former; and yet, 120 to crush this a little,[67] it would bow to me,[68] for every one of these letters are in my name. Soft! Here follows prose: [*reads*] 'If this fall into thy hand, revolve.[69] In my stars I am above thee, but be not afraid of greatness: some are born[70] great, some achieve greatness, and some have greatness thrust upon 'em. Thy Fates open their 125 hands;[71] let thy blood and spirit embrace them. And, to inure[72] thyself to what thou art like to be, cast thy humble slough[73] and appear fresh. Be opposite[74] with a kinsman, surly with servants; let thy tongue tang[75] arguments of state; put thyself into the trick of singularity.[76] She thus advises thee that sighs for thee. Remember who 130 commended thy yellow stockings and wished to see thee ever cross-gartered.[77] I say, remember. Go to, thou art made, if thou desirest to be so. If not, let me see thee a steward still, the fellow of servants, and not worthy to touch Fortune's fingers. Farewell. She that would alter services[78] with thee, the Fortunate Unhappy.' Daylight and 135 champaign[79] discovers not more. This is open! I will be proud, I will read politic authors, I will baffle Sir Toby, I will wash off gross acquaintance, I will be point-device[80] the very man. I do not now fool myself, to let imagination jade[81] me; for every reason excites to this, that my lady loves me. She did commend my yellow stockings 140 of late, she did praise my leg being cross-gartered; and in this she manifests herself to my love, and with a kind of injunction drives me to these habits[82] of her liking. I thank my stars, I am happy! I will be strange,[83] stout,[84] in yellow stockings, and cross-gartered, even with the swiftness of putting on. Jove and my stars be praised! 145

---

66 Riddle.
67 To force (or rearrange) the sequel of letters slightly.
68 'It would yield to me', that is, 'it would support my reading' or 'reveal my name'.
69 'Turn (it) over in your mind', and therefore 'consider (this)'; many actors playing Malvolio exploit the comic potential of this line and actually turn around (see Warren and Wells, p. 149).
70 The First Folio edition (Further Reading, **p. 189**) reads 'become'; this common emendation, which is confirmed by the variant version of this line, repeated by Feste in Act 5, Scene 1, was first introduced in the Douai Manuscript (1694–5), which includes transcripts of six Shakespearean plays, including *Twelfth Night*, and by Nicholas Rowe in his 1709 edition of Shakespeare's *Works*.
71 Are generous with you.
72 Accustom.
73 The skin periodically shed by a snake.
74 Hostile, adverse.
75 Bellow out.
76 Affect eccentricity and originality of character.
77 Wearing garters crossing behind the knee and tied just above it.
78 Change places.
79 Countryside that affords open views.
80 Precisely, in every point.
81 Deceive.
82 'Items of clothing', but also 'mental dispositions', or 'customs'.
83 Proud, aloof.
84 Resolute.

Here is yet a postscript: [*reads*] 'Thou canst not choose but know who I am. If thou entertainest[85] my love, let it appear in thy smiling: thy smiles become thee well. Therefore in my presence still smile, dear my sweet, I prethee.' Jove, I thank thee. I will smile; I will do everything that thou wilt have me.   150

Exit

FABIAN   I will not give my part of this sport for a pension of thousands to be paid from the Sophy.[86]

SIR TOBY   I could marry this wench for this device.

SIR ANDREW   So could I too.

SIR TOBY   And ask no other dowry with her but such another jest.   155

Act 3, Scene 1, lines 1–59: Folly and foolery

The transition between Act 2, Scene 5 and Act 3, Scene 1 reveals an intriguing link between Malvolio's attempt to rearrange the letters in 'M.O.A.I.', so that they can be made to look like an abbreviation of his name, and Viola's remark that 'They that dally nicely with words may quickly make them wanton' (12–13). Although the sequence of letters is not in the right order, Malvolio still identifies himself with the 'M.O.A.I.' who sways Olivia's life (2.5.85). The act of interpreting signs, as both Act 2, Scene 5 and Act 3, Scene 1 suggest, does not lead to the discovery of meaning, because meaning is not unequivocally *conveyed* but rather *produced* by language. Language, in turn, can be described as an unstable system of signs. The definition of sign offered by Swiss linguist Ferdinand de Saussure at the beginning of the twentieth century seems particularly useful to understand how Shakespeare turns 'dallying with words' into witty, entertaining drama in Act 2, Scene 5 and Act 3, Scene 1.

According to de Saussure, words, like any other sign, are the product of the combination of a material element, or *signifier* (the actual sound of a spoken word, or the conventional translation of that sound into the letters which make up a written word) and an abstract element, or *signified* (the general notion, idea, or category conjured by the signifier). For example, the word 'pet' exists materially as a combination of the following sounds or letters: 'P', 'E' and 'T'. Its signified is a category of animals allowed to live in our homes, as opposed to animals that live in our parks or in the wild. De Saussure usefully pointed out that the link between the signifier and the signified is *arbitrary*, because there is no reason why 'P.E.T.', rather than 'T.E.P.', should be used to indicate such a category of animals. The link between the signifier and the signified is also *unstable*, because different cultures notoriously disagree on what animals should be regarded as pets rather than served as food on our tables. Both Saussure and

---

85 Welcome.
86 Shah of Persia (see Critical History, **pp. 45–6 and pp. 48–9**).

Malvolio would agree that interpretation is not an act of objective discovery of a pre-existing meaning but a projection of our own expectations, assumptions and desires. Words, as Feste would put it, are soft and malleable as kidskin and can be turned inside out and made to produce several, sometimes contradictory, meanings.

If Malvolio 'crushes' the sequence of letters 'M.O.A.I.' to rearrange them into an abbreviation of his own name, Feste 'crushes' words for a living. Probably played by Robert Armin, a comic actor renowned for his penchant for puns, wordplay and witty repartees, Feste aptly describes himself as a 'corrupter of words', who skilfully exploits the slippery nature of language to twist what other characters say. At lines 22–25 in the following extract, for example, Feste uses Viola's remark, 'thou [. . .] carest for nothing' – that is, 'you have no care in world' – to insinuate that Viola means 'you have no regard or liking for anyone or anything'. Hence, Feste's reply: 'Not so, sir, I do care for something, but in my conscience, sir, I do not care for you. If that be to care for nothing, sir, I would it would make you invisible'. It is worth stressing that Feste is not simply being rude to Viola. Feste is actually challenging Viola to stand by what she said, by insinuating that if 'not caring for Viola' means 'caring for nothing', then Viola *is* nothing. Feste is simultaneously wishing that Viola was nothing (and that she would make herself invisible), because he sees Viola's intimacy with Orsino and Olivia as a threat for his own position within both households, *and* that Viola is 'nothing' or 'no-thing' (Elizabethan slang for female genitals, patronisingly defined by the absence of 'the thing', or the male member). Is Feste insinuating that Viola lacks virility? Or, can Feste see through Viola's disguise? Some directors have exploited this possibility in interesting ways. In Trevor Nunn's 1996 film adaptation, for example, Feste watches Viola emerge from the sea from the top of a nearby cliff and, therefore, knows that Cesario is Viola all along (see The Work in Performance, **p. 111**).

Feste's 'dallying with words' is not only funny, witty and revealing. It is also disquieting because it makes words 'wanton', that is 'equivocal' *and* 'lewd' (13–17). Like lovers, words breed and generate legitimate offspring (official, intended meaning). Alternatively, when words become 'lewd', 'playful' and 'transgressive', they spawn a progeny of bastards (unforeseen, unsettling, unacceptable meanings). Feste establishes a further connection between transgressive coupling, slippery signification *and* coins, which, as Viola points out, also breed if 'put to use', that is if they are 'invested to produce interest'. More specifically, Feste compares the breeding of coins to the coupling of Troilus and Cressida[1] and his role in 'putting his coins to use' to Cressida's uncle, Pandarus, whose name (pander) has become synonymous for pimp or procurer. Feste's remarks reflect early modern views according to which interest, or, the profit generated by lending capital, was immoral, if not devilish, because it makes money out of money instead of generating wealth through the production or the exchange of goods. The emergence of a capitalist economy

---

1   See Footnote 2 on p. **82** and Footnote 23 below.

during the early modern period generated a tension between these traditional views and the lure of economic gain. Feste develops his witty comparison between the circulation of coins and words even further by pointing out that the lending of capital depends on legal written documents, or bonds, which make words (verbal agreements) 'good'. However, the circulation of money, as well as words and sexual desires, seems utterly out of control in Illyria. Antonio's money, which he has at least partly accumulated through his involvement in trade wars against Orsino, ends up in Sebastian's pockets. Olivia cynically plans to spend her money to buy Viola's affection, 'For youth is bought more oft than begged or borrowed' (3.4.3). Sir Andrew squanders his money, while Maria, who has no money, gets an aristocratic, if profligate, husband by becoming the ultimate 'corrupter of [written] words'. W. H. Auden controversially associated 'the cynicism about money' in *Twelfth Night* with a world where 'women have become dominant [. . .] and take the initiative' (see Modern Criticism, **p. 63**). Although Auden conservatively conflates monetary and (female) sexual disorder, his views helpfully highlight how *Twelfth Night* in general, and Act 3, Scene 1 in particular, explore the interplay of transgressive sexual, economic and linguistic transactions, which, according to critics since Auden, contributed to darken Shakespeare's comic vision.

Enter VIOLA *and Clown* [FESTE, *playing his tabor*].

VIOLA   Save thee, friend, and thy music. Dost thou live by[2] thy tabor?[3]
FESTE   No, sir, I live by the church.
VIOLA   Art thou a churchman?
FESTE   No such matter, sir. I do live by the church, for I do live at my
house, and my house doth stand by the church.   5
VIOLA   So thou mayst say the king lies by a beggar, if a beggar dwell
near him, or the church stands by[4] thy tabor, if thy tabor stand by
the church.
FESTE   You have said, sir. To see this age![5] A sentence is but a cheveril[6]
glove to a good wit: how quickly the wrong side may be turned   10
outward.
VIOLA   Nay, that's certain. They that dally[7] nicely with words may
quickly make them wanton.[8]
FESTE   I would therefore my sister had had no name, sir.

---

2   The witty repartee in the first five lines of this extract rests on the double meaning of the verb 'to
     live by', that is 'to earn a living by' and 'to live next to'.
3   Drum.
4   As with 'to live by' (see Footnote 2), Viola is using 'to stand by' to mean both 'to be next to' and
     'to be maintained by'.
5   Feste ironically complains about the fact that other characters are better at fooling and wordplay
     than the fool himself.
6   Kidskin.
7   'Play', but also 'flirt', in keeping with the double meaning of 'wanton' (see Footnote 8).
8   'Changeable, unstable', hence 'ambiguous', but also 'lewd', in keeping with the double meaning of
     the verb 'to dally' (see Footnote 7).

VIOLA   Why, man?   15

FESTE   Why, sir, her name's a word, and to dally with that word might make my sister wanton.[9] But indeed, words are very rascals since bonds disgraced them.[10]

VIOLA   Thy reason, man?

FESTE   Troth, sir, I can yield you none without words, and words are   20 grown so false, I am loath to prove reason with them.

VIOLA   I warrant thou art a merry fellow and carest for nothing.

FESTE   Not so, sir, I do care for something, but in my conscience, sir, I do not care for you. If that be to care for nothing, sir, I would it would make you invisible.[11]   25

VIOLA   Art not thou the Lady Olivia's fool?

FESTE   No, indeed, sir. The Lady Olivia has no folly. She will keep no fool, sir, till she be married, and fools are as like husbands as pilchards[12] are to herrings: the husband's the bigger. I am indeed not her fool, but her corrupter of words.   30

VIOLA   I saw thee late at the Count Orsino's.

FESTE   Foolery, sir, does walk about the orb like the sun: it shines everywhere. I would be sorry, sir, but[13] the fool should be as oft with your master as with my mistress. I think I saw Your Wisdom[14] there.   35

VIOLA   Nay, an[15] thou pass upon me,[16] I'll no more with thee. Hold, [giving a coin] there's expenses for thee.

FESTE   Now Jove, in his next commodity[17] of hair, send thee a beard.[18]

VIOLA   By my troth,[19] I'll tell thee, I am almost sick for one[20] – though I would not have it grow on my chin. – Is thy lady within?   40

FESTE   [holding up the coin] Would not a pair of these have bred,[21] sir?

VIOLA   Yes, being kept together and put to use.[22]

---

9 Feste exploits the double meaning of 'to dally', which means both 'to play' *and* 'to flirt', and 'wanton', which means both 'equivocal' *and* 'lewd', thus proving his point that any sentence, like Viola's statement at lines 12–13, can be turned inside-out like 'a cheveril glove'.

10 Words can no longer be trusted since bonds (legal *written* documents) were introduced to make vows, pledges, and other *verbal* agreements 'good'.

11 For lines 23–5, see headnote above.

12 Sea fish, similar to herrings, but smaller.

13 Unless.

14 Ironic, reinforcing Feste's insinuation in the previous line that folly is as common in Olivia's household as in Orsino's.

15 If.

16 Judge me.

17 Supply.

18 Straightforward remark on Viola's young age, or ironic remark on the fact that no beard will naturally grow on Viola's cheeks, if we are to assume that Feste sees through her disguise (see headnote above for further commentary on this line).

19 Truth.

20 Sick with desire for Orsino's beard.

21 Generated a third coin.

22 'Invested to produce interest' but also, 'made to copulate'.

FESTE   I would play Lord Pandarus of Phrygia, sir, to bring a Cressida
to this Troilus.[23]

VIOLA   [*giving another coin*] I understand you, sir; 'tis well begged.   45

FESTE   The matter,[24] I hope, is not great, sir, begging but a beggar;[25]
Cressida was a beggar.[26] My lady is within, sir. I will conster[27] to
them whence you come. Who you are and what you would are out
of my welkin.[28] I might say 'element', but the word is overworn.

Exit

VIOLA   This fellow is wise enough to play the fool,   50
And to do that well craves a kind of wit:
He must observe their mood on whom he jests,
The quality of persons and the time,
And, like the haggard, check at every feather
That comes before his eye.[29] This is a practice[30]   55
As full of labour as a wise man's art;
For folly that he wisely shows is fit,[31]
But wise men, folly-fallen, quite taint their wit.[32]

Act 5, Scene 1, lines 45–128, 206–77, 367–404: This most happy wreck

After Act 3, Scene 1, Acts 3 and 4 focus on the gulling of Malvolio and on
Sebastian's arrival in Illyria. Although Sebastian represents a key element in the
dramatic economy of the comic resolution in Act 5, his arrival in Act 3, Scene
2 leads to more confusion, including predictable mistakes of identity and farcical incidents. Most memorable are the unforeseen developments of the duel set
up by Sir Toby once Sebastian joins the fray in Act 4, Olivia and Sebastian's hasty

23   Panders are named after Pandarus, who acted as go-between for Troilus and his niece Cressida.
     Shortly after *Twelfth Night*, Shakespeare wrote a play about their famous love story, which was set
     during the siege of Troy and figured prominently in Homer's *Iliad*, Virgil's *Aeneid* and was adapted
     by Chaucer in his poem, *Troilus and Criseyde*. By proposing to 'play Lord Pandarus' Feste is
     effectively asking for another coin to pair it off with the first one that Viola gives him at line 37,
     while possibly offering his help to bring another Troilus (Orsino) and another Cressida (Olivia)
     together in return.
24   Amount.
25   Begging on behalf of a beggar, that is, on behalf of the coin which Feste calls Cressida.
26   In Robert Henryson's sequel to Chaucer's poem, called *The Testament of Cresseid*, Cressida
     becomes a leper and a beggar (see Lothian and Craik, p. 77).
27   'Construe', 'explain'. Feste is using a pompous register here, because common words, as he com-
     plains in his next statement, are 'overworn'.
28   Sky.
29   Wild hawk, trained to 'start at, respond sensitively to, the slightest thing' (see Warren and Wells,
     p. 156).
30   Occupation.
31   Suits the purpose, is to the point.
32   'Wise men, who give in to folly, spoil their wit.' Possibly an allusion to the gulling of Malvolio in
     Act 2, Scene 5.

exchange of marriage vows which takes place off stage at the end of Act 4, Scene 1 and Viola's failure to recognise Antonio when the latter is arrested at the end of Act 4, Scene 3. By the time the main characters are on stage in Act 5, all the elements are in place for what C. L. Barber calls 'release to clarification' (see Modern Criticism, **pp. 64–7**). The comic resolution, the 'most happy wreck' (263) through which the twins are reunited and paired off in Act 5, reverses the devastating effects of literal and metaphorical shipwrecks. As it turns out, neither Viola nor Sebastian died at sea. Similarly, Olivia and Orsino survive their determination to drown their sorrows in brinish tears or in a solipsistic love that 'Receiveth as the sea' (see Key Passages, **p. 141**).

And yet, the vast majority of late-twentieth-century critics and directors have found the logic of this happy ending far from *restorative*, either because it fails to *restore* the main characters to psychological and emotional health by fulfilling their desires or because there is no *restoration* of the norms that those desires infringe. Antonio, for example, finds no fulfilment in Act 5. Like his namesake at the end of Shakespeare's *The Merchant of Venice*, Antonio is left out of the final celebrations. In Peter Gill's 1974 production of *Twelfth Night* (see The Work in Performance, **p. 107**), Antonio was left stranded on stage as Feste sang his final song, while in Trevor Nunn's 1996 film (see The Work in Performance, **p. 111 and pp. 130–1**), Antonio leaves Olivia's house carrying his suitcase and walks out into the cold followed by Malvolio and Sir Andrew Aguecheek. Even those who are lucky enough to benefit from the 'most happy wreck' of Act 5 do not necessarily get what they wanted. Orsino's attempt to reassure Olivia that Sebastian's blood is 'right noble' (261) does not change the fact that Olivia has married the wrong twin. Sebastian's entrance at line 206, when the twins are finally on stage together for the first time, elicits a gleeful response from Olivia – 'Most wonderful!' – who is suddenly faced by the prospect of having two identical husbands. However, recent productions have emphasised the potential for humiliation and disappointment that the 'comic' resolution implies for Olivia (see The Work in Performance, **p. 128**). Similarly, Orsino fails to win Olivia, and, although his feelings for Olivia were gradually replaced by his growing intimacy with Cesario, Orsino does not get Cesario either, because the 'lamb' (127) that Orsino loves turns out to be a woman.

Besides granting either partial or no fulfilment at all to the main characters, the comic resolution in Act 5 fails to neutralise transgressive desires. Malvolio is harshly punished for his secret passion for Olivia and his dream of becoming 'Count Malvolio', but Maria ends up marrying her lady's uncle. Curiously, Maria and Sir Toby's match has attracted some harsh criticism from early commentators. Émile Montégut, for example, refers to Maria as a 'sly waiting woman' (see Early Criticism, **p. 55**). Montégut's response may be due to the fact that, as Karin Coddon has pointed out, 'Sir Toby's offstage marriage to Maria is a reminder of the instability of rank and order that persists outside the world of the play' (see Modern Criticism, **p. 74**).

Instability of rank is matched by an unresolved ambiguity of sexual identity. Stephen Greenblatt has, for example, pointed out that because Cesario's transformation into Viola is not enacted, Orsino's impromptu marriage proposal is far from normative (see Modern Criticism, **p. 87**). Orsino himself seems happy to postpone that transformation until 'golden time convents' (378), and keeps calling Viola 'Cesario' (381) or 'boy' (264). Even more interestingly, Viola seems happy to postpone the time when she will switch back to her 'maiden weeds' (252), possibly because, as Juliet Dusinberre points out, 'she is diminished by a return to a world where she must be Orsino's lady' (see Modern Criticism, **p. 82**) and where, as Greenblatt explains, 'a passage from male to female was coded ideologically as a descent' (see Modern Criticism, **p. 90**). The restoration of normative heterosexual bonds is also undermined by the climactic reunion between Viola and Sebastian. William Dodd, for example, believes that the audience is led through Sebastian's gaze to 'embrac[e], with growing intensity, first a heterosexual object [when Sebastian sees his newly-wed wife Olivia at line 206], then a homoerotic object [when Sebastian sees his friend Antonio at line 215], and lastly an androgynous self-image [when Sebastian finally sees his twin sister Viola at line 223]' (see Modern Criticism, **p. 94**). Building his argument on the significant length of the 'recognition' sequence (223–55), Dodd concludes that 'the dramatic focus [of the final scene] does not point foward to individuation and maturity, but rather "backward" towards a merger with the narcissistic object' (see Modern Criticism, **p. 96**). This fascinating reading of the final scene in *Twelfth Night* takes us back where we started, to the opening scene and Orsino's self-absorbing obsession for Olivia. Narcissistic recognition seems to be what everybody wants, or '*What You Will*'. The experience of falling in love, in other words, may not fulfil a wish to encounter the other but the need to find our own (twin) image in the eye of the beloved. As T. S. Eliot put it, 'We shall not cease from exploration / And the end of all our exploring / Will be to arrive where we started / And know the place for the first time'.[1]

Enter ANTONIO *and officers*.[2] [iii]

FIRST OFFICER   Orsino, this is that Antonio
    That took the Phoenix and her freight from Candy,[3]
    And this is he that did the Tiger board
    When your young nephew Titus lost his leg.
    Here in the streets, desperate of shame and state,[4]   60
    In private brabble[5] did we apprehend him.
VIOLA   He did me kindness, sir, drew on my side,
    But in conclusion put strange speech upon me.[6]
    I know not what 'twas but distraction.[7]
ORSINO   Notable pirate, thou salt-water thief,   65

---

1 T. S. Eliot, *The Four Quartets* (London: Faber and Faber, 2000), p. 38.
2 Orsino, Viola, Curio and Fabian are already on stage.
3 Candia, modern-day Crete.
4 Careless of his honour and his position.
5 Brawl.
6 Spoke to me strangely.
7 Unless it was madness.

What foolish boldness brought thee to their mercies,
Whom thou in terms so bloody and so dear[8]
Hast made thine enemies?
ANTONIO   Orsino, noble sir,
Be pleased that I shake off these names you give me.
Antonio never yet was thief or pirate,   70
Though, I confess, on base and ground enough,[9]
Orsino's enemy. A witchcraft drew me hither.
That most ingrateful boy, there by your side,
From the rude[10] sea's enraged and foamy mouth
Did I redeem. A wreck past hope he was.   75
His life I gave him and did thereto add
My love, without retention[11] or restraint,
All his in dedication.[12] For his sake
Did I expose myself, pure[13] for his love,
Into the danger of this adverse[14] town,   80
Drew to defend him when he was beset;[15]
Where, being apprehended,[16] his false cunning,
Not meaning to partake[17] with me in danger,
Taught him to face me out of his acquaintance,[18]
And grew a twenty years' removèd thing[19]   85
While one would wink, denied me mine own purse,
Which I had recommended[20] to his use
Not half an hour before.
VIOLA   How can this be?
ORSINO   When came he to this town?
ANTONIO   Today, my lord, and for three months before,   90
No interim, not a minute's vacancy,[21]
Both day and night did we keep company.

Enter OLIVIA *and attendants.*

ORSINO   Here comes the Countess. Now heaven walks on earth.
But for thee, fellow – fellow, thy words are madness:

---

8 Dire.
9 'Base' is here synonymous with 'ground'; hence 'on solid grounds', 'for good reasons'.
10 Rough.
11 Reservation.
12 Wholly devoted to him.
13 Purely.
14 Hostile.
15 Antonio is referring to the duel set up by Sir Toby in Act 3, Scene 4.
16 Arrested.
17 Share.
18 To deny he knew me.
19 Distant, estranged acquaintance, who has been out of touch for twenty years.
20 Entrusted.
21 Interval.

Three months[22] this youth hath tended upon me.   95
But more of that anon. Take him aside.

OLIVIA   [to ORSINO] What would my lord, but[23] that he may not
have,[24]
    Wherein Olivia may seem serviceable? –
    Cesario, you do not keep promise with me.

VIOLA   Madam?   100

ORSINO   Gracious Olivia –

OLIVIA   What do you say, Cesario? Good my lord –

VIOLA   My lord would speak, my duty hushes me.

OLIVIA   If it be aught to the old tune,[25] my lord,
    It is as fat and fulsome[26] to mine ear   105
    As howling after music.

ORSINO   Still so cruel?

OLIVIA   Still so constant, lord.

ORSINO   What, to perverseness? You uncivil[27] lady,
    To whose ingrate[28] and unauspicious[29] altars   110
    My soul the faithfull'st off'rings have breathed out
    That e'er devotion tendered. What shall I do?

OLIVIA   Even what it please my lord that shall become[30] him.

ORSINO   Why should I not, had I the heart to do it,
    Like to th'Egyptian thief at point of death,   115
    Kill what I love?[31] – A savage jealousy
    That sometime savours nobly. But hear me this:
    Since you to non-regardance[32] cast my faith,
    And that I partly know the instrument
    That screws[33] me from my true place in your favour,   120
    Live you the marble-breasted tyrant still.
    But this your minion,[34] whom I know you love,
    And whom, by heaven I swear, I tender[35] dearly,

---

22 When Viola enters disguised as Cesario for the first time at the beginning of Act 1, Scene 4,
    Valentine points out that Viola and Orsino have known each other for three *days*. The double
    time scheme (three days in Act 1, Scene 4 have become three months by Act 5, Scene 1) allows
    Shakespeare to simultaneously stress how quickly Orsino has grown fond of his new servant in
    Act 1, Scene 4 and how much better Orsino and Viola must know each other by the beginning of
    Act 5, Scene 1.
23 Except.
24 That is, 'Olivia's love'.
25 If what Orsino is about to say has anything to do with his old suit.
26 Gross and distasteful.
27 Unkind.
28 Ungrateful.
29 Unpropitious, not disposed to be favourable.
30 Suit.
31 Orsino is referring to the story of an Egyptian thief, who tried to kill his beloved in order to prevent
    her from falling into their captors' hands. This story is included in Heliodorus' *Ethiopica*, which was
    translated from Greek into English by Thomas Underdowne in 1569 and was still very popular in
    the early 1600s.
32 Indifference.
33 Wrenches.
34 (Sexual) favourite.
35 Value, esteem.

Him will I tear out of that cruel eye[36]
Where he sits crownèd in his master's spite. –   125
[*to* VIOLA] Come, boy, with me. My thoughts are ripe in mischief.
I'll sacrifice the lamb[37] that I do love
To spite a raven's heart[38] within a dove.[39]

> As Orsino and Viola are about to leave, Olivia calls Viola 'husband'. Viola
> denies to have ever exchanged marriage vows with Olivia and the priest is
> called in to confirm that Olivia is telling the truth. Orsino's rage threatens to
> break out again, when Sir Andrew and Sir Toby enter to announce that Viola
> has brutally attacked them. The farcical mistakes of identity are brought to an
> abrupt end as Sebastian enters at line 206.

Enter SEBASTIAN.

SEBASTIAN   [*to* OLIVIA] I am sorry, madam, I have hurt your
    kinsman;
    But, had it been the brother of my blood,
    I must have done no less with wit and safety.[40]
    You throw a strange regard upon me, and by that
    I do perceive it hath offended you.   210
    Pardon me, sweet one, even for the vows
    We made each other but so late ago.
ORSINO   One face, one voice, one habit,[41] and two persons!
    A natural perspective,[42] that is and is not.
SEBASTIAN   Antonio! O my dear Antonio,   215
    How have the hours racked and tortured me
    Since I have lost thee.
ANTONIO   Sebastian are you?
SEBASTIAN   Fear'st thou that, Antonio?
ANTONIO   How have you made division of yourself?
    An apple cleft in two is not more twin   220
    Than these two creatures. Which is Sebastian?
OLIVIA   Most wonderful!
SEBASTIAN   [*sees* VIOLA] Do I stand there? I never had a
    brother,
    Nor can there be that deity in my nature

---

36 Out of the five senses, sight, and, therefore, the eye, was believed to be Cupid's prime target; the
    image of the beloved is often described by early modern writers as reaching the heart through the
    eye. See also Footnote 59 on **p. 152.**
37 Viola.
38 Olivia's black (cruel) heart.
39 Olivia's fair appearance.
40 Taking reasonable care of my own safety.
41 When Antonio calls Viola 'Sebastian' at the end of Act 3, Scene 4, Viola explains in a short aside
    that her disguise imitates Sebastian's 'fashion, colour [and] ornament' (3.4.374).
42 The twins are described as an optical illusion produced by nature. Perspective (or distorting)
    glasses were a popular Renaissance invention.

Of here and everywhere.[43] I had a sister,   225
Whom the blind waves and surges have devoured.
Of charity, what kin are you to me?
What countryman? What name? What parentage?

VIOLA   Of Messaline. Sebastian was my father,
Such a Sebastian was my brother too.   230
So went he suited to his watery tomb.[44]
If spirits can assume both form and suit,[45]
You come to fright us.[46]

SEBASTIAN   A spirit I am indeed,
But am in that dimension grossly clad,
Which from the womb I did participate.[47]   235
Were you a woman, as the rest goes even,[48]
I should my tears let fall upon your cheek
And say, 'Thrice welcome, drownèd Viola!'

VIOLA   My father had a mole upon his brow.

SEBASTIAN   And so had mine.   240

VIOLA   And died that day when Viola from her birth
Had numbered thirteen years.

SEBASTIAN   O, that record[49] is lively in my soul:
He finishèd indeed his mortal act
That day that made my sister thirteen years.   245

VIOLA   If nothing lets[50] to make us happy both
But this my masculine usurped attire,
Do not embrace me till each circumstance
Of place, time, fortune, do cohere and jump[51]
That I am Viola; which to confirm   250
I'll bring you to a captain in this town,
Where lie my maiden weeds,[52] by whose gentle help
I was preserved to serve this noble count.
All the occurrence of my fortune since
Hath been between this lady and this lord.   255

SEBASTIAN   [to OLIVIA] So comes it, lady, you have been mistook;[53]

---

43 Divine prerogative of ubiquity.
44 Sebastian was wearing the same items of clothing when he drowned.
45 Physical appearance and clothing.
46 Viola, taking Sebastian for the spirit (or ghost) of her dead brother, questions his intentions, as much as Hamlet wonders whether the spirit of his dead father is 'a spirit of health or goblin damned', bringing with him 'airs from heaven or blasts from hell' (1.4.21–2).
47 The body was believed to weigh down the soul, which naturally yearned to rejoin its creator. See also Hamlet: 'what dreams may come / When we have shuffled off this mortal coil' (Hamlet, 3.1.68–9).
48 As every other detail agrees (with what Sebastian remembers about Viola and their family background).
49 Memory.
50 Hinders.
51 Fit and agree.
52 Clothes.
53 Mistaken.

But Nature to her bias drew in that.[54]
You would have been contracted to a maid,
Nor are you therein, by my life, deceived:
You are betrothed both to a maid and man.   260
ORSINO   [*to* OLIVIA] Be not amazed, right noble is his blood.
If this be so, as yet the glass[55] seems true,
I shall have share in this most happy wreck.
[*to* VIOLA] Boy, thou hast said to me a thousand times
Thou never shouldst love woman like to me.   265
VIOLA   And all those sayings will I overswear,[56]
And all those swearings keep as true in soul
As doth that orbèd continent, the fire[57]
That severs day from night.
ORSINO   Give me thy hand,
And let me see thee in thy woman's weeds.[58]   270
VIOLA   The captain that did bring me first on shore
Hath my maid's garments. He upon some action[59]
Is now in durance,[60] at Malvolio's suit,
A gentleman and follower of my lady's.
OLIVIA   He shall enlarge[61] him. [*to attendants*] Fetch Malvolio hither. 275
And yet, alas, now I remember me,
They say, poor gentleman, he's much distract.[62]

Malvolio shows Olivia the letter he found in Act 2, Scene 5 and demands
an explanation. Olivia recognises Maria's handwriting and promises to compensate Malvolio for the wrongs he has suffered. Fabian explains that Maria
wrote the letter and that Sir Toby and Maria have in the meantime got married
off-stage.

OLIVIA   [*to* MALVOLIO] Alas, poor fool, how have they baffled[63]
            thee!
FESTE   Why, 'Some are born great, some achieve greatness, and some
        have greatness thrown upon them'.[64] I was one, sir, in this interlude,[65]

---

54 A bowling metaphor, hinting at the fact that the weight inside the bowl causes it to swerve. Whether
   Sebastian is implying that nature 'by indirections find[s] directions out' (*Hamlet*, 2.1.65), or whether
   he is more radically implying that it is natural for men and women to 'swerve' off the straight path
   when they fall in love, is open to debate (see, for example, Modern Criticism, **pp. 82–90**).
55 The perspective glass, or natural perspective, mentioned by Orsino at line 214.
56 Swear again.
57 As the sun keeps and preserves its fire.
58 See Footnote 52.
59 Legal charge.
60 In prison.
61 Release.
62 Deranged.
63 Disgraced, cheated.
64 Feste is teasing Malvolio by repeating what he read in Maria's letter in Act 2, Scene 3.
65 Dramatic entertainment; on the meta-theatrical quality of Malvolio's gulling, see Jason Scott-
   Warren's essay (The Work In Performance, **pp. 117–19**) and headnote to Act 2, Scene 5, **pp. 165–6**.

one Sir Topas, sir, but that's all one. 'By the Lord, fool, I am not   370
mad!'[66] But do you remember, 'Madam, why laugh you at such a
barren rascal? An you smile not, he's gagg'd'.[67] And thus the
whirligig[68] of time brings in his revenges.

MALVOLIO   I'll be revenged on the whole pack[69] of you!

[Exit]

OLIVIA   He hath been most notoriously abused.   375
ORSINO   Pursue him and entreat him to a peace;
       He hath not told us of the captain yet.
       When that is known, and golden time convents,[70]
       A solemn combination shall be made
       Of our dear souls. [*to* OLIVIA] Meantime, sweet sister,   380
       We will not part from hence. [*to* VIOLA] Cesario, come –
       For so you shall be while you are a man;
       But when in other habits you are seen,
       Orsino's mistress and his fancy's queen.[71]

Exeunt [all except FESTE]

FESTE (*sings*)
       When that I was and a little tiny boy,   385
           With hey, ho, the wind and the rain,
       A foolish thing was but a toy,[72]
           For the rain it raineth every day.

       But when I came to man's estate,
           With hey, ho, the wind and the rain,   390
       'Gainst knaves and thieves men shut their gate,
           For the rain it raineth every day.

       But when I came, alas, to wive,
           With hey, ho, the wind and the rain,
       By swaggering[73] could I never thrive,   395
           For the rain it raineth every day.

       But when I came unto my beds,
           With hey, ho, the wind and the rain,

---

66 This is, if not verbatim, what Malvolio says to the Fool when he is locked up in the dark room in
     Act 4, Scene 2.
67 Feste summarises the harsh and unflattering remarks which Malvolio makes about professional
     fools and those who laugh at their jokes at 1.5.79–85.
68 Roundabout.
69 Another echo of the bear-baiting motif and the hunting metaphor; see Footnote 57, p. 170.
70 Comes about (see Warren and Wells, p. 220).
71 For a link between this line and Shakespeare's 'Sonnet 20', see William N. Dodd (Modern
     Criticism, **p. 95**).
72 This line could simply be a tautology, since 'foolish thing' and 'toy' are synonymous; or, 'if *thing*
     has the likely overtone of "penis", then the line roughly means: "a little penis was only a toy" – i.e.
     was useless – when I was a child' (see Warren and Wells, 1994, p. 220).
73 Insolent, aggressive attitude or behaviour.

With tosspots[74] still had drunken heads,
    For the rain it raineth every day.   400

A great while ago the world begun,
    With hey, ho, the wind and the rain,
But that's all one, our play is done,
    And we'll strive to please you every day.

                                  [*Exit*]

---

74 Drunkards.

4

Further Reading

Further Reading

Recommended Editions

Twelfth Night was first printed in the First Folio edition of *Mr. William Shakespeares comedies, histories, & tragedies* (1623).[1] The text preserved in the Folio edition has been described as 'remarkably free from textual corruption and obscurity, mislining of verse, and wrong attribution of speeches' (see Lothian and Craik, p. xviii). Although we cannot be absolutely certain about the origin of the manuscript used by the compositor who set the Folio text of *Twelfth Night*, in 1975 Robert K. Turner confuted earlier theories according to which the printer's copy was a theatrical manuscript and explained why he thought *Twelfth Night* was set from a transcript of Shakespeare's own papers. Turner pointed out that a few inconsistencies in the Folio text suggest that the printer's copy preserved changes that occurred during composition. Shakespeare, for example, seems to have changed his mind about Orsino's rank: although he appears as '*Duke*' in stage directions and speech prefixes, he is often referred to as 'count' or 'Count Orsino' by the other characters in the play. Similarly, Fabian replaces Feste in Act 2, Scene 5, although at the end of Act 2, Scene 3 Maria announces that Sir Toby, Sir Andrew and Feste will spy on Malvolio as he reads her forged letter. Rather than a full-scale revision, Shakespeare seems to have introduced these and a few other changes as he was writing the play.[2] Although the Folio text of *Twelfth Night* is relatively unproblematic, recent editors and textual scholars have highlighted a few interesting cruxes and have questioned the way in which earlier editors intervened to emend them. For a full discussion of the Folio text and its editorial transmission, see the 'Critical Editions and Textual Studies' listed below.

Critical Editions and Textual Studies

Donno, Elizabeth Story (ed.), *Twelfth Night*, The New Cambridge Shakespeare (Cambridge: Cambridge University Press, 1985).

---

1 A full facsimile can be found in *The First Folio of Shakespeare*, prepared by Charlton Hinman, with a new introduction by P. W. M. Blayney (New York: W. W. Norton, 1996).
2 For further details, see Robert K. Turner, 'The Text of *Twelfth Night*', *Shakespeare Quarterly* 26 (1975), pp. 128–38.

Elam, Keir (ed.), *Twelfth Night*, The Arden Shakespeare, 3rd series (London: Thomson Learning, forthcoming).

Osborne, Laurie, 'The Texts of *Twelfth Night*', *English Literary History* 57 (1990), pp. 39–61. Analyses interesting textual crux at 2.2.31–2.

Warren, Roger and Stanley Wells (eds), *Twelfth Night*, The Oxford Shakespeare (Oxford: Oxford University Press, 1994).

Student Editions

Gibson, Rex (ed.), *Shakespeare, Twelfth Night*, Cambridge School Shakespeare, 2nd edn (Cambridge: Cambridge University Press, 2005).

Gill, Roma (ed.), *Twelfth Night*, Oxford School Shakespeare (Oxford: Oxford University Press, 1992).

Film and Television Versions

Twelfth Night, 1980, British Broadcasting Company/Time-Life Television: Shakespeare Plays. Producer: Cedric Messina; Director: John Gorrie.

Twelfth Night, 1988, Renaissance Theatre Company. Producer: David Parfitt; Director: Kenneth Branagh.

Twelfth Night, 1996, Fine Line Features. Producer: David Parfitt; Director: Trevor Nunn.

Twelfth Night, 2003, Channel Four. Producer: Rachel Gesua; Director: Tim Supple.

Useful Websites

Internet Shakespeare Editions. Offers full text of the play, both in the original Folio edition of 1623 and in a modernised version, as well as performance records and useful introductions to 'Shakespeare's Life and Time', <http://internetshakespeare.uvic.ca/index.html>. (Accessed 29 August 2007.)

World Shakespeare Bibliography Online. Provides comprehensive annotated records of Shakespeare-related scholarship and theatrical productions published or produced worldwide since 1963, <http://www.worldshakesbib.org>. (Accessed 29 August 2007.)

Collections of Essays and Casebooks

The following books complement the critical extracts included in this guide (especially those gathered in the Early Criticism, Modern Criticism, and The Work in Performance sections).

Ford, John R. *Twelfth Night: A Guide to the Play*, Greenwood Guides to Shakespeare (Westport, Conn., and London: Greenwood Press, 2006). General introduction to *Twelfth Night*, includes the following chapters: 'Textual History', 'Contexts and Sources', 'Dramatic Structure', 'Themes', 'Critical Approaches', 'Twelfth Night in Performance', and 'Suggested Readings'.

King, Walter N. (ed.), *Twentieth-Century Interpretations of 'Twelfth Night': A Collection of Critical Essays* (Englewood Cliffs, NJ: Prentice-Hall, 1968). Similar in scope to Palmer (1972).

Palmer, D. J. (ed.), *William Shakespeare: 'Twelfth Night'* (Basingstoke and London: Macmillan, 1972). Includes early responses and eleven essays by early and mid-twentieth-century scholars.

Wells, Stanley (ed.), *Twelfth Night: Critical Essays* (New York: Garland, 1986). Offers a wide range of critical materials (theatre reviews, critical and theatre-orientated studies).

White, R. S. (ed.), *Twelfth Night: Contemporary Critical Essays* (Basingstoke and London: Macmillan, 1996). Covers recent critical approaches to *Twelfth Night* from the early 1980s and to the early 1990s.

Contexts

The books listed below complement the Contextual Overview and the Contemporary Documents sections by giving detailed accounts of several aspects of Elizabethan England.

Bray, A., *Homosexuality in Renaissance England*, 2nd edn (London: Gay Men's Press, 1988). Revisionary exploration of the simultaneous condemnation and diffuse ubiquitousness of homosexuality in the early modern period.

Melville, A. D. (trans.) and E. J. Kenney, ed., *Ovid: 'Metamorphoses'* (Oxford: Oxford University Press, 1986). Accessible, well-annotated translation, includes useful glossary and index of names.

Norbrook, David (ed.), *The Penguin Book of Renaissance Verse, 1509–1659* (London: Penguin, 1993). The introduction provides a useful overview of the cultural, political and social significance of the main poetic forms and conventions in the period.

Outhwaite, R. B. (ed.) *Marriage and Society: Studies in the Social History of Marriage* (New York: St Martin's, 1981). Useful essays relevant to the period include Kathleen M. Davies, 'Continuity and Change in Literary Advice on Marriage', pp. 58–80.

Smith, Bruce, *William Shakespeare, Twelfth Night: Texts and Contexts* (Boston, Mass. and New York: Bedford and St Martin's, 2001). Illuminating discussion of the following contexts: romance, music, sexuality, clothing and disguise, household economies, puritan probity, clowning and laughter.

Todd, Margo, *Christian Humanism and the Puritan Social Order* (Cambridge: Cambridge University Press, 1987). Todd departs from earlier social historians like Christopher Hill and Lawrence Stone in arguing that humanist influences were as important as ideals of Puritan probity and orderly life in changing early modern views on marriage.

Woodbridge, Linda, *Women and the English Renaissance: Literature and the Nature of Womankind, 1540–1620* (Urbana, Ill.: University of Illinois Press, 1984). A comprehensive analysis of the 'Woman Controversy' between 1540 and 1620 and of the interplay between social practice and literary conventions.

Recent Critical Interpretations

Callaghan, Dympna. '"All is Semblative a Woman's Part": Body Politics and *Twelfth Night*', *Textual Practice* 7 (1993), pp. 428–52. Investigates women's exclusion from the early modern stage and the effects of such exclusion on dramatic representations of the female body.

Elam, Keir, 'The Fertile Eunuch: *Twelfth Night*, Early Modern Intercourse and the Fruits of Castration', *Shakespeare Quarterly* 47 (1996), pp. 1–36. Historicises Viola's unfulfilled plan to disguise herself as a eunuch in Act 1, Scene 2, by identifying both the dramatic-diachronic and the social-synchronic dimensions associated with this social and literary type.

Jardine, Lisa, 'Twins and Travesties: Gender, Dependency, and Sexual Availability in *Twelfth Night*', in *Reading Shakespeare Historically* (London and New York: Routledge, 1996), pp. 65–77. Argues that erotic attention is triggered by submissiveness, rather than 'the sex of the possibly "submissive" partner' (p. 77).

Kahn, Coppélia, *Man's Estate: Masculine Identity in Shakespeare* (Berkeley, Calif. and London: University of California Press, 1981). Regards homoerotic desires as a temporary stage towards the emergence of normative heterosexual bonds.

Malcolmson, Cristina, '"What You Will": Social Mobility and Gender in *Twelfth Night*', in Valerie Wayne (ed.), *The Matter of Difference: Materialist Feminist Criticism of Shakespeare* (Hemel Hempstead: Harvester Wheatsheaf,

1991), pp. 29–57. Considers Shakespeare's representation of class and gender in relation to 'socio-economic . . . as well as sexual-familial structures' (p. 31).

Piquigney, Joseph, 'The Two Antonios and Same-Sex Love in *Twelfth Night* and *The Merchant of Venice*', *English Literary Renaissance* 22 (1992), pp. 201–21. Useful contrastive analysis of two of the four characters named Antonio in Shakespeare's plays.

Traub, Valerie, 'The (In)Significance of Lesbian Desire', in Jonathan Goldberg (ed.), *Queering the Renaissance* (Durham, NC: Duke University Press, 1994). Historicises the place of transgressive female sexuality in the early modern period.

Production History

Billington, Michael (ed.), *RSC Directors' Shakespeare: Approaches to 'Twelfth Night'* (London: Nick Hern Books, 1990). RSC directors Bill Alexander, John Barton, John Caird and Terry Hands discuss their productions of *Twelfth Night*.

Edmondson, Paul, *Twelfth Night*, The Shakespeare Handbooks series (New York and Basingstoke: Palgrave Macmillan, 2005). Offers a detailed commentary of the play in performance.

Brown, John Russell (ed.), *Twelfth Night* (New York and London: Applause, 2001). The text of the play glossed with theatrical commentary.

Greif, Karen, 'A Star is Born: Feste on the Modern Stage', *Shakespeare Quarterly* 39 (1988), pp. 61–78. Examines the roots of Feste's popularity on the twenty-first-century stage.

Hattaway, Michael, 'The Comedies on Film', in Russell Jackson (ed.), *The Cambridge Companion to Shakespeare on Film* (Cambridge: Cambridge University Press, 2000), pp. 85–98. Discusses Trevor Nunn's film adaptation.

Jones, Nicholas R., 'Trevor Nunn's *Twelfth Night*: Contemporary Film and British Theatre', *Early Modern Literary Studies* 8 (2002). Available online at <http://www.shu.ac.uk/emls/emlshome.html>. Focuses on Ben Kingsley's Feste. (Accessed 29 August 2007.)

Potter, Lois, *Twelfth Night*, Text and Performance Series (London: Macmillan, 1983). Detailed study of staging issues and four major productions.

Thompson, Peter, '*Twelfth Night* and Playhouse Practice', in *Shakespeare's Theatre*, 2nd edn (New York and London: Routledge, 1992). Examines the material conditions of production on Shakespeare's stage and reflects on the interpretative implications that such conditions have for *Twelfth Night*.

Trewin, J. C., *Shakespeare on the English Stage, 1900–1964* (London: Barrie and Rockliff, 1964). Useful survey of early to mid-twentieth-century productions.

Wells, Stanley, *Royal Shakespeare: Four Major Productions at Stratford-upon-Avon* (Manchester: Manchester University Press, 1976). Includes one chapter on John Burton's production of *Twelfth Night* (1969–72).

Index

Related titles from Routledge

World-Wide Shakespeares
Edited by Sonia Massai

World-Wide Shakespeares brings together an international team of leading scholars in order to explore the appropriation of Shakespeare's plays in film and performance around the world. In particular, the book explores the ways in which adapters and directors have put Shakespeare into dialogue with local traditions and contexts.

The contributors look in turn at 'local' Shakespeares for local, national and international audiences, covering a range of English and foreign appropriations that challenge geographical and cultural oppositions between 'centre' and 'periphery', 'big-time' and 'small-time' Shakespeares. Their specialist knowledge of local cultures and traditions make the range of appropriations newly accessible – and newly fascinating – for world-wide readers. Drawing upon debates around the global/local dimensions of cultural production and on Pierre Bourdieu's notion of the 'cultural field', the contributors together demonstrate a significant new approach to intercultural appropriations of Shakespeare.

ISBN13: 978–0–415–32455–7 (hbk)
ISBN13: 978–0–415–32456–4 (pbk)

Available at all good bookshops
For ordering and further information please visit:
www.routledge.com

Related titles from Routledge

Accents on Shakespeare Series
General Editor: Terence Hawkes

Books in the Accents on Shakespeare series provide short, powerful, 'cutting-edge' accounts of and comments on new developments in the field of Shakespeare studies. In addition to titles aimed at modular undergraduate courses, it also features a number of spirited and committed research-based books.

The *Accents on Shakespeare* series features contributions from leading figures and the books include:

- *Shakespeare and Appropriation*
  Edited by Christy Desmet and Robert Sawyer
- *Shakespeare Without Women*
  Dympna Callaghan
- *Philosophical Shakespeares*
  Edited by John J. Joughin
- *Shakespeare and Modernity: Early Modern to Millennium*
  Edited by Hugh Grady
- *Marxist Shakespeares*
  Edited by Jean E. Howard and Scott Cutler Shershow
- *Shakespeare in Psychoanalysis*
  Philip Armstrong
- *Shakespeare and Modern Theatre: The Performance of Modernity*
  Edited by Michael Bristol and Kathleen McLuskie
- *Shakespeare and Feminist Performance: Ideology on Stage*
  Sarah Werner
- *Shame in Shakespeare*
  Ewan Fernie
- *The Sound of Shakespeare*
  Wes Folkerth
- *Shakespeare in the Present*
  Terence Hawkes
- *Making Shakespeare*
  Tiffany Stern
- *Spiritual Shakespeares*
  Edited by Ewan Fernie
- *Green Shakespeare*
  Gabriel Egan
- *Shakespeare, Authority, Sexuality*
  Alan Sinfield

Available at all good bookshops
For a full series listing, ordering details and further
information please visit:
www.routledge.com

Related titles from Routledge

Alternative Shakespeares 3
Edited by Diana E. Henderson

This volume takes up the challenge embodied in its predecessors, *Alternative Shakespeares* and *Alternative Shakespeares 2*: to identify and explore the new, the changing, the radically 'other' possibilities for Shakespeare Studies at our particular historical moment.

Alternative Shakespeares 3 introduces the strongest and most innovative of the new directions emerging in Shakespearean scholarship - ranging across performance studies, multimedia and textual criticism, concerns of economics, science, religion, and ethics – as well as the 'next step' work in areas such as postcolonial and queer studies that continue to push the boundaries of the field. The contributors approach each topic with clarity and accessibility in mind, enabling student readers to engage with serious 'alternatives' to established ways of interpreting Shakespeare's plays and their role in contemporary culture.

The expertise, commitment and daring of this volume's contributors shine through each essay, maintaining the progressive edge and real-world urgency that are the hallmark of *Alternative Shakespeares*. This volume is essential reading for students and scholars of Shakespeare who seek an understanding of current and future directions in this ever-changing field.

Contributors include: Kate Chedgzoy, Mary Thomas Crane, Lukas Erne, Diana E. Henderson, Rui Carvalho Homem, Julia Reinhard Lupton, Willy Maley, Patricia Parker, Shankar Raman, Katherine Rowe, Robert Shaughnessy and W. B. Worthen.

Diana E. Henderson is Professor of Literature at MIT.

ISBN13: 978–0–415–42332–8 (hbk)
ISBN13: 978–0–415–42333–5 (pbk)
ISBN13: 978–0–203–93409–8 (ebk)

Available at all good bookshops
For further information on our literature series, please visit
www.routledge.com/literature/series.asp
For ordering and further information please visit:

www.routledge.com

Related titles from Routledge

THE NEW CRITICAL IDIOM

Series Editor: John Drakakis, University of Stirling

The New Critical Idiom is an invaluable series of introductory guides to today's critical terminology. Each book:

- provides a handy, explanatory guide to the use (and abuse) of the term
- offers an original and distinctive overview by a leading literary and cultural critic
- relates the term to the larger field of cultural representation

With a strong emphasis on clarity, lively debate and the widest possible breadth of examples, The New Critical Idiom is an indispensable approach to key topics in literary studies.

'The New Critical Idiom is a constant resource – essential reading for all students.' – Tom Paulin, University of Oxford

'Easily the most informative and wide-ranging series of its kind, so packed with bright ideas that it has become an indispensable resource for students of literature.' – Terry Eagleton, University of Manchester

Available in this series:

The Author by Andrew Bennett
Autobiography by Linda Anderson
Adaptation and Appropriation by Julie Sanders
Class by Gary Day
Colonialism/Postcolonialism – Second edition by Ania Loomba
Comedy by Andrew Stott
Crime Fiction by John Scaggs
Culture/Metaculture by Francis Mulhern
Difference by Mark Currie
Discourse by Sara Mills
Drama / Theatre / Performance by Simon Shepherd and Mick Wallis
Dramatic Monologue by Glennis Byron
Ecocriticism by Greg Garrard
Elegy by Greg Garrard
Genders by David Glover and Cora Kaplan
Genre by John Frow
Gothic by Fred Botting
Historicism by Paul Hamilton
Humanism by Tony Davies
Ideology by David Hawkes
Interdisciplinarity by Joe Moran

Intertextuality by Graham Allen
Irony by Claire Colebrook
Literature by Peter Widdowson
Magic(al) Realism by Maggie Ann Bowers
Metre, Rhythm and Verse Form by Philip Hobsbaum
Metaphor by David Punter
Mimesis by Matthew Potolsky
Modernism by Peter Childs
Myth by Laurence Coupe
Narrative by Paul Cobley
Parody by Simon Dentith
Pastoral by Terry Gifford
The Postmodern by Simon Malpas
The Sublime by Philip Shaw
The Author by Andrew Bennett
Realism by Pam Morris
Rhetoric by Jennifer Richards
Romance by Barbara Fuchs
Romanticism by Aidan Day
Science Fiction by Adam Roberts
Sexuality by Joseph Bristow
Stylistics by Richard Bradford
Subjectivity by Donald E. Hall
The Unconscious by Antony Easthope

For further information on individual books in the series, visit:
www.routledge.com/literature/nci

Related titles from Routledge

Shakespeare: The Basics
Second Edition
Sean McEvoy

The way in which Shakespeare's plays are studied has undergone considerable change in recent years. The new edition of this bestselling guide, aimed squarely at the student new to Shakespeare, is based on the exciting new approaches shaping Shakespeare studies. This volume provides a thorough general introduction to the plays and a refreshingly clear guide to:

- Shakespeare's language
- The plays as performance texts
- The cultural and political contexts of the plays
- Early modern theatre practice
- New understandings of the major genres.

Sean McEvoy illustrates how interpretations of Shakespeare are linked to cultural and political contexts and provides readings of the most frequently studied plays in the light of contemporary critical thought.

Now fully updated to include discussion of criticism and performance in the last five years, a new chapter on Shakespeare on film, and a broader critical approach, this book is the essential resource for all students of Shakespeare.

ISBN13: 978–0–415–36245–0 (hbk)
ISBN13: 978–0–415–36246–7 (pbk)
ISBN13: 978–0–203–012758 (ebk)

Available at all good bookshops
For further information on our literature series, please visit
www.routledge.com/literature/series.asp
For ordering and further information please visit:
www.routledge.com

Related titles from Routledge

Twelfth Night
New Critical Essays
Edited by James Schiffer

This volume in the Shakespeare Criticism series offers a range of approaches to *Twelfth Night*, including its critical reception, performance history, and relation to early modern culture.

James Schiffer's extensive introduction surveys the play's critical reception and performance history, while individual essays explore a variety of topics relevant to a full appreciation of the play: early modern notions of love, friendship, sexuality, madness, festive ritual, exoticism, social mobility, and detection. The contributors approach these topics from a variety of perspectives, such as new critical, new historicist, cultural materialist, feminist and queer theory, and performance criticism, occasionally combining several approaches within a single essay.

The new essays from leading figures in the field explore and extend the key debates surrounding *Twelfth Night*, creating the ideal book for readers approaching this text for the first time or wishing to further their knowledge of this stimulating, much loved play.

Contributors: James Schiffer, Christa Jansohn, Ivo Kamps, Marcela Kostihova, Cynthia Lewis, Catherine Lisak, Laurie Osborne, Patricia Parker, Elizabeth Pentland, Alan Powers, Nathalie Rivere de Carles, David Schalkwyk, Bruce R. Smith, Goran Stanivukovic, Jennifer Vaught.

ISBN13: 978–0–415–97335–9 (hbk)

Available at all good bookshops
For further information on our literature series, please visit
www.routledge.com/literature/series.asp
For ordering and further information please visit:
www.routledge.com